# The Boo
# Better Roads

## How to $ave Your Crumbling Roads with Practical Pavement Management

*To Bobby Go Green.*

by **Blair Barnhardt,** APM

http://www.thebookonbetterroads.com

The Barnhardt Group
Kennesaw, Georgia

This book was made possible by a partnership agreement between Auburn University and The International Pavement Management Association.

**Regarding the use of trademarks (™ or ®) in this book:**

The Barnhardt Group claims ownership of certain names and has added the ™ to clarify that fact. There is no legal requirement to add the mark every time the name is used, and we feel it gets in the way of our message to do that. Therefore, the following list is the names TBG claims. The ™ is added here, but it will not be added in the text of the book:

IPMA™, Accredited Pavement Manager™, APM™, PDH Power Hour™, RockSTARS™, Better Roads Radio™, Three Legged Stool™, Tip of the Week™, The Better Roads Bus™.

Other companies/products are discussed that use trade marks. They are listed here, but their mark will not be repeated in the text:

MicroPAVER™, StreetSaver®, PAVER™, Cityworks®, HA5® (High Density Mineral Bond) and Re-HEAT®.

## Special Thank You . . .

This book was made possible by a partnership agreement between Auburn University and The International Pavement Management Association.

Blair Barnhardt and Wanda Lambert, Marketing Director of the Samuel Ginn College of Engineering, Auburn University, hold the new IPMA Academy diploma for Accredited Pavement Managers.

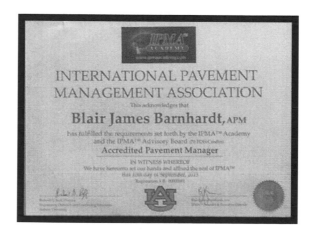

# Comments from Readers

***The Book on Better Roads*** provides the most comprehensive source of expert information regarding all things pavement management. I highly recommend the book to anyone seeking to expand their knowledge or just become acquainted with pavement management. It's time we all become better stewards of public funds and manage our crumbling infrastructure more wisely!

Brian A. Frix, EIT, MSc, APM, Traffic/Transportation Engineer, Rockdale County, Georgia

Blair has an amazing ability to get people focused and listening about a topic that usually people are not very interested in until they are directly affected by poor road and crumbling infrastructure, which is when it is too late and costs too much to fix. Blair has created an easy read!

Diane Sheesley, Project Engineer, City of Tacoma, Washington

As you travel the nation spreading the word on better roads, don't be discouraged if you look in the rear view mirror and see no one; you are not traveling alone, there is a large convoy behind you headed in the same direction. Some trail behind because they are unfamiliar with the road, others are weighed down by old habits and lack of innovation.

And then some of us actually obey the speed limit . . . .

Miguel Valentin, PE, APM, Transportation Director, Rockdale County, Georgia

Blair's straight-forward, no nonsense advice will surely strike a chord with many in our industry who have pleaded with agencies and politicians to challenge "conventional thinking" and "standard approaches" when it comes to pavement management. Public Works Directors and County Highway Supervisors should read this and then read it again! With reduced pavement maintenance budgets becoming the norm for the foreseeable future, agencies must re-think how they are doing things. The leaders among them are the ones always trying new methods or, simply, methods that are "new" to them but used throughout the country for decades.

Patrick Gallagher, Gallagher Asphalt Corporation, Chicago, Illinois

# Acknowledgements and Dedications

First of all, thank you . . . **Joy,** . . .

for taking this journey with me and always being the voice of reason, even when I didn't want to hear it. Your love and support is everything.

And **Brooke, Andrew** and **Lyndsey,** the best kids a Dad could ask for. You inspire me every day. I could not be more proud.

Lastly, I'd like to dedicate this book to two men who helped shape my life and taught me to dream big,

**John Lawley** and **D.L. Stephens.**

Until we meet again.

I would also like to thank my mentors for making this book, as well as our mission, a reality. Here is a bigger than life shout out to **Brendon, Frank, Jeff, Joe, Mike, Paul, and Tim.**

And to all those on *The Book on Better Roads* team: Thank you!: **Ben, Brock, Lea, Rocco, Tracey,** and, of course, **Joy**!

Better Roads Bus Buds — Jason Sorenson, Montana DOT, and Blair

**This book is written for:**

— All of those struggling city and county engineers, township officials, politicians, and every day residents who are struggling to cope with crumbling roadways in the USA and the World.

— All of these local agencies not knowing where to turn for reliable unbiased information on how to do more with less and who, without better ways, are set up to fail due to the budget constraints they have inherited.

**The Three-Legged Stool™ System of Pavement Management**

Throughout the book there will be references to the **Three-Legged Stool of Pavement Management**. This is a system, devised over the last decade, whichs saves local agencies millions of dollars by marrying: 1. a proactive pavement management program with 2. eco-efficient, in-place, asphalt recycling and 3. pavement preservation.

# Foreword

I am writing this foreword to acknowledge first and foremost the contribution of Blair Barnhardt to the field of pavement preservation and preventive maintenance.

As the State of California has invested trillions of dollars on the huge network, it is imperative that we acknowledge the importance of preserving our investment and highlighting all the tools that are available in the tool box. Blair's efforts described in this book clearly articulate this Vision.

Basem E. Muallem, P.E.
Director, District 8, California Department of Transportation

District 8 is the largest of the 12 Caltrans districts, with over 7,000 lane miles of roads. District Director Muallem manages a staff of 1,280 with an operating budget of $181 million. He oversees all facets of design, construction, operation and maintenance of the state highway system in the greater Inland Empire region.

Basem Muallem has been with Caltrans for 29 years (since 1985). He has experience in Construction, Design, Operations/Encroachment Permits, Surveys, Maintenance, Program/Project Management, and Right of Way. He most recently was the District 8 Deputy District Director for Program/Project Management and Deputy District Director for Right of Way.

Previously, he was the Deputy District Director for Maintenance in District 8 and also served as the interim HQ Division Chief for Maintenance and Division Chief for Right of Way.

Mr. Muallem holds a Bachelors of Science degree in biology, and he has Bachelors and Masters of Science degrees in Civil Engineering. Basem began his career in Los Angeles (District 7) as an entry level Civil Engineer.

**Blair and Basem Muallem**

THE PHOTO AT THE TOP OF THE PAGE AND THE INFORMATION ABOUT DISTRICT EIGHT IS FROM THE CALTRANS WEBSITE.

# Free Resources for YOU

Here is a chance to go deeper into all things saving YOUR crumbling roads. Whether you are an elected official simply scanning Part One and handing this book off to your city or county engineer, or a seasoned pavement manager with decades of experience, this simple book registration process will unlock hours of video, audio and written training material for you to further your knowledge.

Because you took the initiative to purchase this book, you are entitled to several FREE gifts, including:

- A free video training series on **The Three Legged Stool System of Pavement Management**.

- A webinar with real life "what's working now" success stories of elected officials, city and county managers, state DOT officials, and pavement Engineers across the world who are implementing **The Three Legged Stool System** to do more with less money and less carbon footprint.

- PLUS, we promise to continue to lead the world in all of the best practices in pavement management, in-place pavement recycling and pavement preservation. As such, we will always keep you up to date with the most current best practices available to all, but known to few.

Simply click on the following website to register your book to stay current and to receive your free Bonus material: www.thebookon-betterroads.com/register

We promise to never send unsolicited bulk messages (SPAM). We will do our best to keep you current on all the great things that are happening as we work together to resurrect our economy and make better roads for all!

* HYPHEN CAUTION: If a link includes a hyphen as it goes to the next line of text, when you retype the link into your computer **do not include the  hyphen**.

# Driving America Drove Me to Write This Book . . .

Along the journey you will take with me as you read this book, there will be several references to the things I do as an entrepreneur. Understand that it is not my intent to barrage you with unneeded, ineffective information, to sway you into hiring me, joining any association, or doing anything you don't want to do.

That being said, I can say that, had I not jumped behind the wheel of my RV and driven 83,000 miles, I never would have had the perspective or passion to share what I discovered. Even with 30 years of heavy, civil construction experience, and with two decades of teaching university and college level curriculum on this book's subject, I wouldn't have had the courage to stand up and say what needs to be said if I hadn't driven the roads and seen it all myself.

Even after several years as a board member on a very influential industry trade association, and routinely dealing with high ranking FHWA (Federal Highway Administration) and state DOT (Department of Transportation) folks, had it not been for the **Driving America for Better Roads** series of videos, I don't think I would have ever had the gumption to stand up and say the things that need to be said.

You see, even after travelling across this country several times, teaching FHWA National Highway Institute curriculum, developing new curricula, helping to write and rewrite the texts that go along with this curricula, it wasn't until I put myself in that seat in the **Better Roads Bus** and forced myself to drive 1,000 miles a day, and saw first hand the billions of dollars being wasted away, that I really, actually, GOT IT.

Our infrastructure is crumbling in this country (and, if you are reading this book in another country, your infrastructure may be crumbling, too). **During my travels, I saw the stupidity of what we are doing first hand.** There, I wrote it, and it feels good to get it out of my system.

---

I was told a long time ago to go to your boss with a problem only when you have a solution. Well today, as I write this book, I will say that the problem is we are paying for 1956 solutions with today's dollars. We are wasting billions of dollars on rebuilding our 4 million miles of road like it is 1956!

Some state DOTs and trade associations insist on putting up walls around local agencies and limiting the information about innovative technologies. They are keeping the information away from the city and county engineers and elected officials who rely on them for their advice. These local agencies hang on their every word as to what is right for their roads. Well, here it is — I am going to write it once and for all.

Yes, a few states share innovation technology information. And many cities and counties learn about these options themselves. But as long as there are state DOT officials, FHWA officials, trade associations, and naysayers out there limiting the flow of information and sabotaging the efforts of those who want to be better stewards of their infrastructure, then I will continue to fight the fight.

I will continue **Driving America for Better Roads**, until I see change. Until the day comes when every single road that I travel is a road that is recycled in-place, or better yet, preserved from the day it was built so it never falls in to a state of disrepair, I will continue to drive.

And while I have already dedicated this book, here goes a big shout out to the naysayers: **Thank you!** Without you I may have never developed the fire in my gut to put pen to paper and finish this book.

Beware the naysayers, because if you are a local agency waiting to hear from your state DOT officials or trade association about cost effective and innovative ways to take care of your aging infrastructure, you may only hear of one or two methods, even though there are many more.

You may never be introduced to the entire tool box of cost effective methods. And while there may never be enough pages in a single book to direct you to the right resources, know that we have built an entire library of ways for you to get more information as you go forward on your journey to become a better pavement manager or a more educated elected official.

Again, I want to remain on the high road and never want to bash any specific person, state agency, or trade association. But, I also can't be a weak "Casper Milquetoast" or we simply will never see change. That is what driving 83,000 miles does for a person. It has motivated me by forcing me to see both the worst road maintenance programs and the best.

Regarding some of the best: I got to hear the amazing success stories from the **APM Accredited Pavement Managers**. I got to see cities and counties all across the country that are implementing successful pavement management programs and saving millions.

* HYPHEN CAUTION: If a link includes a hyphen as it goes to the next line of text, when you retype the link into your computer **do not include the  hyphen**.

You can hear many of these success stories, too. Stories of in-place pavement recycling like Kenny Horak's from the City of Richmond, VA, in Episode 4, Better Roads Radio, www.betterroadsradio.com. He describes how he did 250,000 SY of hot in-place asphalt recycling and loves the results. Many more case studies are available in Part Two.

But think about this again if you will. How can all of these techniques successfully work in some states and their respective cities, townships and counties, and yet in other states, state DOT officials, local contractors and often industry trade associations are adamant about keeping these same cost saving treatments and contractors out?

Here is what I have learned in my three decades in construction activities and teaching how to maintain better roads: In America, FHWA writes policies. The latest is MAP 21 (Moving Ahead for Progress in the 21st Century), our transportation funding bill, strongly states that we should sustain and preserve our infrastructure. They even go as far as to say local agencies and state DOT officials can hire sole source suppliers and service providers, provided there is an inherent cost saving benefit and the treatments are congruent with MAP 21 and the objectives of the transportation bill.

You can read it yourself. Here is a link to the memo from King W. Gee, Director of Engineering at AASHTO (American Association of State Highway and Transportation Officials): http://www.preventpotholes.com/fhwa-policy/ and a direct link to the details regarding the US DOT's take on the subject here at the FHWA website http://www.fhwa.dot.gov/programadmin/contracts/011106qa.cfm .

So whether you are just looking to read through Part One as an elected official, or read the book several times over as a pavement manager, you MUST KNOW THIS:

FHWA makes funding policy, but based on my interpretations from conversations I have had with them over my career in the industry, they cannot DICTATE what state DOTs do with their funds. So herein lies the dilemma. While some state DOTs are following MAP 21 and are even re-recycling roads that they recycled 22 years before, some state DOTs are doing everything in their power to KEEP THESE INNOVATIVE TECHNIQUES OUT. Yes, you read it right . . .

Some state DOTs have an entire data base full of proven techniques they share with their staff and encourage their cities and counties to do the same cost effective and eco-efficient treatments. They get it!

And while this is going on, some other state DOT officials haven't changed or added anything significantly new, eco-efficient, or cost saving to their specifications books for decades. You see, these states are not willing to budge. Somehow they think they are different than the rest of the country and the world. They seem to be stuck in 1956.

"How do you know this, Blair?" you may ask. Because I have spent 30 years in this industry and have put the miles in to back it up. I have traveled and taught, walked the walk, and talked the talk. I am not saying this to be boastful or arrogant, but simply to reassure you that each and every page you read in this book is written to be a conduit of change for this country and the world. **We don't have to have crumbling roads.** I am convinced that what we teach as an army of pavement management **Rock-Stars** (you'll learn more about **RockStars** later) across the nation is a win, win, win situation. Nobody suffers as a result of **The Three Legged Stool System of Pavement Management.**

In fact, your agency could be saving millions right now, but you may have to stop listening to the folks whom you think you should be listening to for professional advice. Beware the naysayers. Beware the naysayers, for they are uninformed, misdirected or shortsighted. They will be exposed, thanks to people like you who have dedicated the time to learn new ways.

Again, I want to reiterate there are many pavement management professionals who I regard with great respect and appreciation — I have learned from them, taught them, or worked for them as their pavement manager consultant. They, and others, are fighting the fight and winning the battle, I commend you.

---

Ben, our webmaster guru, has done an amazing job of putting all of the details about what I do on our websites to promote this movement for better roads. You can find most everything on this website: www.drivingamericaforbetterroads.com. Once you have had the opportunity to read this book and have registered it at www.thebookonbetterroads.com/register, you may want to drop back occasionally to see what is going on at the mothership, **Driving America for Better Roads**.

While I have invested 30 years in this great industry, it really was the past year steering the **Better Roads Bus**, meeting great folks, learning, strategizing, and dreaming about how we could JOIN together and resurrect our flailing economy that made this book come together. A simple plan did it for me!

Take a look at what my friend and colleague Stevan Gorcester, Executive Director of Washington State Transportation Improvement Board, has done with his pavement management challenges: www.tib.wa.gov/tibdashboard.

## Here are some quick links to all that we do:

www.drivingamericaforbetterroads.com

www.ipma.co

www.ipmaacademy.com

www.betterroadsradio.com

www.thebookonbetterroads.com

www.thebarnhardtgroup.com

www.blairbarnhardt.com

www.ipma.co/marketplace

www.drivingamericaforbetterroads.com/press

https://www.youtube.com/user/ipmaTV

https://www.youtube.com/user/barnhardtgroup

https://www.facebook.com/DrivingAmericaForBetterRoads

https://www.facebook.com/blairbarnhardt

https://twitter.com/blairbarnhardt

https://twitter.com/drivingamerica4

http://www.linkedin.com/in/blairbarnhardt

# Comments from Readers

Blair will admit that he's not for everyone. Personally, I like what they are doing over at The International Pavement Management Association (IPMA). I enjoyed going through the Accredited Pavement Manager (APM) program and learned some good practical things - usable things - even though I've been around the industry for a quite a while. As a long-time practicing Pavement Manager, this was right down my alley. Blair is a good presenter and the subject matter does a good job bringing newer folks up to speed, shortening the learning curve, while filling in the blanks, connecting dots and tying things up nicely for those of us that have been around for a while.

I think emphasizing and elevating the Pavement Manager role is a very good thing that can benefit many agencies. I highly recommend the APM accreditation, or other similar program, if you can find one. Thing is, I don't know of anything even remotely similar out there. I've attended quality seminars for years without coming away with nearly as much gain. I found the APM program invigorating and it amped-up my game.

Jon Heese, APM, Arapahoe County, Colorado

# Table of Contents

## For Elected Officials, Media
## and the Everyday Normal Person — Part 1

## For the Pavement Manager & Engineer — Part 2

## Bonus Chapters —

# Introduction -- What if?

**What if we didn't have the trillions of dollars in debt in this great country?**

**What if we could resurrect our economy and clear up our backlog deficit of crumbling roadways that are never going to get fixed if we keep doing what we are doing now?**

**What if we didn't have to grind up our paved roads and turn them back into dirt roads any longer because we are literally running out of money to take care of them?**

**What if we stopped wasting billions of dollars milling up our "worn out" roadways and dumping this valuable resource? We are dumping 200 million-year-old rocks that we bought and paid for into a desert ditch in the middle of nowhere!**

**What if there is a tried-and-true method of resurfacing/recycling these same roads that take a tenth of the amount of time, cost around 50% less and decreases up to 62% of the normally generated carbon emissions?**

**What if, going forward, we would stop letting our roadways get to the point of no return, and actually start preserving them early in their life?**

**Dare to Imagine our network of roads improving instead of watching them crumble before our very eyes. Could we actually see a steady, gradual improvement of our entire network?**

We always start early with preservative upkeep on automobiles, buildings and ourselves. We don't wait until things start wearing out. Yes, it's kind of like going to the dentist to get our teeth checked. We all know how important that is to keep our mouths healthy and teeth shiny. In fact, I could go on with many analogies. They all work, and they all save us money, and they all produce better results. But when it comes to taking care of our most valuable transportation asset, many agencies seem to ignore preventive maintenance.

Even though the Federal Highway Administration proved pavement preservation techniques work well and cost substantially less, the majority of elected officials and pavement engineers that I talk to on a regular basis DO NOT practice, or are not allowed to practice, these very techniques.

While I will do my best to take the high road on this journey, there will be occasions when I have to "tell it like it is" in order for you as a reader (and future torch carrier) to become the best change agent possible in your organization. In taking the positive, high road, I will avoid using specific names of individuals, companies or associations.

It is not my intention to call out specific naysayers that are standing in the way of our country benefiting from better, safer roads at a fraction of the cost of conventional rehabilitation methods, but I will have to give you pertinent information about the walls that must be broken down for the **Three Legged Stool System of Pavement Management** to save our transportation infrastructure.

And, before I take you on this marvelous journey of understanding where we have come from, where we are, and what the solution is, a short disclaimer is needed: The views in this book are those of my own, not that of **IPMA, IPMA Academy, The Barnhardt Group**, or any individuals who are associated with any of the aforementioned firms such as Auburn University, **IPMA** Charter Members and Partners.

There are no affiliate commissions coming our way for any of the products or services mentioned in this book, and I am not writing to endorse or promote any specific firm, product or service. At the time of writing this book we have no corporate sponsors offering tens of thousands of dollars to get us to say nice things about them.

There are great books on the subject of pavement management, but most are very technical and do not cover the balancing act of combining pavement preservation and in-place pavement recycling. The purpose of this book is to give the reader a quick reference on how to save crumbling roads for less money and in less time.

Those seeking more information to enrich their learning experience will have a chance to do so in a live format during *The Book on Better Roads* Book Tour that will be announced to those who register their book at www. thebookonbetterroads.com/register. Also those who register their books will receive all links to the videos, podcasts and other BONUS training material mentioned as well as all new material as it is released.

There is more legalese covered in the final bonus chapters, and you may want to review our terms on our website at www.ipma.com.

The book is divided into two parts. Part One is for the normal, everyday person to get a grip on where we are with our crumbling roadways. Your elected officials, residents and media should read Part One.

Part Two is for YOU, the one who knows there is a better way. And the one who is presently set up for failure with your city, county, township, HOA, state (or wherever). This book is your guide out of the failure spiral and gives you simple steps to implement a plan for a better road network.

Please share and enjoy, and don't forget to register your book before you get started.

Register at: www.thebookonbetterroads.com/register.

# Part 1

# For Elected Officials, Media, and the Everyday Normal Person

# Chapter 1 – In the Beginning

What business could keep doing things the same way they have been since 1956 and still be in business today? Does anyone still use a rotary dial-up phone? Anyone still listening to 8-track tapes, vinyl records, or cassette tapes (excluding those studying historic sound reproduction)? How about your camera? Anyone still buying rolls of film? Just the other day while at Torrey Pines Beach, the kids used their iPhones with some high-tech device to print photos like we used to do with the big clunky Polaroid cameras.

And yet, each week as I drive the **Better Roads Bus** across North America, I see literally billions of dollars being wasted on milling up asphalt roads, breaking up concrete roads, dumping our resources into the desert ditches or piling the rubble up into mountainous stockpiles. As a former Vice President of a paving and reclamation firm, I used to bid upwards of 50 million dollars of work each year. And as a college instructor, estimating is something I am able to do in my sleep. So imagine how painful it is for me as I drive through a construction site seeing the wasted dollars being spent on unnecessary tasks! And don't forget I am risking my life as I am being forced to drive at 60 mph on a narrowed-for-construction, two-lane section of interstate, and the only thing between me and the oncoming 18-wheeler truck is a 40 lb reflective dellneator barrel.

This is so wrong!

If we were a private business that cared for 4 million miles of roadways, and we knew we could take care of it for 40% less money in half the time, wouldn't we have done it? Of course we would have, because like we see so often in the private sector, when firms don't stay innovative and keep up with current technology and best practices, they simply go bankrupt and expire.

So here is where we are in the simplest form I can put this. If we don't change the way we take care of our roads (don't even get me started on our bridges), we are on a downward spiral toward total failure.

According to www.smartgrowthamerica.org, we are spending 57% of our GDP on 1.3% of our roadway system building additional lanes. If you do the math that means we are spending a measly 43% of the GDP on the other 98.7% trying to take care of it all. Everything.

When we began building the Dwight D. Eisenhower National System of Interstate and Defense Highways, I don't suspect much thought went into how we were going to preserve it. And now, with the little bit of revenue generated from the gas tax, we are faced with an incredible plight of having to maintain, preserve, and rehabilitate our aging Interstate System and roadways.

Now, I can't control what went on in the past with our forefathers, and how they rehabilitated the roads in this country (and the world), but I sure am not going to sit here and watch us waste billions of dollars when I KNOW we can be doing more with less money, and less carbon footprint, in half the time. I made a promise to one pavement engineer that I would not pick on what agencies have done in the past, like before there were milling machines, etc. But there is absolutely NO REASON why we are not following **The Three Legged Stool Pavement Management System** today and into the future.

Now let me do some explaining. I want to make it perfectly clear that, while you are reading this book and referring back to it regularly, there are pavement management champions actively implementing everything that I am teaching. These champions are generally going to have **APM** after their name or have the knowledge that comes with this **Accredited Pavement Manager Certification**. These are the pavement managers, consultants, vendors, material suppliers, equipment manufacturers who have invested the time to digest 70 hours of online training to become better stewards of their infrastructure.

In addition to the **APM** Alumni and those currently enrolled, there is also a small army of people who embrace all the elements that are taught in **IPMA Academy**. Moreover, several large state DOTs, and industry trade associations understand this book and the message and vision that it contains.

It is unfortunate, however, that these champions cannot single handily resurrect our economy and our infrastructure. Currently our roadways sit at a decrepit D+ rating according to ASCE's (American Society of Civil Engineers) Report Card. Even with FHWA promoting all things sustainable and preservable in their transportation bill, MAP 21, there are still some high ranking US DOT officials, along with industry trade association staff, and even state DOT officials, who are sabotaging efforts to do anything different than a thin virgin HMA overlay, or a medium virgin HMA overlay or a thick virgin HMA overlay.

In simplest of terms, the naysayers rebel against change and all of the ecological and economical benefits associated with doing things differently and better. Ironically, in **The Three Legged Stool System of Pavement Management**, the hot mixed asphalt producers, Portland concrete road builders and bridge builders will actually get substantially more work by freeing up the funds that are being wasted doing things the same old 1956 way — the year that highway interstate construction began.

As I mentioned in the introduction, I am taking the high road and sticking to it wherever possible . . . .

Imagine if you will, I have spent the last two decades of my life teaching and saving agencies millions and millions of dollars doing pavement management, in-place pavement recycling and pavement preservation. I have taught National Highway Institute Workshops, developed and delivered curriculum for three prominent universities, **IPMA,** NWETC, APWA, LTAP, TTAP, and on and on. A few short months ago, I was standing in front of a US DOT official who blatantly told me that he thought a lot of these processes were "snake oil" and wasn't sure they were going to work.

Huh?

We have some state DOTs going back now and re-recycling roads that they recycled 22 years ago or more. These agencies have saved at least 600 million dollars so far. FHWA has spent tens of thousands sponsoring the NHI Workshop developments, and redevelopments and many thousands more on the **Basic Asphalt Recycling Manual**. And this man stands in front of me, with my tax dollars paying his salary, and says he thinks it is "snake oil"?

REALLY?

A few days after our consulting side of the business delivered an absolute rock solid pavement management plan for getting a county agency onto better roadways for less money with pavement preservation and in-place pavement recycling, a local state DOT staffer and a "concerned citizen" of the county, convinces the Chairman and his Commission that my professional advice is not good. Those treatments I speak of are not proven, and they really should consider doing either thin overlays, medium overlays or thick overlays, and chip seal. After all, it had worked in the past.

A recommended preservation treatment this "concerned citizen" called "not proven" was used during the a high profile international paving event in his state. (It was a significant project of 600,000 SY or more.) TRB report which was written by his state officials went on record touting the benefits of the preservation treatment.

So there you have it, that is the motivation for me to sit here and write this **Book on Better Roads** for you. Had it not been for that day, I may have procrastinated forever and never served up this simple guide to resurrecting our infrastructure and economy. If we can put a man on the moon, we sure as heck can have better roads!

Now on a positive note, several state agencies, Utah DOT, and Caltrans to name a few, invite me out each and every year to train their staff. I was recently asked by a Utah DOT official to do the keynote speech for their annual meeting. They get it! Big shout out to folks like Reed Ryan at UAPA, Utah Asphalt Pavement Association — They get it! Their paving contractor members took very little time to figure out that with the **Three Legged Stool System of Pavement Management**, they could increase their annual business by 20%!

I implore you, as an elected official, ratepayer, or everyday normal citizen, to learn all there is to know about what is going on with the local contractors and your agency staff about all things pavement management, preservation and in-place pavement recycling. They may simply not know about these options. Ask them questions about it. If you want to do more with less, you have got to be open to doing something different.

In a time where agencies are grinding up their hard-topped surfaces and reverting them back to dirt roads, you must understand that in the beginning, there may have not have been a solution — but today there is, and you have no excuse to keep doing things the same old way.

In Part Two of this book, there will be countless case studies to prove to you there is hope. But you have to take action. It is not enough to just watch the videos and read the book.

---

Even after you have registered your book at www.thebookonbetterroads.com/register, you will have to empower your pavement managers and engineering staff to make the critical changes to your pavement management system. And if you don't have a system in place, for 2 cents a square yard you can. Contact me. On average, you can save ten bucks a square yard by proper selection of the requisite treatments recommended by the pavement management system. That is a $9.98/SY net gain in my books, and I am not the brightest light bulb in the fridge!

---

The bean counters of your agency — the city managers, CFOs, and county managers — always perk up a bit and have a sparkle in their eye when I mention that doing pavement management annually, or at least every three years or so, gives the GASB 34 (Government Accounting Standards Board Statement 34) auditors reason to give your city or county a better bond rating!

The bottom line in this chapter, if I have said it properly, is that if it weren't for the naysayers out there backstabbing the efforts of the champions, our country (plug in your country if you are outside of the USA) could have much better roads for less money and less carbon footprint!

I am hoping that by 2024 we will be able to remember back to 2014 this way: In the beginning, there was a crumbling roadway system. Then folks started to read **The Book on Better Roads**. In fact, some angry ratepayers started mailing several hundreds, and sometimes thousands of copies of Amazon.com's **Book on Better Roads** to their public works policy makers and elected officials, and then **60 Minutes** and **20/20**, and news makers started filming as truckloads of boxes of **The Book on Better Roads** were delivered daily down to their city halls and county commissioners' offices . . . . you can write your own headline here.

---

The best way to predict the future is to create it. We don't have to have crumbling roads any longer. Please join our movement by registering your copy of this book and visiting www.drivingamericaforbetterroads.com to see how you can get further involved at any level. Help us change this country for the better.

---

If you would like to watch a video of me doing a live presentation from Purdue Road School on **The Three Legged Stool System of Pavement Management**, simply click here to register your book and get access to the free BONUS material: www.thebookonbetterroads.com/register

---

That's it for this chapter, I will take the high road from here as I am sure you all feel my pain in writing this book for you to enjoy!

## Chapter 2 – How Bad Can This Really Be, Blair?

Asphalt is the number one recycled product in America, and we recycle 100 million tons a year back at the plant but only about 3% of our roads are actually recycled in-place. Our awesome asphalt producers put out about 600 million tons of hot mixed asphalt per year, and about 93% of our roads in the USA are paved with hot mixed asphalt.

Blair holds up a 10-inch core of HMA at Purdue Road School

Unfortunately, even though we have been taught that asphalt paved roads have a 20 year life cycle, for whatever reason, some of the roads I core when we do the pavement distress evaluations have upwards of 10 inches or more of asphalt on them, which is made up of 6 or 7 sequential overlays. And the road is less than 25 years old based on the back calculations we do from the date on the fire hydrants.

You can watch this little **IPMA Tip of the Week** after registering as a free BONUS after registering your book at www.thebookonbetterroads.com/register if you are interested in learning how we do this calculation.

To make matters worse, a very low percentage of normal, everyday folks know what pavement preservation is. Yet, we all know how important it is to fix our roof when it leaks and change the oil on our cars. But we somehow figure it is OK to let billions of dollars worth of roadways literally "die on the vine," so to speak. You see, if we would have preserved our pavements early on in their life, we wouldn't have had to spend as much over their lives. Our Network Level Pavement Condition Indexes (NLPCI) would be higher, and the money we saved could have been spent improving our backlog deficit of bad roads that most agencies will never get to.

As you will learn in **The Three Legged Stool System of Pavement Management**, hot mixed asphalt contractors will put down 800 million tons of hot mixed asphalt a year, up from 600 million tons annually. Further, it will take them the 215 years to eliminate the backlog deficit of bad roads at 800 million tons a year. Meanwhile, the local agencies will be able to free up funds that have been typically wasted on doing sequential overlays and start to preserve their good roads so they last longer and don't fall into the dreaded red zone of PCIs below 55.

"So how bad can it really be, Blair?" At the rate we are headed, according to ASCE Report Card, our USA roadways are currently rated at D+, and we are headed for a three trillion dollar backlog deficit of bad roads in 2040. While it may be hard for the average citizen to fathom the severity of this, just for a second or two imagine you not being able to drive your grand kids down to McDonald's to get a hamburger because of the enormous debt load our country will be carrying and all because nobody took the time to consider how easy it could be to implement **The Three Legged Stool System of Pavement Management** two or three decades ago.

Again, I want to reiterate for those of you who may be thinking: "How bad can things be, Blair?" Right now we have local agencies pulverizing their hard-top roads and turning them back into dirt roads because they don't have the money to maintain them as hardtop roads. As I told one local agency, if your county commissioners insist on having you spend all of your money paving dirt roads without preserving the existing hardtop roads, you may as well start planning on pulverizing existing paved roads. That is where you are headed, and it's right around the corner!

This is not a book about "perhaps," or "maybe," things are bad. I can say that with confidence based on thirty years of being in the industry, at the rate we are going, and with the current Department of Justice ADA (Americans with Disabilities Act) clarifications that have just been legislated, your city or county, township or state DOT is headed for a path of bankruptcy if you don't implement a plan that ties practical pavement management together with eco-efficient and cost saving in-place pavement recycling and pavement preservation.

While the average citizen may not be fully aware of the financial impact on the recent US Department of Justice pavement treatment type clarifications, you as a city manager or county manager have to realize what they have legislated.

All rehabilitation and preservation projects are now considered "alterations" not "maintenance". So, along with budgeting for pavement work in older neighborhoods that have old style curbs, sidewalks, truncated domes (detectable warnings between sidewalks and the street for the visually challenged), wheelchair ramps, you will need to upgrade them to meet current ADA standards. On the long run, it certainly is good legislation. Making neighborhoods ADA compliant adds long term value in many ways. But

8

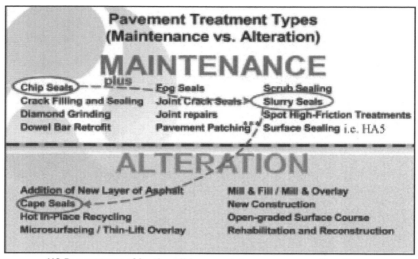

US Department of Justice slide on maintenance versus alteration

when the needs are so overwhelming, it's an added financial burden that could not come at a worst time. Note the slide above from a recent DOJ/FHWA webinar presentation:

Now, for clarification's sake, let me use an example of a fairly large city in the Pacific Northwest where the PW Director emphatically stated during a presentation at Northwest Pavement Management Association Meeting that the cost of each of his projects just doubled literally overnight. This may not be the case if you are a county manager, or elected official with little or no sidewalk or curb and gutter in your network of roads, but if you are in a city, this is a key factor in everything you do going forward with your pavement management system.

Also, for the record I am not here to do disservice to anyone with disabilities; This is the law and I support it totally. I knew that this DOJ Clarification would have significant impact on already struggling local agencies cash strapped for roadway funding.

Bottom line here is we were already faced with crumbling roads in America and the world, with little funding to spend to maintain their current condition. Now the situation, especially for cities with curbs, gutters and sidewalks just got even worse. Now more than ever, we must take heed of the warning signs and do everything we can in our power to educate our communities about the road ahead (pardon the pun).

In Part Two I will lay out a simple plan for your city and county engineers to follow in Part Two of this book. For now I want to make absolutely sure that you, as elected officials, media and normal everyday citizens, understand how severe the situation is and how we got here. Now, how the heck we are going to get ourselves out of it?

Let's take a minute and do this simple example to find out what your budget should be for maintaining your roadway network for your local agency. Now for those of you just getting used to what I am talking about, we will use a PCI or Pavement Condition Index of 100 as a brand new or freshly rehabilitated road. A PCI of 0 means a road has reached the end of its useful life. Typically, a city or a county will strive to have their roads in decent shape, but if the pavement network was running at its best, the average network level PCI would be about 85. This is about as good as it gets across the network.

So the first step for us folks who are not city and county pavement managers and engineers is to find out how many center lane miles of roadway that you have. Let us assume, for this example, that your city or county has 500 center lane miles of roadway.

---

CL Miles = 500 miles

---

Now, we won't bother getting into specifics about whether these roads are all 2 lane roads or some 4 lane. Let's assume that all 500 CL miles of roadway are 2 lane roads. Since a typical county road is about 22 feet wide, I usually plug in 13,000 square yards for each CL mile of road.

---

500 CL Miles x 13,000 SY = 6,500,000 SY Total

---

We will take the total square yards above and multiply it with a number that it would typically cost to replace the entire section of pavement along with some estimated prerequisite engineering costs. In some states this could be $48/SY, and in other states this could be $78/SY. The final price depends on factors such as how much aggregate is readily available in your region, how many asphalt producers are there, ready mixed concrete plants and other production related details.

---

In this example, we will plug in a modest $60/SY for our hypothetical local agency. Thus we have: 6,500,000 SY x $60 = $390,000,000 worth of network replacement value

---

10

This figure could be more or less for your city or county depending on how much concrete sidewalk, curb and gutter you have, whether the roads are asphalt pavement or Portland concrete pavements, etc.

So in this example, our little city or county has a whopping $390,000,000 worth of replacement value over the life-cycle of the present pavement, using current techniques, not allowing anything for inflation. Few, if any, of the residents know this. In fact, most of the elected officials I talk to, and many of the city and county engineers, don't know the enormity of value in their network of pavements.

As with most assets, we can assume 2-3% of the overall network level value as the investment amount required annually to maintain the current PCI for your city or county. Again, depending on where you start with the implementation of your pavement management program, this multiplier could vary.

For this example, we will use 3% hence:

---

$390,000,000 x 3% = $11,700,000 annual amount required to maintain PCI.

---

Two things here. First, the 3% is required just to maintain, not improve, your network level PCI ratings. Therefore, if you start with a network level PCI rating of 38 or 51, it may take a multiplier of 5% to 7% before you can see the network level PCI climb to a better range such as 70 – 75.

Second, the above exercise does NOT take into account the requirements of the DOJ ADA clarifications mentioned above. So if you are in a city with a lot of non-compliant ADA ramps, nonexistent wheelchair ramps and the likes of that, you may have to run the costs on a year or two of work that you have planned and then back-calculate the multiplier that you will need.

In any case, in our hypothetical city or county above, it is clear that 11.7 million dollars is needed to maintain the current PCI rating. As a general rule in my world, dealing with local agencies on a daily basis across the country, the norm is typically that the pavement manager or who ever is in charge of spending the money and fixing the roads, is getting a tenth to a third of what he or she actually needs based on the above formula.

So the trend we see with folks who are actually managing their pavement is their PCI is declining, their backlog deficit of bad roads is increasing and the amount of money they are spending on their roads is declining. Now to make matters even worse, the pavement engineers who have adequate funds, or less than adequate, are not always well-versed on the most appropriate treatment at the right time on their roads.

In fact, I would urge you to consider this little phrase each and every time. Ask yourself as you put the work out to bid: **Are we using the right treatment on the right road at the right time with the right contractor and for the right reason?** Are you overlaying your roadways just because it is an election year? Could you be using a treatment that costs $2/SY instead of $8/ SY?

And, on top of all this, consider that even if your engineering staff is doing everything in their power to follow and implement **The Three Legged Stool System of Pavement Management**, there is always a chance that the naysayers (you know who you are) will swoop in and try to convince your elected officials and ratepayers that none of the treatments Blair writes about and that a well-established community of pavement managers already uses works.

In some states you may be surprised to find out just how adamant the local contractors, state DOT, even FHWA officials are about keeping certain treatments out of their proverbial "backyard." They often try to discredit the contractors and vendors providing these services.

Fortunately, the power of social media will always trump the naysayers. In fact, this book will be chuck-full of case study after case study on successful programs that have gone on for decades. Again, I am taking the high road. With over 300 million new users of the internet and smart phones coming online over the near future, we are living in a time where the truth cannot be suppressed, and the naysayers are about to be found out.

It is not my intent to damage anyone's reputation by the printed pages in this book, but as Tony Robbins said, "Words can be used as daggers; they are very powerful tools."

---

As read this book, whoever you are, and you take the time to dig into the BONUS material available when you register your book at www.thebookonbetterroads.com/register and when you dig deeper into finding out about all of the possibilities of your new pavement management program, you will find the power of your newfound education.

---

Just about that time, one of these naysayers, whether they are with a trade association, a DOT office, or just a normal citizen who is uninformed about your game plan, will enter your office and may try to convince you that some things in this book don't work. What will you do? Will you laugh that person right out of your office? Will you report him or her to their upper management? Whatever you do, just know that there is an entire army of **Accredited Pavement Managers (APM)** being assembled in part by this book, by word of mouth and/or through our 70 hours of online training at www.ipmaacademy.com to support you.

---

Feel free to call on that army of pavement managers whenever you wish to, I know I can speak for them here; they will be there to help you save your crumbling roads at your local agency.

---

# Chapter 3 –

# Ok, I Get It. Now, How Do I Get The Money?

Like my friend and colleague, Dr. Gary Hicks, said to me after a presentation I did for Utah Asphalt Pavement Association, "Blair, I get the **Three Legged Stool**. Now, how do the agencies get the money?"

At the risk of sounding like I am passing the buck here, I can help educate you, your elected officials, ratepayers, normal everyday citizens and engineering staff on how to save money by doing more with less; however, I can't go over to the money tree and pick more money for your agency to spend on these techniques.

We all know that the gas tax in this country is not providing us with enough revenue to preserve and rehabilitate our roads, and some of us know that we are wasting billions milling up asphalt on Interstates, city and county roads and piling it in the middle of the desert when we could be easily recycling them in-place for half the money.

I hear each and every day about how strapped we are for funds and how bad the roads are. Yet, each and every day as I drive 83,000 miles a year in the **Better Roads Bus,** I see billions of dollars being wasted.

My biggest fear is even if we come up with alternate funding vehicles, if we don't spend the additional money wisely, we are going to wind up no better than where we started or in a worse spot than we came from.

During a live classroom setting, I will often get the attendees to stand up and pledge to me that they will NEVER, NEVER, NEVER again dig up a roadway and haul it away to a landfill site and bring all new material back again. This is ludicrous. There is no possible reason why we have to be milling up our most valuable resource, our 4 million miles of roads in America (plug in your own country here if you are reading this abroad).

Your local agency will do well to adopt this pledge and make some simple guidelines that will provide the threshold for all work that you plan on doing going forward. You must empower your pavement managers to use in-place recycling and pavement preservation wherever possible and follow the recommendations made by your soon-to-be-implemented pavement management program which we will cover in Part Two in detail.

If you make this one simple pledge: to NEVER, NEVER, NEVER dig up an entire section of roadway, and promise, at most, you will only do Full Depth

Reclamation (FDR) in-place recycling for hot mixed asphalt pavements and Rubbleization for your PCC pavements, you will be leaps and bounds ahead of most struggling agencies in this world. Moreover, for the **Three Legged Stool System of Pavement Management** to work its wonders and to get the hot mixed asphalt industry laying 800 million tons of HMA a year, this simple pledge is crucial to their success.

While you are developing a strategy on how to generate more revenue to take care of your roads and figuring out the most effective way to spend those funds, take a few minutes to read the following transcript of a Better Roads Radio Podcast interview that I did with Hans Larson and his team of engineers at City of San Jose.

Hans discusses his pavements, and severe shortfall of funding along with some alternate methods of funding that they are considering.

Note that Hans and his team are already successfully managing their pavements like many agencies (in this case they are using MTC Street-Saver software as they are part of the Bay Area Metropolitan Planning Organization), using in-place pavement recycling and pavement preservation techniques. In other words, they are basically following all things **The Three Legged Stool,** and like many agencies, they just happen to be severely underfunded.

You can read the transcript here in this Chapter and listen to it at www.betterroadsradio.com, Episode 5.

## Transcript begins

Blair Barnhardt: . . . The City of San Jose won this amazing award from the **International Pavement Management Association** for using eco-efficient in-place asphalt recycling.

. . . It was cold in-place recycling with the foamed asphalt and . . . Hans Larson, the Director of Transportation for the City of San Jose and his team provided an amazing array of comments that really resonated with myself and Michael Arikat, one of our **IPMA** Charter Members, who joined me from FMG.

We presented the **IPMA Award of Excellence** to Hans and his staff, and I wanted to go ahead and share this information with everybody who is listening here at www.betterroadsradio.com.

. . . Hans is the Director of Transportation for City of San Jose. He is a Professional Engineer in the State of California as well.

---

Remember you can find us on www.betterroadsradio.com, iTunes https://itunes.apple.com/us/podcast/better-roads-radio/id783779335?mt=2 and Stitcher Radio http://www.stitcher.com/podcast/better-roads-radio?refid=stpr radio or whatever favorite podcast mechanism that you like to listen to on your drive into work.

---

And we are in beautiful downtown San Jose. We are in this magnificent tower of city hall here, and I wish you could see the view as I look out across the scenic of mountain range and all the palm trees. It is very beautiful. Hans is the Director of Transportation in the City of San Jose. We have Hans, we have Ricardo, Henry, Patty, and Noi. So Hans is going to go ahead, and you guys are welcome to comment on anything about the cold in-place recycling efforts.

I will say that Jeralee Anderson from The Greenroads Foundation, www.greenroads.org, also awarded San Jose. It was the very first award ever. Wasn't it a Bronze Certification? Wasn't it for the City's cold in-place recycling efforts. I know Jearlee came down and presented that prestigious award personally.

So I will turn this over to the group here . . .

Hans: Blair, thank you for the recognition of the City of San Jose and our team with the Department of Transportation and the Public Works Department. This is very meaningful for us primarily because we don't have enough money to properly take care of our roads. To get recognized for using our limited resources in the most efficient way possible is very meaningful to us and our community.

I think why it is important to bring attention to the issue of pavement maintenance and pavement management is that there is a need for our communities and the public to invest in rehabilitating our transportation system. In the last 50 years we have built a lot of roads, but they are now aging, and they need to be rehabilitated. Probably one of the most expensive or valuable assets that

\* **HYPHEN CAUTION**: If a link includes a hyphen as it goes to the next line of text, when you retype the link into your computer **do not include the  hyphen**.

17

our community has is our roadway network. Our Department of Transportation and our Principle Construction Inspectors, appreciate this award.

Blair: You do get what you inspect. Not what you specify, right?

Hans: (John) was the Lead Inspector on the Monterrey Highway Project.

Blair: You've got to keep an eye on these contractors, John. (Laughter).

Hans: I'm going to give my little overview pitch on the investment crisis we have. We have 2400 miles of roads in San Jose. If you line them all up, you have a road from here past Chicago. Unfortunately, just due to age and the lack of investment in adequate preventative pavement maintenance, we find ourselves with a 400 million dollar backlog of deferred maintenance needs.

Almost 25% of our streets are in poor condition. We only have about 20% of the money we need to adequately take care of our streets. There is a very active level of advocacy to educate our elected officials in the community about the need to invest in pavement maintenance.

. . . It really helps to reaffirm to our elected officials in the community that, with the limited dollars we have, we are being creative and resourceful and using it in the most effective way possible. The cold in-place recycling technique which, with the Monterrey Highway, we tried it out for the first time about 2-3 years ago. Now we are very successful with it. It is well received, both in the terms of cost savings benefits—it was almost 25% savings if I recall—and just the quality of the finished product. Plus it was a benefit with the ease of construction and minimizing the impact to the community.

Then, for all the green elements of it: the amount of energy saved, avoiding grinding it out, trucking it off, and then bringing it back; it is just a superior technique in terms of sustainability.

Blair: With traffic the way it is, you just never know if you load up a dump truck with millings it may never get to the job site. It may never come back in time. With traffic and the congestion, we have to do things in-place. It's a huge cost savings. As soon as you put a milling machine in there, and if you mill off a bunch of asphalt and haul it all away, then you expose the subgrade to wet conditions, and, before you know it, you have a lot more dump trucks pounding away at that subgrade. Before you know it, you are 1 million dollars over in a change order to do deep patching. Kudos to you guys for doing that.

Hans: Monterrey Highway was the first time we tried that out. The following year, we did it on four, five, six additional roads with success. We have our projects for 2014 rolling out to get bids, and we've got some more streets we will be doing this year.

Blair: When you do the cold in-place, are you putting asphalt on all the job, or have you tried putting some microsurfacing down as a wearing surface?

John: Asphalt.

Blair: Feel free to use 0.40 for a layer coefficient for the cold in-place.

The Virginia Department of Transportation did I-81 Interstate with the exact same train and the cold in-place plan. Brian Diefenderfer, Ph.D., P.E., let that sit for several months with truck traffic running on the cold in-place mat before they put the asphalt on top of it. They went out and they cored it (a lot).

They did falling weight deflectometer and rut testing and he gave me the results of the rut test, [It was excellent.] I knew that it was a high Marshall stability with a flexible mat, but I didn't have any idea that it would stand up that well under truck traffic—An Interstate Highway.

---

(Note: to see a Free BONUS Video of Brian talking about this project be sure to register your book at www.thebookonbetterroads.com/register)

---

Feel free to consider going forward into this season based on your 400 million dollar backlog. In **The Three-Legged Stool System**, we say take the hot mixed asphalt, where possible, and move it over to the full-depth reclamation roads. When you are doing your FDR projects on the really, really bad roads, take hot mixed asphalt and move it there. Put microsurfacing on the cold in-place jobs wherever possible. I'm not telling you guys to do it; I'm saying it is a viable option.

Hans: Mike Bitowski, the Senior Engineer, said he wanted to try some sort of microsurfacing, or even slurry seal, or something like that, but the roads we are doing are pretty high traffic.

Blair: Okay, in that case, you want to have the [additional] structure.

Hans: We need a wearing course. We need something more than a microsurfacing. We want something that will last.

Blair: Hans, you are hitting the nail right on the head!

Hans: We have been actively trying to get the public to engage—and our elected officials—in more investment in transportation, particularly with road maintenance. Education and communication on the topic—particularly endorsement of San Jose being efficient and creative—is something that serves our efforts to try to build public confidence to tax themselves or raise revenues in a variety of different ways.

We have a whole financial strategy we put out there. It all revolves around tax increases in one way or another.

Blair: So, have you, in the past, run local option sales tax to try to come up with more money for roads?

Hans: Two days ago, we had a study session with our City Council on the topic of taking to the voters in San Jose a 0.5 cent sales tax increase. The two things that are on the mind of most of the public is improving police services for public safety and pavement maintenance.

Blair: Great! . . . You hit the nail right on the head! Yesterday when Michael and I were talking, I said if we take 4 million miles of roads in America, 25% of them are a deficit backlog of bad roads that we are never going to get to. Every agency only has 20% of the money they need to spend. We are making 600 million tons of hot mix each year. If we just take the hot mix and try to move it over to the FDR roads, it will take 215 years to clear up that backlog deficit of bad roads. At 800 million tons per year!

Clearly you summarized the entire state of America's crumbling roads right there, 400 million dollar backlog, and this is right on the streets. This is scientific evidence right? You run these plots all day long—prediction models—and the good news is now at least we are using cost effective green technology to try to keep up with the curve.

Hans: The troubling thing is, there's a community issue in terms of declining quality of the streets in our city, but there's a kind of fiscal concern out there, too. The longer you wait, the more deterioration you are going to have. If you are not doing preventative maintenance, the right treatment in a timely manner, you are facing the issue of having to pay a lot more later because the roads will continue to deteriorate.

We projected, using our StreetSaver tools, that we are here, in 2014, with a 400 million dollar backlog and only 20% of the money we need. It is not enough. **By the year 2020, just 6 years from now, that 400 million dollar backlog of deferred maintenance is going to cost us 870 million dollars.** So, it **is** huge. If you don't think you can't afford to deal with it now, it is not going to get any better. I think we all know in the profession if you are not doing the timely sealing treatments in the streets, it costs five times more . . . to have to come back and rehabilitate or replace it later.

Blair: Let me ask you guys . . . Last August or September the Department of Justice drew a line in the sand and . . . said now every time you do microsurfacing or hot in-place or cold in-place or full-depth reclamation or mill-and-inlay thou shalt . . . do every single ADA upgrade on that project as well. Have you guys run any preliminary budgets on some of the projects you have for 2014? Have you found the costs doubling?

Ricardo: No, it doesn't double, but we take into consideration those standards and the costs. It impacts the project but it doesn't double the final costs.

John: It is in the tens of hundreds of thousands. It varies on . . . how many corners that haven't been improved.

Blair: That's a good point. If you are in an intersection that has already been upgraded, then it is not as significant.

Hans: One thing we've done in San Jose with our elected officials and with raising awareness that we only have 20% of the money we need to maintain all 2400 miles of the streets. There was an effort done a couple of years ago that asked what is the best place to put this investment? The city council adopted our recommendation. The best thing we can do is to make sure that the streets that are most heavily traveled are the ones that we're putting our maintenance investment into and can, at least, keep those in good condition.

We adopted a policy that essentially said we have 900 miles of major streets and 1500 miles of neighborhood streets. All of our pavement maintenance investment is targeted towards keeping our major streets in good condition. But we don't have enough to do all 900 miles. We are essentially only covering half of those, which we call our priority street network. They are the four lane and six lane arterial streets.

I think a lot of those have been upgraded with ADA ramps and most of our needs for ADA ramps are in our neighborhoods that were built before the 70s. We are still catching up with some of them on the major streets.

The troubling thing is, 60% of the money we have comes from State and Federal gas taxes that come to the city to help maintain our pavement. The crisis we are facing is that the gas tax is not a funding source that is keeping up with the cost of pavement maintenance work.

Blair: Exactly. Yeah.

Hans: At the Federal level it has been flat for over the last 20 years. The last time it was adjusted was 1993. We are getting, for the last 20 years, the same level of federal support, but costs are 3, 5 or 10 times more. We have some numbers on that on the increase. We are getting less value for the money, and there's a National Policy that says, hey, we need to convert to electric vehicles and more fuel efficient vehicles and so the gas tax is going the way of the dinosaur. It is a declining source of money, and we've got a problem of costs going up and our tax base that supports transportation is significantly declining.

Blair: What's the answer to that? Some states have tried to implement their own tax outside the fuel tax. Oregon has tried to collect at the pump and the likes of that. Is there a solution outside of waiting for the Feds to change something along the way? Outside of the local option sales tax, how are we going to get the other 80% of the money to start addressing those roads?

Think about this, if you will—everyone in the room is set up for failure. How do you go to city council and the mayor and say we are really doing a great job of taking care of the roads. We are not! We are scratching the surface, and you guys must feel horrible because you have to walk in the grocery store, and people are telling you about the pothole out there. In your mind you are thinking, it's a residential road that you are never going to fix.

That's the deal. We are taking care of the priority streets, but we can only do half of the 900 miles. What we want to say is: unless you go to Home Depot and get yourself a bag of cold mix, we are never going to see that road in the pavement management system. It is never going to come up on our priority list.

Hans: I think that has been the message you were talking earlier about, just the education process on this, and that it takes a long time for things to sink in on really how dire the situation is. The message is, in San Jose our neighborhood streets are getting no money for pavement maintenance.

We don't have the money for it, and, unless something changes from investment side, your street, even though it is falling apart, is not going to get any attention other than safety repairs. If it is a pothole, we will fill potholes within 48 hours. I say we will provide safe streets, but we can't provide smooth streets.

Blair: Do the residents accept that? Do they understanding the situation?

Hans: I think people do, but it takes time for that sort of message to sink in. I think that is why we are seeing for the first time pavement maintenance is increasingly becoming a priority issue for the community. We've fallen behind. Police, fire, parks, libraries, and other issues like that have captured the community's attention, and, with pavement maintenance, you can kick the can down the road another year and the deterioration is not as perceptible compared to closing a fire station or reducing services at community center or a library.

If you cut their budgets, the community sees it immediately. If you defer money for pavement maintenance it does not really show up, or you don't notice it over the course of time, but, all of the sudden, you wake up and my neighborhood street looks like crap. What are we doing about it? It's an education process and talking about the strategies Obviously we've spent a lot of time of this issue.

Blair: Strategy is a key element.

Hans:  We need 20 million a year.  We should be spending 60 million on a preventative maintenance program, so we have an annual shortfall of 40 million dollars.  We deferred maintenance, and have a backlog of 400 million. Streets that are beyond preventative maintenance, streets that we need to rehab or replace, those are part of the 400 million.

We have a 40 million annual short fall and a 400 million dollar annual backlog.  We put together for our city council a strategy on how we would address that.  A 0.25% sales tax is allocated for street maintenance. Our council is actively considering a 0.50% sales tax for public safety and other services, but hopefully a big chunk of that can go to local pavement maintenance needs.

We were hoping that California would put on the ballot an increase to the vehicle license tax. They were actively looking at raising the vehicle registration tax in California by 1% and that would bring into San Jose another 19 million dollars per year.

Blair: That would be a big start.

Hans:  It would help the state, it would help the counties, it would help the cities, and there is some money to deal with you know maintenance needs on our transit systems, but their polling indicated that they would have a hard time getting majority state approval for a road repair measure like that.  The idea is that people who have a vehicle need good roads and would pay for it.

Someone driving an electric car today is paying zero in gas tax, and this is a more equitable way of being able to fund the update of our road system.  But I think it comes down to public awareness. The need to invest isn't at a high enough public awareness level yet where you could put something out there statewide.

Blair:  So it never went to vote?

Hans: It did. The State Attorney General filed for getting the Title and the Summary of the Measure. Then they did some polling on that, and they decided to withdraw it for the year 2014.  Their message and timing wasn't right for California. Voters had approved a temporary sales tax increase and the public needs to feel confident that other recent tax increases are being used effectively. They didn't see the timing was right for this year.

Blair: Unbelievable. If we go back to your discussion earlier that the 400 million dollar backlog is about to grow to 800 million, it is pay a little now or pay a whole lot later. In five years if we rerun that vote, we may have to collect 3%.

It is an alarming situation to be in. I was at Wal-Mart this morning and I looked at the 8.75% tax. If I'm living in San Jose and paying an additional 1% or 2% local option sales tax, if I knew the money was dedicated to the roads, and I saw that the roads were getting improved, I could understand that. But would the average rate payer understand that? Would they accept 10.5% in 2014 knowing that they are not going to have to pay 6% additional tax in 2017 or 2019?

Hans: I just want to correct for the record we are not looking at numbers that high. I think for what we are talking about if we can get a 0.25%, it would have a significant impact.

Blair: I guess, even that would have a significant impact.

Hans: 0.25% sales tax in San Jose is about 35 million dollars in a year.

Blair: So, we are getting 20 million now but, if we got up to 80, that would be starting to eliminate our backlog deficit, would you say? If we start chipping away at that 400 million dollar deficit?

Hans: Yes, that would be a big help. We would like to have a preventative maintenance program. We need 60 million and we have 20 million. When we find a way to bring in 40 million a year, it gives us a fully funded preventative maintenance program for all of our streets. Then we have a one-time need of 400 million to deal with the backlog.

Our strategy on that has been to do a property tax based bond measure. San Jose voters have approved bond funds upwards of 600 million dollars to deal with improving libraries and fire stations and community centers.

In California those require 2/3 approval, and we have polled on doing a property based bond measure. We have not been able to get 2/3 approval on any of our polling, so it has been a challenge.

One of our strategies is we are actively working on state legislation that would allow reducing the 2/3 threshold to 55%, which is something that schools have for their bond measures. Lowering the approval threshold for important things like transportation infrastructure may work. There is active legislation on that now, and there seems to be growing interest. We've gotten some feedback in the last month that tells us the timing may not be quite right. That is disturbing when you know it is just going to get more expensive later.

There are three strategies out there attempting to get more statewide benefits for cities. We recognize we need more investment with ongoing money as a city, and now we need a source to deal with the 400 million.

Blair: With that backlog.

Hans: We try to make our council aware of it, kind of like here's the three-pronged strategy that will cover it. All of them require voter approval.

Blair: I went through this in my county back in Georgia. They passed a 1% local option sales tax and passed it 51%. I wrote this long editorial article about pavement management, three points a year decline and where we are headed if they don't pass that.

I guess obviously another key concern is people need to know that there is accountability, and, I'm not pointing a finger at you guys, Hans, but if they know that all that money that went into that pot—that 0.25%—did go to my roads and they see improvements, that's great. But too often the police get their hands into that money, or the community gets new fire trucks and new ambulances and new baseball fields, and before you know it, it is the same thing all over again. So if we could, can you just talk about the cold in-place benefits?

Think about this, if you will, Hans, when I go back out on the road next week, I'm going to stop in, and I'm going to see an engineer in Tucson, Flagstaff, or somewhere. They are going to look at me with a deer-in-the-headlight-stare and say, "Blair, I know you always have these visions about cold in-place recycling, but I'm not sure this is going to work for our city or our county." What would you say if they are looking at you, Hans? What would you say based on your experience here in the city?

Hans: We tried it out. We are one of the leaders, particularly in California and The Bay area. There are some great stories of experiences in other parts of the country (and maybe even the world) with this, so we are not the bleeding edge of a technology that isn't well understood. We used it on a project on our Monterrey Highway. When was it? Two years ago?

John: Yes, two years ago.

Hans: We bid the project out using both methods — cold in-place recycling and conventional methods — just to verify there would be some cost savings associated. In the event it was equal we would have been willing to try CIR because that is what we do here in Silicon Valley—we like to be innovative. Also because of the green benefit of it reducing energy and being efficient with materials.

We got, however, between 20-25% savings in overall construction of the project with CIR. That was huge for us!

Also, we are a city that has a green vision. We support goals on sustainability using our resources efficiently, and we have some incredible numbers in terms of the amount of energy saved and construction vehicle trips avoided by using this method.

Then the thing that was also a huge benefit to the community was just how fast the in-place construction went. Basically, to go through there and you can put traffic on it right away meant the minimized disruption to the community from the construction side was incredible. We overlaid it with recycled rubber tires and put 18,000 tires back on the street.

Blair: Amazing. Amazing. So happy to hear that!

Hans: And the quality of it is excellent. It is smooth and quiet, and it drains well. The quality is fantastic.

Blair: That was the project that won the bronze green roads award?

Hans: There were three elements of the project that led to that award. It was using the CIR method. It was overlaying it with recycled rubberized asphalt, and we also upgraded the streetlights. Another one of our innovative things we are doing here.

We replaced it with white LED lights which provide energy savings of 40% over most of the lights we have out there now. Something else we developed here in the San Jose Silicon Valley is the idea of the dimmable street lights so our street lights . . .

Blair: You have dimmers on the lights! That's cool.

Hans: Our street lights don't run full power all night from midnight to 5:00 AM in the morning when you really don't need to light up the street. We worked with industry here in Silicon Valley to develop the dimmable street light. The light reduces to 50% power between midnight and 5:00 AM. We save an additional 20%.

Blair: Unbelievable. Did they patent that?

Hans: There's a number of companies here in the Valley that produce streetlights that meet our standard. We were the first in the country to develop a standard for dimmable lights. We have three lighting vendors that produce the lights. The control system that manages the dimming piece of it is from an overseas company. We are working to raise awareness of this new opportunity. We also encourage competition and improvement. Hopefully others will get in the dimmable light business as well.

Blair: What would it have taken to get to gold certification (with www. greenroads.org)? Would it have been feasible on that project? Would you have had to do some bridge decks or something with some innovative green concrete? Does the value of the project or the amount of recyclables have to go up another big exponential step to get to gold? I'm just curious.

Ricardo: That's an excellent question. I guess it would be related to the size of the project. I am speculating at this point and time.

Blair: We'll get with Jeralee (www.greenroads.org) afterwards on that and maybe the next project we can shoot for gold.

Hans: I think our staff who worked on the application are no longer working in this program so they might know. I think it gets into the quarter half water efficient landscaping, and I think there's a whole kind of larger breadth of types of things for the Green Roads Foundation Certification. I think some of them include when you are building a new facility. Are there other things you are considering in the whole transportation corridor part?

Blair: Well, I tell you what. I can't be more happier to present you guys with the **IPMA Certificate of Excellence** award here for the City of San Jose.

## Transcript ends

For those of you who have read Part One and choose to act on it, I commend you for becoming change agents for your agency or media firm. Please remember to register your book so you can receive all of the bonus content at www.thebookonbetterroads.com/register.

I am always happy to discuss pavement management with those who have more questions. If you are with the media and wish to do a TV or Radio Interview, you can contact joy@ipma.co to schedule an appointment. At this time you can keep your copy of your book for reference, or walk into your city engineer or county engineer's office and ask them to read the entire book. Once they have gone through the entire book, there will be plenty of DVD, CD, live workshops and online training available for them to learn at a deeper level of understanding going forward.

To learn more about all that we do be sure to check out all the details over at www.drivingamericaforbetterroads.com. Not only is the website chuck full of all the details of our existence and mission, you can watch a multitude of videos and listen to all of our podcasts to familiarize yourself with the massive potential for change that is possible when you choose to JOIN our movement and spread the word.

# Part 2
# For the Pavement Manager & Engineer

# Chapter 4 —
# The Three Legged Stool System of
# Pavement Management — Part I

Each of us wants to learn from those who walk the walk and talk the talk. Well, just know when I am not writing books, recording videos or podcasts for **IPMA, IPMA Academy** or **Driving America for Better Roads**, I am basically out there on local agency roads, down on my knees, assessing them. If you would tell me you're out fixing something now, I would likely recall seeing the exact same thing that you are describing.

I believe one of the things I saw frequently in Lee County, GA, for example, was this soil treated base, a soil cement base, under the hot mixed asphalt layer. Now, in this case, it almost looks like when the housing industry was booming, and, as the houses were being built, the builder's paving contractor might have been skimping a bit. As such, an asphalt wearing course and a soil cement base typically provide 15 to 20 years of service life. There may have been a little bit of skimping going on during the construction stages of this example.

That's all I'm going to say with the asphalt thickness. We diamond core drill at the network level for each and every road. It's a part of what we do when we manage the pavements for local agencies. It is also part of what we teach at **IPMA Academy,** www.ipmaacademy.com. We feel that the network level diamond coring is an instrumental step in the selection for the proper and most effective rehabilitation treatment for the requisite candidate selection of a roadway.

When I think about the whole Lee County Pavement Management implementation in this example above, I remember seeing a lot of really great cement treated bases holding up to the loading of heavy cotton trucks and the big tractors. The surface treated roads were holding up really well as well, but, along the way, the newer subdivision roads got a little thin on the asphalt wearing surface. I suspect the inspection staff probably know this. It may be that during times of expeditious building of these subdivisions, the County inspection staff may have been stretched fairly thin. It is evident when you go to fix a pothole, you notice those locations are also the same places that it got really thin in terms of the asphalt pavement wearing surface.

We say that at **The IPMA Academy** the learning experience is funducational. So whether we are doing a live event, video, podcast or book for that matter, I made a conscious promise to keep things like a candid conversation you or I may have while driving around your city or county. There are plenty of really technical books out there that cover pavement preservation, pavement management and in-place pavement recycling. However, few if any resources will be as straight forward as this book or as accessible for real-world pavement management practitioners, who, do to the demands of field work, are not able to spend a lot of time in the office reading.

You see, this is not rocket science, folks. It is simply going out and surveying your roadways, entering those results into simple-to-use software, and populating a decision tree with several different treatment options that are triggered to be done at the right time.

Also, try to resist the urge to fast forward through the book, as I laid it out in a manner that will take you through the vision of the **Three Legged Stool System**, present you with the top 10 things that the room full of engineers at the IACERS meeting in Boise, ID, decided needed to be in the book, give you a bunch of case studies that cover a myriad of treatment options, breakdown the list of treatments and recycling methods that are available, and cover some frequently asked questions.

---

For all of the BONUS material, you simply register your book at **www.thebookonbetterroads.com/register.**

---

If you've ever wondered about an SMA paving or open grade friction course? Doctor Michael Heitzman can explain it later on in this book via a link to a video of him teaching at an **IPMA Academy LIVE Training Event.** That topic could be a whole class on its own, so just know we've got some pretty good knowledge coming your way throughout the book.

---

If you are a public works official, or elected official, or hold any similar position, such as an army engineer, fighter pilot, basically any position that is not private sector, you can JOIN the **International Pavement Management Association (IPMA)** at no charge right here, **www.ipma.co**. In doing so you will know about everything that is coming down the pipe well in advance of our general audience. Also, you will receive a free PDH **Power Hour Training**

**Session** on all things pavement management each month. (CEUs and PDH Certificates will be offered at a low cost if you wish to hang these in your office).

---

For those of you who are just meeting me, I spend a good amount of time on the road in the RV. So I basically have hunkered down for a hundred and twenty days on the road this past year in a 23 ft by 7 ft Sprinter Van. It's put a strain on my marriage, granted, but we needed to get out there on the road and figure out what the heck was going on in this great country. Right now we are on our way to being about 3 trillion in debt of backlog deficit with back roads in America. By 2040, our grandkids won't even be able to drive the roads.

Why? Because the roads in this country, and the world, are crumbling. I don't know how many—let me see a show of imaginary hands as you are reading this book—how many people have noticed the roads are getting really, really bad. So it's everybody, right? All of you agree? Ok, so it's amazing to think about that in this great county, and the world, for that matter. We have all the resources at hand. We have the knowledge, and yet, for whatever reason, the priorities have never shifted into getting more money for road work.

We can put a man on the moon, and make self driving cars! Why can't we figure out how to stop our roads from crumbling?

Because everyone of you pavement managers and engineers out there, you may not know this yet, but you are being put into a position to fail. Even if you manage your pavements, you preserve them, and you recycle them, the biggest challenge you face is that there is never enough money to go around.

And as a result, the contractors have missed out on a lot of opportunity to make more profit and produce more tonnage and cubic yards from their HMA and ready-mixed concrete plants. You see, some of the hot mix asphalt and Portland cement concrete paving contractors are thinking preservation, recycling and pavement management is a bad thing, when, in fact, it will actually grow their business.

And after driving around for so long and shooting these videos for **www. drivingamericaforbetterroads.com** and putting together **www.ipma.co** and the **www.ipmaacademy.com**, and being with a bunch of smart people across America, and hanging out with these local agencies from Washington State, all the way down to Florida and California, all the way back to Maine and everywhere in between, I've learned a few things along the way.

Now I may not be the brightest light bulb in the fridge, but when I constantly get phone calls and e-mails every day from local agency engineers saving millions and doing more with less, I CAN'T continue to keep this a secret. I WANT TO TELL THE WORLD!

And one of the underlying things we all know is our roads are crumbling. Well, granted, there are likely some folks who don't see it. After all, the average person commuting to work 29 miles a day, one way, might not know a milling machine from a road grader. They may not know the contractor is milling up perfectly good asphalt material and dumping it into a ditch only to replace it with something that is three times the cost of what they could be doing. They may not realize the potential for saving America. Some states are resistant to make the switch, while others states have switched and are thriving because of it.

---

So as you listen to some of the free BONUS material when you register your book at **www.thebookonbetterroads.com/register,** you'll hear some thoughts from the speakers from our **IPMA Academy LIVE** events from Georgia and California, and we're going to try to highlight what's going on in other areas with some positive case studies and the likes of that.

---

Some state DOTs specifically ask me to speak for them, to train their employees, to do keynote speeches. Other state DOTs are trying to stab me in the back, trying to make it sound like **The Three Legged Stool System of Pavement Management** is not for them. They say the motor grader operators of their local cities and counties can do the pavement distress evaluation. There is free software you can get them that will tell you when it is time to do a thin overlay, medium thick overlay or thick overlay. Why would you want a professional working on your roads for $.02/SY, saving you $10/SY with those "snake oil" techniques, that work for everyone in America, when you could do it yourself?

Oh, and check with some of those state DOTs, because the things they are trying to get local agencies to do—like your grader operator to do the pavement distress evaluation, and use simple free software—they likely hired someone at their office to do their own pavement assessment with some fancy automated survey vans and software that cost $200,000.or more.

Again, trying to take the high road here as promised, but for too many years I have watched as hold-out states have tried to get in the way of

* **HYPHEN CAUTION:** If a link includes a hyphen as it goes to the next line of text, when you retype the link into your computer **do not include the hyphen.**

progress for whatever reason—you can figure that out—when they could be saving their ratepayers millions of dollars in eco-efficient savings.

Yet, please note that each and every one of these state DOT officials attend the big fancy conferences and pay the $10,000 to be members of the big fancy groups. The only difference is while listening to some of the biased information coming from these big fancy groups, some state DOT officials actually implement. Others simply go back to their office and convince their staff, and the city and county engineers that listen and follow their advice, that this "snake oil" should be avoided, and we should keep doing things the same old same old way. Now I use the word "snake oil" here to represent the words spoken to me by a high ranking US DOT official.

That person will not be named here. Realize that the term "snake oil" could be used broadly to represent any and all of the treatments available to us as pavement managers. In its simplest form, some state DOTs will not advance in their pavement management. They refuse to teach others about the benefits of using alternate methods of pavement management, in-place pavement recycling and pavement preservation.

I will go one step further, and emphatically state that during their so-called training sessions, some US DOT officials, state DOT officials, contractors and industry associations spread ill-informed and short-sighted information about these same treatments that work worldwide to save crumbling roads. Even though, as previously mentioned, FHWA has put an emphasis in MAP 21 on sustainable and preservable resources.

I accept the challenge of acting as America's watchdog on our transportation economy, and take full responsibility for the statements that I am making. We cannot resurrect our economy and have better roads for all, if the naysayers are allowed to continue in their current roles.

Just know that if we do the **Three Legged Stool System of Pavement Management**, it is a win, win, win for everybody. Nobody loses. You as an agency engineer will have more money available for key projects. Contractors will be making more profit, putting down more tonnage and placing more cubic yards. The world will be a better place. I know that sounds rosy, but it can actually happen. I have been to the new land; it is great there. Recall that I have been doing this since 1995, and watched some agencies save millions, perhaps billions. This works!

I am happy to say it's already starting to happen in a lot of the areas we've visited around this country. So, I always say this to the contractors, if you want to get 10% more tonnage out the door and 20% more profit, listen closely; this is not rocket science.

Local agencies—that's you guys reading Part Two, cities, townships and counties—you want to do more with less, with less carbon footprint, this is your answer. Like Hans told me from the City of San Jose, he said, "Blair, even if it was the exact same amount of money to either recycle roads in-place or to do the conventional rehabilitation method, I would choose to recycle the roads in-place. It's more eco-efficient." It's 65% more eco-efficient, and a smaller carbon footprint.

Ok, a quick disclaimer reminder here: we are not here to promote any one product, service or company.

We'll talk about MicroPAVER and StreetSaver, pavement management software, on the consulting side of the business. We set up about 14 or 15 local agencies in the Southeast with StreetSaver pavement management software. We also used MicroPAVER to do pavement management for the US Corp of Engineers at Dugway Proving Ground in Utah. On the teaching side we cover both software in detail in **IPMA Academy www.ipmaacademy. com,** and do customized training on both. There may be many different ways to evaluate and manage your pavements. These two software programs may be the only two that follow ASTM 6433 verbatim. The reader is encouraged to look at all of the options, not just the ones that we list.

That being said, know that many cities and counties across this country and the world use these two programs with great success.

The City of Oakland, Georgia, for example, was one of the very first agencies to use StreetSaver in the Southeast. We also do a lot of work for the U.S. Army Corp and other local agencies with MicroPAVER which is also used by the largest municipality in USA, City of LA. And we actually go out, Scott McDonald and I, and teach MicroPAVER training for 2½ days, LIVE. We just did a session in Richmond, VA, as a matter of fact.

---

For those of you who are interested, you can listen in to **www.bet-terroadsradio.com,** the only podcast on the planet dedicated to saving our crumbling roads. In Episode 3 hear a session by Blair and Scott as they discuss the key elements of setting up your pavement management system successfully.

---

* **HYPHEN CAUTION:** If a link includes a hyphen as it goes to the next line of text, when you retype the link into your computer **do not include the hyphen.**

I have included the transcript of our podcast session here in the off chance that you are sitting by the pool side in Punta Cana, DR, and have to put your right hand on your forehead and left leg up in the air to attempt to connect to the world wide web with little or no reception.

---

Better Roads Radio Episode 3 — Covers: Pavement Management Computer Systems, Pavement Types

---

Blair Barnhardt: . . . So glad you could join us for another episode here in the struggle to try to save our crumbling roads here, not only in America, but the rest of the world for that matter. I'm so glad you could join us. Today we have **IPMA Academy Advisory Board Member www.ipma.co**/advisory-board, Scott McDonald, with us. Scott McDonald, go ahead and introduce yourself. So glad you could be here.

Scott McDonald: Hey, Blair, good to be here with you. We are in Richmond, Virginia, doing some training for the CIty of Richmond this week. I work for Atkins North America, but I also provide all the technical support and training to the American Public Works Association, www.apwa.net, user community for the PAVER software system. Blair and I are kind of splitting up the duties in terms of providing the City of Richmond with some information that is going to help them do a more effective job of managing their pavement.

Blair: Really amazing when you think about a city of this size and 900 center lane miles. There is a lot of financing behind them to get this job done, and get it set up. A lot of people are involved with this loop—a lot of very smart people—but there's still a lot of missing elements. It is always amazing when we sit down with these folks to get the questions they come up with and the concerns they have: It may be a GIS professional, or the inspection people looking at the new hot-in place job last year, or it could be the people actually doing the work planning going forward.

There is a variety of different people involved with the pavement management system. We started to draw that on the whiteboard and saw the integration between the GIS (Geographical Information System), the PAVER system, and the Cityworks Software in this case.

It really made me realize the high level of expertise that is required to get this up and going, and, to be quite honest, it can be overwhelming even to us in the industry. So, what advice do you have for someone at a local agency?

What advice, Scott, do you have for the first time implementation of a pavement management system? What elements are critical elements the local agencies absolutely have to have, if they do it themselves, or if they hire somebody to do it or use some hybrid situation?

Scott: When you mapped out internal connections on the board this morning, it made me realize to have a successful pavement management system implementation, it really requires buy-in from everybody who is even remotely going to be involved in the process. So you've got Public Works, you've got Engineering, you've got GIS personnel. You've got the people who are actually going to be going out on the streets doing the repairs if that is all happening internally. The good news here at Richmond is that there is buy-in from all the important players. I think is the first step.

Once you get that established, it is also important to understand that a system is made up of several components, not the least of which is having a good software system at the core. We are here talking about PAVER today.

I represent PAVER for the American Public Works Association. I've been involved with PAVER for years and I believe in what it does. I think a couple of things about PAVER that makes it powerful are: It is the ASTM standard of practice in terms of calculating the pavement condition index, and the price is right on it because a lot of the development costs are being sponsored by the Department of Defense.

Blair: That was a great point. It is $999 for APWA members. I don't know what software you can buy that is going to run a 100 million dollar infrastructure for $999?

Scott: You mentioned Cityworks a minute ago. Cityworks went through the trouble to integrate a link with PAVER so they trade information back and forth. If a city needs to utilize the information that Cityworks can manage, you've got a link automatically connected to PAVER, and PAVER also links to GIS. Internally you can take all the information that you are using in PAVER and link it easily externally, so there's a lot of flexibility there.

Blair: Yeah, great point.

Scott: You know you asked about some of the important points as far as getting it implemented. So many things come to mind, but, there has been a lot of rework done from people who initiated the process and didn't really pay attention to some of the important initial requirements. We are talking about PAVER at the moment, but, you really need to make sure to the best of your ability, the organization needs to collect information about its pavement network with respect to how it wants to segment it. So you are talking about sectioning.

What's the best way to section it? Not always is that intersection to intersection, which is the way the GIS maps are going to break it down, but if you can think about how you would section it from a pavement management approach. We also want to talk about the age of those segments. What is the surface type of those segments? And, what PAVER calls the section rank—what's that functional use of the section? Is it an arterial? Is it a residential? Is it a parking lot?

You break all of that down, and, if you can collect that information, you've got some very solid information to get started with.

Blair: You are dealing with 100, 200, or 300 million dollars' worth of infrastructure in any one city. You send the crew out there, and you collect this data—whether you use semi-automated methods or boots on the ground methods. Scott, I think when we crunch these numbers, it always amazes me that an agency is only spending 2 or 3 cents per square yard.

At the end of the day, even with all the people who have gotten involved in this loop for a mere 2 or 3 cents per square yard, to implement a pavement management system and correlate all that back at their office, and have this network level inventory of all the roads, just like you said, with the functional class codes, what do we have for pavement types? What they heck are we going to do in 10 years, what are we going to do in 20 years?

Well, the bottom line is, in the case of Richmond—if they use the suggested eco-efficient, preservation, in-place recycling techniques, and save 20-30% — they are saving $8 or $9 per square yard on any one given project. So, by spending $.03/SY to get the information, that looks to me like a $7.97 net gain.

It is almost like they cannot afford to not implement a pavement management system. What are your thoughts of people sitting on the fence and saying, well, that's for fancy cities. You've been with a lot of small cities. You've been with a lot of big cities and counties and states. What is your advice on people sitting on the fence?

Scott: I've known Blair for a while, and both of us have been involved in assisting people in implementing pavement management systems at all different levels, from managing the entire process to just going in and providing just initial training and guidance.

What is going to make it effective and what is going to make the difference is when an agency makes an honest determination about what they are capable of doing themselves.

Blair: Good point.

Scott: Determine what resources you have and what resources don't you have. I've this contention that if you can employ the services of somebody who knows what they are doing, you are going to get a much better bang for your dollar.

. . . Not in every case is the lowest bidder the best person to get on your team, and that is true in all facets of business from manufacturing to service sector related types of things.

If you can find somebody who knows what they are doing, and if PAVER becomes the central hub of your management system, find somebody who knows what they are doing with PAVER. Get their help to whatever level you need. It has been a personal experience of mine, from the time I spent at the University of Illinois supporting a variety of organizations to now, having the opportunity to work with some directly, you won't have to go back into a lot of rework. Do it right the first time. Save yourself a lot of money. With the right buy-in from the right people, cost effectiveness is the name of the game throughout the process. That includes investing some funds to get the assistance necessary to make that management system get up and running effectively.

Blair: You have seen many agencies set PAVER up, get all the books, get Dr. Shahin's book, get all the manuals, and go out and do the evaluation. They get all that data into the computer, and, then it is 8 years later, they are calling you and saying, well, we really haven't kept up, Scott, what should we do now?

It must be a real heartbreak for you to get someone set up and running, and then only to have everything sit and collect dust on a bookshelf. Or maybe there's a transfer of the guard, or maybe the county engineer goes to another location, and so forth. A new County Engineer comes in and she is not familiar with PAVER. All of the sudden everything goes out the door.

Is there something that can be rekindled or do you almost have to go in and start fresh each and every time?

Scott: We have seen plenty of cases where people come in and they become the point person, and then they move on to other things. If they take all the information with them, the process has to start all over again.

In other cases, an organization wanted to have some continuity with their pavement management system. That is sure the best way to go. If an organization is moving into implementing a system and wants think through all of the steps, I would highly advise them to call somebody who has done this before and get their help to talk through it.

People ask me, "Can you give me the names of some organizations that are using MicroPAVER?" Not in every case are they always the best reference, and I don't mean that in a negative sense. It's not that they may not be doing MicroPAVER the right way. They may have customized it to fulfill their specific organizational needs.

I would encourage you do a quick needs assessment of where you are and also build an inventory of what you have to work with. That will really help launch the pavement management process and give you a way of moving forward in the most cost effective way. And certainly building a good contingency plan so you don't get caught down the road with not doing a good hand off or transfer to somebody else who can carry it on.

Blair: So let's talk about the person who came in eight years ago and set up the program. They've gone through a little bit of training perhaps. They've gone ahead and used their own methodology of setting up section names and section ID numbers and the likes of that.

Somebody comes in now eight years later, the data sat on a shelf and nobody has manipulated any predication modeling or work planning or anything. Let's say the system has sat sort of stagnant so to speak. What would be the procedure? Would it be the same procedure for someone starting out from scratch as someone coming in with data that is 8 years old?

Scott:  People want to know how they can take advantage of an existing data set. With respect to PAVER there is a template that has been put together that helps guide you through the process of what you need to have at a minimum from the standpoint of a set of inventory data. So nine times out of ten you are going to be able to utilize some of the data you've got.

If you have existing data, it is in one of three formats. It could be data that PAVER needs and it is in the correct format. Number two is data that PAVER needs, but it is in the wrong format. Or three, it is data that PAVER does not need. So, when you can make the determination of what you've got and make up the difference, it usually is not that difficult. But, as we discussed with the City of Richmond this morning, the most difficult information to collect is going to include the last construction date—which identifies the age of the pavement—which essentially is defined as the last time you did something structural to that segment of pavement and the surface type. The surface type can exist in a lot of different hybrid forms. So, to have those two pieces of information about all the segments in their network moves them forward quite a long ways towards being able to put together a nice, up-to-date, complete set of inventory.

Blair:  Okay, so let's drill down on those three or four key elements. If you are new in setting up a system, or whether you have been given the job, and many of you agency people may be on the move now, and, at the time of this recording, you know you may be at a certain location. By the time this gets listened to over the next couple of years, you might have been moved onto another location, and put into a brand, new implementation of PAVER. So let's walk through a hypothetical situation.

Someone has set up PAVER at a city, and, 6 months later, they get a job at a county and they say, "Hey, I think we should come in here and set up a new PAVER pavement management system for the county." They are a virgin user. They have never done anything. That person sits down, and they try to get the buy-in.

He or she tries to get the buy-in from the county folks and the county commissioners, trying to convince them it will be a great decision for the County to do pavement management. Let's talk about the three or five key elements, and how we go about collecting that data and setting up the database from day one, so it can provide the most robust and accurate results.

Scott: Okay, you first want to put together an inventory set. In PAVER, that consists of 13 to 15 data elements per segment. PAVER also has created a module that allows you to create a PAVER database from a GIS map. So, ideally because GIS is becoming the way of the world everywhere, if you have a GIS map of your pavement network, and, for every one of the records or segments you can identify these 13 or 15 fields of information, you populate that GIS file set. That becomes a shape file.

You can actually type or upload that to PAVER, and PAVER will automatically create a database. At that point you will have your inventory established again, assuming you are able to collect good last-construction data information, good surface-type information, and good section ranking information for every segment. Once you get that done, and you get the inventory established, then the next step, which is a very important one, is making the first round of inspection data collection.

The first time you do it is going to be pretty invasive because you are going to have to do every segment. From that point forward, you may choose to stagger the re-inspection effort. You are then spreading the paint out over a series of two or three years, or whatever the case might be, and the ASTM standard has a lot of governance in terms of how it recommends doing that.

For those who are not familiar with PAVER: It is a sampling inspection process so you are typically inspecting only about 10% of the network. That saves you a lot of time. Once you are able to get the pavement management wheels under you, your inspectors become familiar with the distresses, which is another critical link to the effectiveness of the process.

The inspectors need to be familiar with the distress identification process and carry a manual (**The PAVER Distress Identifica-**

44

*tion Manual*) with them. Once you create that first inspection event, now you've got a baseline you can use to build prediction models and do work planning. Then you are off to the races from the second level.

Blair: Good point on the inspection. Let's talk about that just for a second. Let's take the assumption that the inspection crew has sat through some training, like you mentioned. And again Scott is reiterating training here for those of you who have not had any experience in this genre. Not everyone has the luxury of going into **IPMA Academy (www.ipmaacademy.com)** and doing the online training, but, if you can get a 1 or 2 day training class, it will help your field inspection crew recognize those distresses and get accurate information back into your program.

That is one of the most important things of all, Scott. You can't just rely on hiring a bunch of interns, or part-time help, or maybe the neighbors kids, or something like that for the summer. You need to have somebody who has experience with road building and understands the difference between block cracking, alligator cracking and such. As you go through collecting this data, you are getting about 10% of the network. Now just touch on that for a second if you will.

Even as early as last year, I had people coming up to me and saying, "We are fixated on doing 100% sampling." I tell them you really don't need to do that unless you are doing the keel section of a runway for an Air force base or Hartsfield Jackson Airport (Atlanta, GA), or something like that.

Can you just touch on the importance of the random systematic sampling of 10% of the overall network? Put people's minds at ease, people who are adamant that they need to do 100% sampling on their city blocks.

Scott: This system was designed by the US Army Corps of Engineers. They are phenomenal people who do a tremendous job, and they have been at this for many, many years. This is a tried and tested process. It has an ASTM standard of practice compliance, which says a lot about the rigor they went to in order to establish a repeatable and objective system.

When you establish a section in PAVER, and the boundaries of the section are determined by a pavement manager, 9.5 times out of 10, the distresses within that section tend to be very homogeneous. It really lends itself well to representative sampling.

Because a typical section in PAVER has distresses that are propagating relatively evenly, you would really be wasting your time if you did much more than a 10% inspection. From one sample area to the next, you are going to be collecting the same distress information. You are not collecting any new information from one sample to the next, and you are really wasting your time in the inspection effort.

The way that the PCI (pavement condition index) calculation process is set up, if you have good representative samples, they will calculate a very accurate PCI. The whole process, from a network level management perspective, is designed to help save you time and help save you money without compromising the quality of the data you are going to be working with.

Blair: Good point. And again we are dealing with a lot of cities and counties that may historically have done nothing more than drive the roads once per year, and, you know what I mean, Scott, I'm not here to point the finger and say how bad are you if you are just doing a "windshield survey" (just looking at the roads from the seat of your truck without getting out).

No, I'm saying if you are doing that, it shows you have the intent of having better roads for your city or your county, and kudos to you! Anyone who is out there even with an Excel spreadsheet or a legal pad and an HB pencil, if you are out there doing something proactive, good for you! I guess what I'm saying to these cities and counties that are adamant about getting 100% sampling, there is absolutely no need. It is going to be redundant. If Scott and I were to go out and do the 10%, the PCI ratings results are going to be almost identical as you would obtain if you spent all summer with a group of interns doing 100%.

Scott: And furthermore, in PAVER, the process calculates a standard deviation between PCIs that are calculated for all the samples involved in a section. Without going into all the math and the details that lets you know if more samples are needed in a section that happens to have not such an evenly distributed set of distresses, you always have a back check on that you can use if you are concerned you are not taking enough samples in a specific section.

Blair: Perfect. Okay. So we've covered what I would call mandatory. We want to have, well, let me rephrase, we absolutely have to know a few certain criteria as we set up our database.

Now a database is only going to be as good as the time and effort that is put into setting it up properly. So, we get those samples, locations, and segments. The sections go into the computer, and we are going to have the software staring at us, looking for that last M&R (Major Rehabilitation) date, which is the last time somebody came through and did some sort of major rehabilitation.

Now for those of you who don't know how to collect that data, or use your best guesstimate, or have your staff do the best guesstimate, you know we've had the **IPMA Tip of the Week,** where we've had the fire hydrant, and we taught you guys how to back calculate the base M&R date based on how many overlays we have and when was the subdivision originally built.

---

If you haven't watched that episode, go to our **YouTube Channel IPMATV** and look up that **www.youtube.com/user/Ipmatv segment** on the fire hydrant and back calculating the last M&R date. (as a reminder, if you register your **Book on Better Roads at www.the-bookonbetterroads.com/register** you won't miss a single episode of **IPMA TV**).

---

But, Scott, you did say there was a tool within PAVER that would go back and calculate the last M&R if, for whatever reason, you didn't have that data. Do you want to talk about that for a little bit?

Scott: If you have a lot of sections that don't have last construction data information, and you've exhausted every resource in your organization to try to figure that out, PAVER has a way.

Blair: See they shouldn't have fired that guy who knew it all, right? They should have never let him go.

Scott: (Laughter). PAVER has this tool called the Last Construction Date Back Calculate feature which basically allows you to try to the best of its ability to determine what these last construction dates were by using one of two approaches. One is, you can tell this tool what the average points per year decline of your PCIs are for the families in question, and it will simply back calculate to when it was supposed to be 100, based on that calculation. Then it will change the date to reflect that. Or you can take a model from another organization, or one of the models that are given to you with PAVER, and use that as a model. It will follow that trajectory backwards to the 100 PCI point, and calculate what it thinks that actual last construction date was supposed to be.

Blair: If I understand you correctly, it would be better for the agency to physically go out during the survey and do the best guesstimate on the last M&R date. If they can't do that then let the software tell us its best guesstimate. It is really as simply as going back three or four points each year, and back calculating. If it a road has a PCI rating of 70 now, and you estimate it drops three points per year, it would back calculate 10 years to the M&R. Correct?

Scott: Correct. Correct.

Blair: So a 2015 road with a PCI of 70 would then become a 2005 construction? I'm not that good with math, folks. Sorry and bear with me. So if we've got that out of the way with the last M&R date, we know we have to have the functional class codes. So I guess the City Inspectors who are going out to do the pavement evaluation would do well to have a rollup map of the functional class codes in their van as they go to do that, and then they cross reference it. Can you think of any other method that someone might come up with that data?

Scott: The functional class, or, what the PAVER calls a section rank, is really the easiest of those three items to identify because people largely have that pretty well classified. They know how their collectors, locals, and arterials are all split.

Blair: And common sense has to prevail here. So let me give you an example. If your inspectors go to a job, and they are out there trying to do rut depth measurements, and they can't get on the road because of the amount of traffic going by. Their map says that it is a residential route, but it probably is not a residential route anymore, right?

Let's face it, there are times, Scott, when I go out to do rut measurement, and I literally would take 20 minutes to gather the sample information because I'm darting in and out of traffic trying to not get run over. So, if you question about how your agency has done this functional class code, whether it is arterial, collector, minor collector, etc. or residential, really take a good look at the traffic flow on a Saturday morning or a Tuesday morning at work time. Let's move to the third surface type.

## Surface types.

Blair: I remember Dr. Shahin saying there was a big distinction between an asphalt overlay and how it performed, versus just a simple asphalt on rock base. It is probably a key element if you can get out there and determine that whether you are looking at the curb line to see if it has been overlaid maybe there is some fill of asphalt into the gutter line. How important is that in the overall algorithms as they start to crunch out those PCI numbers?

Scott: It is pretty intuitive for most pavement managers that if you have a full-depth asphalt construction, versus a mill-and-overlay cross section, versus asphalt overlay on top of a concrete slab, versus asphalt on top of some unique base, that there is going to be a difference in terms of how those different cross sections perform over their life cycles.

The purpose of identifying different surface types is to give you the ability to group those sections that have different cross sections into what we call "families," and then allow PAVER to represent those families uniquely using a life cycle model that would be tailored to the dynamics of that specific cross section. That really determines the life cycle model that would be tailored into the dynamics of that specific cross section. And that really increases the level of accuracy with which you are able to perform work planning on all of your segments.

Blair: Sure. So, now you are drilling down to some very specific prediction models based on the functional class code and the pavement section type. With that data going in and being manipulated, as long as we have accurate data in, we can expect to have the most accurate data out at the back end of the program.

Scott: Right.

Blair: Interesting. So, let me ask you this, and I don't mean to put you on the spot here, but you've been doing PAVER for so long and you've dealt with so many agencies, and you've dealt with a lot of users who are just starting, but you've also dealt with some seasoned professionals. Is there any one or two areas that often really surprise you when you are talking to a seasoned MicroPAVER user?

Do you have one tip that you can share that would have an "aha moment"? Share some advice based on your decades of experience here with PAVER.

Scott: I've got one answer that I'll give and I think it would be this: PAVER is designed as an expert system or a decision support tool, and it is designed to replicate what a panel of pavement management experts would do. Understanding that, I think the trap many of us can fall into is if we come into something with too strong of a preconceived idea of how things should be, we may influence the results. And, I think we may limit our ability to really learn, grow, change, and do what would be best in the case of pavement management for our organization.

So, I tell this to people when we get into work planning discussions: I will usually say if you can fine-tune the inputs to the work planning process, which are going to be a quality inventory set, some good solid inspection data, and get your system tables which involve the cost tables, all together nice and tight. Get the prediction models strengthened and make sure everything looks good there. And have inputs to the work planning process. When you look at the outputs of the work plan, you may not like what you see, but let them challenge you.

Blair: Okay!

Scott: Let them suggest to you what you might do better. It is never an issue of things you are doing right now that aren't good, but let's try to do them better.

Blair: Let's use this analogy, Scott. Let's say we have a pretty cool circle of friends who are smart people, a lot of pavement managers and—God knows we've traveled around this country enough to know a lot of really good County Engineers, City Engineers and Pavement Managers. If I could sit down at any one time with a table of 12 expert Pavement Managers, that is what we have with

MicroPAVER. It is literally combining a whole bunch of different recommendations on what could be done with your city's or your county's infrastructure.

Scott: Absolutely.

Blair: So, if you are in a situation where you are used to just doing this, or, maybe doing "worst first" and, all of a sudden, you are presented with this work plan that is doing a whole bunch of things you are not used to considering, I think what I'm hearing here is that you should try to embrace that. Make it a challenge and think of it as if you've just got 12 of your best friend Pavement Managers in a room with you and they are suggesting you do that.

Scott: Absolutely.

Blair: So, at the end of the day, when you do the pavement management implementation, and you follow that work plan that may surprise the agency engineer, all of the sudden there is going to be the big "aha moment". This is what you predict will happen when your advice is followed and the work plan that MicroPAVER suggests year after year, after year is implemented.

Scott: With the PAVER approach to pavement management being what they—US Army Corp and Dr. Shahin—refer to as a Critical PCI method, it simply means that somewhere in the life cycle of your pavement, it becomes more cost effective to think about replacing the pavement as opposed to continuing to try to do some type of repair work on it.

If you can see that concept and understand that in the long run, as you are able to apply the appropriate kinds of funds at the appropriate times during the life cycle, hopefully you know the goal will be to see the positive impact of following the guidelines of MicroPAVER. We hope you will allow some of the specifics of what is happening in your organization to be able to interconnect with it, so it becomes a customized tool to your specific organization. And, hopefully, it will give you better visibility of where you are, where you are headed, and how you can most effectively manage the funds you are dealing with.

Blair: In your experience, anyone who has followed your advice and actually let the work plan dictate what needs to be done, they've had good results.

51

Scott: It is an ongoing process. I think you would be hard pressed to find somebody who has been really trying to use the system that won't say they are really making progress. And they are growing as they add data because it is kind of a feedback loop. They can trim your course of action more effectively. I think they see it happen from year to year as the step-by-step process unfolds.

Blair: So here's a question you might not get that often: What do you do in a city the size of say Richmond, or one of these medium or large sized cities, when you've got five or six people who are going to have access to the database? Do you let one person drive the database and the other people help out? Or do you let four or five people simultaneously manipulate the data and doing things differently?

Scott: That is another one of those "what works best for your organization" kind of questions, but, I would have to say that probably you will be best served if you can find somebody who is your point person. And have somebody who is going to be a "champion," although champion is not the right word because it is already implemented, but you do want to have somebody who is really promoting the cause of your pavement management system within the organization. You need someone being sort of a focal point in terms of the organization's ability to keep everything coordinated and data flow working efficiently. It's especially important if you are going to integrate some of the inspection efforts in-house. You want to manage that probably through one central person.

Other than that, you can store the data on a file server. Many people can access that data and utilize it for a variety of different reasons, running different reports, looking at inventory information, doing a quick check of recent condition, assessment numbers, and accessing data for different reasons and purposes, going into the GIS maps and taking a look at some things.

I think a lot of people can use it, and it is usually better if one person has at least some kind of primary responsibility for it. He or she can keep an eye on it. Then you know, like you mentioned earlier, what happens if this person is going to leave? Let's try to plan for that so we don't get caught short and have to do a lot of stop gap work.

Blair: Great point. So in wrapping up here, Scott, just walk us through, I know we had an intensive day today what with the preservation overall pavement management concept, the **Three-Legged Stool (System of Pavement Management)** and in-place recycling and so forth.

Tomorrow you are going to drill down and walk the city through the 10 or 12 basic steps and make that framework. If you will just in the short amount of time we have, walk through the framework of those 10 top elements in the MicroPAVER program and if anybody has got any more need for more information, they can always contact Scott later. Let's walk through the framework you are going to cover tomorrow.

Scott: In the nutshell, I tell people to look at the toolbar in PAVER from left to right, it is a logical sequence. We start by talking about Inventory and making sure you build an efficient inventory that breaks down your sections or segments logically. That becomes the framework with respect to how PAVER is going to communicate to you. You are going to get PCI information at the section level. You are going to get work plan recommendations at the section level so you want to make sure you break that down efficiently.

Then we talk about Work History. Let's put in some information about what has been done on that segment or section in the past because that is going to tell you why you have the PCI that you have. What have we done or what have we not done? So after talking about work history we move into inspections.

We want to find out how to set up the inspection process, following the ASTM guidelines so we are abiding by the rules and getting good quality PCI data from that effort, making sure our inspectors are very familiar with the inspection, the distress identification catalogues, and from there we talk about the different kinds of reports you can run in PAVER, how can you get different kinds of data out of the program. Then the next major segment really is to build Prediction Models which is going to leverage the organization's data set to build the organization's specific life cycle models for your sections. These take into account things like climate, soil conditions, construction, material types, and all of the unique things that go into how the pavements degrade for that organization.

Once you have the Prediction Models built and tightened up, then we use of system tables to develop good solid cost tables and some maintenance policy tables. Those are all of the things the Work Plan is going to use.

We will wrap it up with a conversation about the Condition Analysis and the M&R Planning Tools, which are really designed to be able to provide the user with the option to run multiple what-if scenarios. It is a very flexible tool, and gives you the option to suggest different budget scenarios, different goal scenarios so you get a good sort of spectrum of things to look at.

PAVER is not a one-size-its-all approach. It is really designed to give you a lot of flexibility to try to take several looks and then decide what your next best steps should be. So that is kind of the sequence we go through.

Blair: Awesome. A pavement management system is not as difficult as it sounds. It is really a straightforward framework. Scott, you did a great job of laying that out. Our advice is—I think we can speak together on this—get some training wherever possible, help to set up your system, don't be daunted by the enormity of the overall scope of setting this up. Once you've got the data into the program you are going to find out it is very easy to crunch some very robust budgets for your city council or for your commissioners.

If anyone has questions how can they contact you? Scott: My e-mail address is pavertechsupport@apwa.net.

Blair: You heard it. Scott McDonald, APM, your **IPMA Advisory Board Member** here. Thanks so much for being part of **IPMA**, the **International Pavement Management Association**. Scott, we sure do appreciate your input and thanks for hanging out with us today on this podcast.

---

Scott is on **Better Roads Radio Session 3**. If you would like to subscribe, you guys know how to do that. You can find us on Sticher Radio, on iTunes or visit us right here at the website **www.betterroadsradio.com**. So glad you could be here. See you next time. Thanks for joining us.

---

There are other types of pavement management software available and, even if you just go out and look at the roads, and rate them on a scale of 0 to 5 or 0 to 10, you might use the Wisconsin Pacers Rating System like the folks in Fayette County, GA, are doing (using the Pacers Rating System from Wisconsin) or at least that methodology.

Be wary though, let's say a DOT has a system called "12345", and they come into your local agency and ask you to consider using it. And they might say your motor grader operator can go out and look at the roads and use their identification techniques. But here is the bottom line, you may have just inherited about 200 million dollars worth of infrastructure. Do you really want your motor grader operator performing pavement distress surveys? (No offense intended, I am a former heavy equipment operator in another chapter in my book of life).

I would highly recommend you get it into a software system that has some history, that's easy to use, that you can print off reports like when the County Commissioner calls you up: the Chairman says, "Hey, I got a extra million dollars to spend." You are going to be able to go in ten minutes or less, and influence that budget scenario.

During our discussion in this book we talk about StreetSaver and MicroPAVER, because these are the two most popular pavement management systems in the world. They are both publicly available, without having to go through a proprietary purchase from a sole source vendor or consulting firm. Furthermore, our consulting side of the business, www.thebarnhardtgroup.com uses these two software systems exclusively for their city and county clients across America.

I specifically like the fact that FHWA recognizes these two systems, and as far as I can tell, they are the only two pavement management software systems that are ASTM 6433 approved.

I would encourage you, as a local agency trying to set up a pavement management system for the first time in your life, to investigate all of the options that are available to you at the time in your specific region and that meet your specific needs.

So, real quick disclaimer here: Again, some of the views we'll talk about in this book are really not views of our Academic Partner (Auburn University), NCAT (National Center for Asphalt Technology) or **IPMA Charter Members**, or the **IPMA Advisory Board**, or any of our members and partners for that matter.

* HYPHEN CAUTION: If a link includes a hyphen as it goes to the next line of text, when you retype the link into your computer **do not include the hyphen**.

Sometimes I might just tell you some personal thoughts as I write this book, and I am open to any and all feedback from readers along the way.

So, we are not here to endorse anyone. I just want to be perfectly clear on that. You see, many of the "non-biased" trade associations and centers we hear from on a regular basis, seem to have their own personal agenda. Believe me, after spending over 30 years in this industry and sitting behind the closed doors of many a board room meeting, it has become all too apparent to me that almost everyone seems to have an agenda.

One difference, my only agenda, as I write this book is to save our crumbling roads, period. As such, I am willing to ripple the water a little bit where necessary to get the results I know we are capable of achieving if we all JOIN together and make this journey happen.

So, what have I learned driving 83,000 miles in an RV? I've banged my head every day for the last 100 days. Well, first of all, because there's not a lot of room inside there. I've learned, perception. You know, I've gone to cities like Flagstaff, Arizona, where they say they have 243 freeze/thaw cycles. So imagine you don't have freeze/thaw to deal with in your particular city or county. What are some of the unique characteristics you may endure in terms of your pavement management in your region? You build a road, and it's going to stay pretty good without the risk of freeze/thaw damage. All of these treatments that are mentioned in this book, whether they are in-place pavement recycling or pavement preservation treatments. They all work!

The pavement management systems work in every city in every county. And along the way I've learned that our US paving contractors can increase their tonnage from 600 million tons to 800 million tons a year (plug in your own country and tonnage increases if you are reading abroad). By simply not allocating funds for sequential overlays and asphalt that is being wasted on the wrong roads at the wrong time for all the wrong reasons, an agency can start moving in the right direction.

Asphalt has a 20 year service life if it's properly preserved. For example, when our **www.thebarnhardtgroup.com** crews go in and do the pavement management, and I take cores with the core drill, it's quite often that I come across a road that's only 22 years old. And it has, 8 sequential hot mixed asphalt overlays on it, based on the core.

If you take 22 and divide it by 8, what is that? Let's round 22 up to 24, 24 divided by 8 is an even 3 years, right? So, I don't know if that was on the election cycle or what, but we cannot continue to do this in America or the world. We're going to be in dire straits if we continue to do that. And there's no reason. And, I brought this asphalt core with me from Canada back in 1999. I actually had to put this through the x-ray at Buffalo Airport.

They said, "What the heck do you have that in your suitcase for?" I said, "Well, man, I'm going to go to America and try to change the world." And I'm still working on it, and all I can say is I don't feel like I'm alone anymore. People like you that have bought this book are helping to support this movement. We have a real movement underway; a growing community of practice for the simple and effective techniques.

This core is 6 inches of foamed asphalt base with two and a half inches of asphalt on top. And I'm not allow to guarantee it or anything for FTC Guidelines, but I could almost guarantee that if I drove back to Wellington

County, where I used to live in Canada, that this road is still in place. And holding up very, very well. And you know what the difference is?

The top one cost about a hundred dollars a square yard (the 10 inch core of sequential overlays). And the bottom one (foamed asphalt base with overlay) costs us about twenty-five dollars per square yard. You guys get the picture?

Gets me to thinking again, by saying, "What if . . . ?" What if there is a better way? What if our grandchildren weren't going to be trillions of dollars in debt? What if the Federal Highways Administration and the White House sent a very strong message down to the local agencies and state DOTs and said, "Thou Must recycle and preserve and manage your pavements instead of, 'You really ought to consider this but here is the money, do whatever you want with it.'"

What if we weren't trillions in debt and we had better roads? What if we didn't have D+ infrastructure with our roadways and bridges crumbling?

What if people weren't dying on unsafe bridges and roads? What if we redirected the funds that we have been wasting on sequential overlays for no reason to placing the hot mixed asphalt overlays on top of recycled and stabilized bases that act as a perpetual pavement so to speak, and here's the kicker, okay?

You may know of a local paving company somewhere in the States or in your own country that goes out and they do a lot of hot mix asphalt paving every day. What if, every time they pulled out of the yard they had a shuttle buggy (MTV or Material Transfer Vehicle) and they were putting 2600 tons a day down? On Full Depth Reclaimed (FDR) roads.

What if? They get more profit. They'll get more tonnage. You know, I think a lot of people in the industry would appreciate more tonnage and more profit. This is happening right now in regions where **The Three Legged Stool System of Pavement Management** is taking off.

For example, I was just in Utah recently doing the Utah Asphalt Pavement Conference, UAPA. Their Executive Director, Reed Ryan, of the Asphalt Paving Association Conference, asked me to come out and bring this message to his contractors. There's perhaps a hundred people in the crowd and half of them were contractors—paving contractors, just like the ones in your city and county.

At the end of the two hours I was presenting I said, "You guys get this?" And they're all like, "Yeah, hell yeah." And they actually came up after and said, "Where can we buy the recycling and preservation equipment? And how many pulverizers should we get?" And yet, other states are resistant to change, and they don't want preservation or in-place recycling or pavement management for that matter. It is common knowledge that even when FHWA puts on a big fancy workshop and they have 17 or so different state DOTs present their findings on how their recycling programs are working, there always seems to be one Negative Naddy in the crowd that stands up in front of all of the other state DOT officials and says something like, "We're not sure that is going to work in our state. We are still doing some research."

REALLY? Should that person even have a job? That is what I would be asking!

So, this **Three Legged Stool System of Pavement Management** is the solution to the problem that I have presented so far in this book. I have the perception from 30 years of construction, 20 years of that teaching, and having flown and driven to every corner of North America. And I know it works. Nevada DOT, right now, to this date, has saved well over 600 million dollars by doing pavement management, in-place pavement recycling and pavement preservation.

I will repeat: They saved 600 million dollars by doing pavement management, in-place recycling and pavement preservation. And now they are going back and re-recycling roads that had been recycled 22 years before. The paving contractors, I guarantee you, are getting the same amount of tonnage or more. Nothing has changed except that their state is doing more with less money, creating a smaller carbon footprint in less time.

"How could it be, Blair, that there are still some hold out states and local cities and counties that are following their dumb ass advice?" you may be asking. One day at a time, the walls will come crumbling down, and each and every state will find their way out of the dinosaur days. They may just put away their 8 track tapes, vinyl records and rotary dial phones, and save their job by doing what is right for this planet. I trust that when you close the last page on this book, and read the case studies I will present to you, that there will be irrefutable proof that we can resurrect our economy and have better roads for all!

Now, I'm going to take you guys back to a few years. Because there is one of my mentors from Federal Highways, Mr. Jim Sorenson. He was a very staunch advocate for pavement preservation, and we sat down in

Jim Sorenson

Charleston, South Carolina, at an expert task group meeting, and he looked me right in the eye and he said, "Blair, if America ever fully gets this . . . ." I think he was alluding to the fact that we feel like we're talking to the proverbial wall.

If we could get people to stop watching the TV, and quit worrying about the Oscars and the Emmys and the Housewives or whatever that show is, if we could get them to think about preserving our infrastructure, our most valuable resource.

Jim emphatically stated to me, "With 4 million miles of roads in America, if this country every fully adopts this pavement preservation thing, there will never be enough equipment manufactured quick enough or enough qualified workforce available!"

And if you folks reading this book have ever tried to hire a motor grader operator lately, you know what it's like, right? It's hard to get qualified labor at any price. Isn't it? Many I know are working in North Dakota now, on the fracking operations. So think about, if you're in Montana and you've got a motor grader operator with your local agency, that can strike a match with a motor grader, he's gone, he's gone over there to North Dakota to work and make a lot of money.

So it's hard to get people to work, it's hard to get the equipment manufactured quick enough, and, right now, a lot of the pavement preservation and recycling equipment is being shipped to other countries. Why? Because they get it. So, heed the warning signs here. You say, "Blair, tell me a little bit more about this theory, why do you think it's going to work?"

Here's the reasoning why. We have 4 million miles of roads here in America. We do 600 million tons a year of asphalt, we recycle 100 million tons of that back at the plant and a little bit in place on the roads, but we really truly only recycle in-place about 3% of our roads. Only a small percentage of the American public knows what preservation is, but we all want to fix the window in our house, or the shingles on our roof if it starts leaking, right?

I'm the first person who wants to fix a window on my house if it's broken, so I did a quick calculation. Because I used to estimate 50 million dollars worth of work a year as the Vice President of a paving and reclamation firm, this is second nature to me. I just always want to figure out numbers and tonnages, and square yards, and all that good stuff everywhere I travel.

If every city and county has a 20% backlog deficit that they are never going to get to, and, trust me when I say that, you may have just inherited it or you may have been saddled with it all your life (refer back to www.better-roadsradio.com episode 5 with Hans from City of San Jose).

If you've got a 10 million dollar backlog deficit of bad roads you're never getting to, that's never going to go away unless we change how we manage our pavements. So based on the **Three Legged Stool System of Pavement Management**, we can increase the tonnage in America to 800 million tons by following the methods outlined right here in this book.

Does everyone understand that? Maybe you can't read my scribbling below. It's like a doctor's prescription here. But it will take 215 years to eliminate the backlog deficit at 20%. This is a very simple prescription for America and for the world.

And like Pat Faster, President of the Asphalt Recycling and Reclaiming Association, told us when he was speaking a while back, some agencies actually have a backlog deficit of 40 to 50%.

---

So, **The Book on Better Roads,** whether you are reading it on your Kindle or listening to it on your CD player, when you get a chance to take a break, check out **www.drivingamericaforbetterroads.com**.

---

If you go to that website, this is what you see: we've got **Driving America**, you can look at some of the free pavement management videos along the

---

* HYPHEN CAUTION: If a link includes a hyphen as it goes to the next line of text, when you retype the link into your computer **do not include the hyphen.**

61

way, from stunning National Parks all over America, and Niagara Falls in Canada. We've got the **IPMA the International Pavement Management Association**, and you are welcome to join as local agency folks at no charge. Just want to remind you that anytime you want to go on there just type in your name and you are a member of **IPMA** no strings attached.

---

As a registered **IPMA** Member you will receive monthly **PDH Power Hour Training Webinars** at no charge as well (PDH and CEU Certificates will be available for a nominal cost). And you will also receive discounted costs for a lot of the other DVDs, CDs, Books, etc. and maybe we'll give you guys a break on the books and that sort of stuff, and occasionally even our **IPMA Academy**, 70 hours of online training, the most comprehensive pavement management, in-place recycling and preservation course curriculum ever built in this lifetime. You get an **Accredited Pavement Management Certification** when you're done. **APM** to put after your name on your business cards or your linkedin profile. On the **www.drivingamericaforbetterroads.com** website, you will also see a link out to **www.betterroadsradio.com**, the only podcast on this planet dedicated to saving our crumbling roads. You can dial into Better Roads Radio 24/7 and listen to a lot of the city and county engineers as we have discussed things along the way.

---

Often, we actually record live podcast sessions from our stages when we are providing live pavement management training. On the same website you will see our link out to *The Book on Better Roads.* We've captured this amazing journey in printed and audio format with the solution out there for all the public to see, and all the city and county engineers in America.

We polled our audience in Boise, Idaho, when we did the conference for IACERS, and they came up with the top 10 things they wanted to see in this book. After that, we sent out an additional request for more information that city and county engineers wanted to see in this book. We got over 250 responses with questions and statements people wanted to hear more about: up-to-date case studies and the likes of that.

We got the **Barnhardt Group Consulting Firm Pacific and Atlantic Division** listed at **www.drivingamericaforbetterrods.com**. **The Barnhardt Group (TBG)** does the pavement management and much of the actual job site work provides the training videos for **IPMA Academy** and the free BONUS content for this Book. TBG is a small boutique firm. We go everywhere in America to do the full-scale pavement management implementation or even QC/QA correlations for local agencies that already have a program in place.

We can take on 6 or 7 jobs a year, period. We book up relatively quickly each year with repeat business. If you are looking at setting up a pavement management system implementation, please let us know as soon as possible. Otherwise, we'll just have to go on a backlog, first come — first served basis.

Also listed under the **Driving America for Better Roads** website is keynote speaking. This is something I really enjoy doing because it gets me out there across this great country, meeting a lot of really great folks. For example, the UAPA conference folks, when I was over there a while back, the guys from Utah DOT asked me to come back in later that season and do a Keynote talk for their annual DOT meeting. They get it.

And finally, **The Marketplace** is where you can buy all the products we are talking about in the book, and the Press Room is where you can find all the latest press releases on all things **IPMA, IPMA Academy,** and **IPMA Academy Live.**

My goal is for the reader of the book to understand all we do back here at headquarters to see how we may be of assistance to your local agency. The placement of this screenshot below is in no way meant to be an advertisement, and if you never hire our firm or join our association, or attend our **APM Training,** that is perfectly okay.

I want you to know me, as I get to know the readership of this book. Along the way, it is only through my network of friends and colleagues in this industry that I have garnered the background information possible to put pen to paper and write this book.

Take for example, Dr. Mike Hetizman from NCAT (National Center for Asphalt Technology). I met Mike up in his laboratory at NCAT a few weeks ago, and he took me for a tour again of that fabulous laboratory just outside the Auburn University campus.

Almost a decade or so ago, Mike and I first met at Iowa DOT. At the time, Mike was the Chief Bituminous Engineer at Iowa DOT, and he was having us provide his staff with the National Highway Institute (NHI) an In-Place Asphalt Recycling Technologies Workshop. Ironically, our journey began when we first met during a tour in his Iowa DOT laboratory. Mike showed me his custom made foamed asphalt testing apparatus.

---

* **HYPHEN CAUTION:** If a link includes a hyphen as it goes to the next line of text, when you retype the link into your computer **do not include the hyphen.**

Screenshot of the www.drivingamericaforbetterroads.com website

Each week I get the opportunity to meet great local agency engineers while we do the pavement management or live training events. In addition, we have the learners enrolled in **IPMA Academy,** and those who provide feedback after purchasing our DVD and CD sets. Then there are the **Better Roads Radio Podcast Sessions**. These are always a bunch of fun!

One of the Podcast Episodes had us in Richmond, Virginia, with Thomas and Kenny. That's podcast episode 4, I believe. Go on and listen to Kenny, Richmond, Virginia, one of the oldest cities in America. "So, Kenny, you did this hot-in-place recycling in Richmond?" He said, "Hell yeah, we did over 240,000 square yards for the very first job here, and we love it."

I promised to stay on the high road for the rest of the book, and I'm never going to talk negatively about the industry, or any one company, or any one state. But I am going to tell it like it is. So I hope you can appreciate that. I'm trying to be perfectly frank. If we all dream big, we can make this happen. But you have to grab the bull by the horns and say, "Damn it, Blair, I get this!" How many people get this so far?

During a talk, I occasionally ask people if they get it. Then I say, "If you do, let me hear you say, "Hell, yeah!" It's usually pretty lame the first time. So I usually say, "Let's do that one more time and pretend we didn't do that last one together." It's always better the second time. If you are ever in one of my audiences, you are now forewarned.

Now further to Chapter 5, if you're wondering how to get more funding for your local agency here's a perfect way to go about doing that. This is an example. I just met with these guys recently when we were in Utah with the City of Provo. They found a way to get more money. Their method is a very innovative way to increase funding and awareness for pavement preservation and rehabilitation.

---

If you want to come up with a few ideas on how to generate more funds for the roads in your local agency, this is a great 6 minute video on the Provo website.

---

Essentially the City of Provo came up with a plan where they tax the residents and businesses differently depending on how many cars a day travel into their businesses, or the library, or the BBQ restaurant, or your house, or the neighborhood. And the tax is going to be like 3 or 4 bucks a month for typical residents.

---

By the way, if you happen to be visiting Utah, and have the opportunity to visit the Arches National Park, or if you'd like to see it, just watch **Driving America for Better Roads Episode 6** right here **http://youtu.be/v8t-kmpozYY**. Most all of our Episodes for **Driving America for Better Roads** are shot inside our National Parks in USA. Next year we will be offering a new book on Amazon called, you guessed it **Driving America for Better Roads – The Journey To Save Our Crumbling Roads.**

---

As with a lot of the core content in this book, during the video episodes of the Driving America series, we talk about pavement management, pavement preservation and in-place pavement recycling along the way. In fact I may be the only person on the road with an RV that packs a guitar and diamond core drill at the same time!

Sometimes when I show up to each at a conference, I also get to play in the band for the reception. Last time I taught at Utah Road School, I got the opportunity to play with the country band on Saturday night, which was made up of the local county commissioners and city engineers. They were amazing musicians with The Intense County Band! You can listen in and watch the video of us playing right here http://youtu.be/rkL2-gYkQ8M.

We're out there every single day trying to spread this message and here's a typical day for me traveling in the **Better Roads Bus**. It's a 950 mile trip.

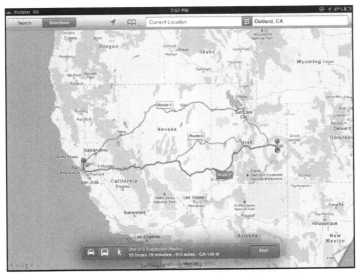

A typical day on the road for the better roads bus

On this particular trip I learned something new. Once you've set your GPS on your iPhone, don't touch it. If you do get to a place with no service, your route immediately goes away and you lose track of where you're going as soon as you hit the refresh button on your IOS device. I've learned, along the way, resist the urge to mess with your GPS route when you are in the middle of nowhere—Death Valley. How many people have heard of Death Valley? So when there is only one diesel fuel station in a 500 mile radius, you gotta get fuel when you can, right? Especially if you are looking for diesel fuel! And the service station can charge whatever the hell they want. The stop for me in Death Valley that day was $5.29/gallon, when at the time, diesel was about a mere $3.50/gallon in civilized land.

66

It's kind of like the guys at Piqua, Ohio, told me. They only have one asphalt contractor and supplier in town. And they have to pay around $130 a ton to get it laid. So what did they do? They did what a lot of you public works officials do. You go out and buy your own paving equipment, right? You buy the asphalt and put it down yourself. So, many turns along the way.

How about this group of signs? There's a one way sign going in, and the exit sign going out is on the same roadway. This is at the Social Security building in Marietta, Georgia. I thought it was kind of cool. I wasn't stopped, and I didn't get a ticket.

Sign, sign, everywhere a sign!

Right outside on the same roadway, I found one of my favorite asphalt situations to photograph (see the core photo on page 68). There is a 7 inch asphalt sequential buildup on the curb and gutter section. It's all fine material, too. You, as publics works managers, may know the same thing I do. Quite often, when we see the built up layers of asphalt, although we like to see a lot of course aggregate down in underlying layers, there isn't any visible. Why? Because we have built up these asphalt roads so quickly over the last 20 years or 30 years, it's all of topping mix. It's susceptible to rutting and shoving as a result, especially in hot climates.

And it's great for making new roads, and making new smooth surfaces to drive on. But, eventually, it causes a lot of grief when we have these deep drop offs. See the photos on page 72.

I ran out of gas in my rental car, and, on my walk down to the gas station, I got a chance to take the photo on page 69. So as you read the book, know that the insanity can stop. No longer should we continue putting overlay, after overlay, after overlay on top of these surfaces and disrupting the hydrology like it was designed for. We can do hot-in-place recycling, cold-in-place recycling, full depth reclamation, soil stabilization on our paved roads. All these treatments work. We can do the rubblization on our PCC concrete pavements, and put a new asphalt wearing surface on.

(If you would like to see a video on the savings that can be had

Effects of sequential fine HMA overlays over time

by using rubblization, remember to register your copy of the book at **www.thebookonbetterroads.com/register** so we can send you content directly to your inbox each week.) We can once and for all save our crumbling roads with eco efficient treatments instead of doing things the same old way.

Best of all these eco-efficient, in-place pavement recycling techniques give us the opportunity to shift the focus from putting asphalt down over, and over, and over where we don't need it. We could be preserving that road with a lesser treatment for half the cost, or a quarter of the cost, take that asphalt and move it over here, and let's start chipping away at our deficit backlog of bad roads.

You guys are going to have the same amount of money to spend, or more. You are going to have a better pavement condition index rating as a

result by using hot-in place recycling, cold in-place recycling and full depth reclamation.

Recall, that putting 83,000 miles a year on in the **Better Roads Bus,** and traveling across this great country teaching, I have also had the opportunity to learn about effective treatments that many engineers have not been made aware of yet. Perception is what I have gained as a result. I have put the miles on so you don't have to. I have met with thousands of city and county engineers in every corner of North America, and spoken to hundreds of pavement managers, world wide. This is an exciting time for everyone involved in pavement management.

I will reiterate, even when you hear about a new treatment for the first time, consider that this very treatment may have already been in use for the last 14 years or more in another region of the country.

---

Any of the free BONUS content that we send you will be of treatments by contractors that have been personally visited by myself or our team. We have spoken to the cities, counties, townships and state DOTs about using these products. They are tried and proven.

---

Don't let the naysayers come into your office and try to convince you these products and services are not going to work in your region. Don't let the naysayers come into your office and convince you that the only thing that works in your area are thin overlays, medium overlays and thick overlays. We no longer have the luxury of depleting our natural resources and

Hot-in-place asphalt recycling with the Re-HEAT train — no overlay required

making new paving products. Take advantage of the in-place recycling techniques, or better yet, preserve your roads from day one, so they don't fall into the critical zone of no return.

There are plenty of high performing pavement preservation treatments that are readily available for you to use. Contractors are stepping up to the plate and building out their network of distributors and applicators. Contractors are spending millions gearing up for the inevitable switch to **The Three Legged Stool System of Pavement Management.**

This systematic approach is working for countless agency engineers across the nation, and for cities and counties just like you readers. So beware of the naysayers for they will soon be exposed for who they are and what they are all about.

Also, if you're a pavement contractor or you're in the paving business, I know you guys with the cities and counties that have your own paving crews would never, ever drive past a pot hole and not put some mix in there, right? How many people reading this book have their own public works paving crew? If you have your own paving crew, and you went up to the job sight after they went through one of the county roads, and they left the road like in the example below, what would you say to them? Is this good job site execution?

Someone's going to get kicked in the ass, right? Hell yeah. And today, on a serious note, 75 people will die on unsafe rural roads in America. And the majority of them will be in the seven southeastern states, mostly due to

Example of poor planning and execution on the job site

these dangerous edge drop offs. See page 72.

It's such a shame. So if you are ever out there paving, I encourage you pavement managers to put some dirt in those shoulders, or RAP (Recycled Asphalt Pavement). A lot of times on the consulting side of the business when we are doing the pavement management, we keep a Top Ten List of items

71

Deadly unsafe edge drop off on paved roadway surface

Example of poor planning and workmanship on paving project

that could be huge liabilities for the county or the city that we are working for. We find edge drop-offs on a regular basis. I encourage you to keep a Top Ten List as well while you are out there doing the pavement distress evaluations.

We always try to let the folks know they need another 10 or 12 loads of dirt out here for shoulder dirt. We can't have what is depicted above any longer. We can't have this type of liability hanging over our heads as department managers at our public works agency.

Don't let the paving crews pave over the manholes and water valve boxes, right? Let's get some riser rings or adjust the manholes accordingly.

Plugged inlet

How about this one? How many readers have seen this before in their city or county? That's an inlet, right? Isn't the water supposed to go in there? Right? You guys are still here reading, right? What do you see there? Water is supposed to shoot across the roadway in the photo below and go into that inlet right? How about that? (Quite often I am down on my hands and knees taking these pictures, and I wonder if someone will run me over one day. Will anyone care or find me?) So, clearly, that's not good. Eventually the water goes right over the sidewalk and into someone's basement, right?

Yeah. So, the core pictured on page 75 was taken next to the drainage disaster! Seven inches of asphalt, sequential overlays over a few short years, and that's the reason why the inlet is all blocked out. We don't need to do that anymore, not with all the knowledge and technology that is possible today!

Example of poor sheet flow due to excessive multiple overlays

If you would like to receive a template of the sheet that we use to do our on the ground pavement distress evaluations be sure to register your book at **www.thebookonbetterroads.com/register** and we will send you weekly tips, tricks and best practices directly to your inbox each week.

I promised one city engineer after he said, "Blair, you really pick on a lot of stuff that's happened over the last 20 or 30 years."

I said "Yes, I am guilty."

He said, "I think you should stop picking on the stuff that's happened in the past."

I said, "OK, I promise I won't pick on stuff that's happened in the past, but I'm damn sure going to try to predict the future. And I'll do my best to change the way we do things with our pavement management going forward!" So I hope you readers are on the same page of music with me.

The photo on page 76 shows a couple of cores that I took out in Utah at U.S. Army Corp's Dugway Proving Ground. They've done a great job over the years of putting very coarse asphalt layers out there, making for a really good pavement matrix and structure. They could drive tanks on this all day long. And they put a lot of crack seal in there, that's good. They preserved

Example of sequential fine overlays over short time span

their asphalt pavements well. The core on the left is probably over 60 years old.

And I'm okay with that, but the point I'm trying to make here is when it comes time to pick the right treatment, to make the rehabilitation technique selection under **The Three Legged Stool System of Pavement Management**, this is when you really need to do network level coring. From the core log, and having done this personally in this case, I could tell this section of roadway was a little delaminated, in other words, the core was coming apart when I took it out.

The best way to take care of this road—it might have been a good hot in-place or cold in-place recycling candidate—but I'd feel a lot better about going through this section of roadway that was cored and evaluated with a full depth reclamation train. Then putting it all back together again into one homogeneous blend—literally gluing it all back together. How about you readers? Same thing? Because if you have a core that you see delamination like you see here, it's always a good idea to put it all back together along the way. Now you may have sections of paved roads that you core, depending on where the delamination shows up, and the road may still be a good cold-in-place recycling candidate as opposed to full depth reclamation, but it will likely never be suitable for hot-in-place recycling in this example.

How about the photograph on page 77? Cracked filling, crack sealing. Little picture here for you to think about. So, maybe a little overboard, right? With the pavement preservation treatment there, right? So if you figure the crack filling crack sealing is a approximately buck a linear foot, there could be upwards of a hundred dollars in any one square yard there. Would you all agree?

We probably could have gone in and done 6 inches of bituminous or chemical base stabilization with 2 or 2½ inch cap on top for about 25 dol-

Coring is essential for the Three Legged Stool ystem to work well

lars per square yard instead of all the crack filling and crack sealing that was wasted here. So, at one point, I definitely want to make sure that we are doing the right treatment on the right road at the right time with the right contractor for the right reason.

---

Any questions so far? If so, shoot me an e-mail to blair@ipma.co.

---

You may be asking, "What are the benefits to spending a few cents per square yard to put this **Three Legged Stool System of Pavement Management** into place, Blair?"

Well, again I say, if I walked up to you and said, "Hey, if you give me two cents, and I gave you back ten bucks would you be happy?"

This is essentially what is happening when you take the time to learn how to implement your pavement management program, and marry it to eco-efficient, in-place pavement recycling and preservation!

Perhaps a little too much too late with the crack sealing operation?

Moreover, because you will soon have a comprehensive computerized data base full of your entire inventory of pavements, functional class codes, and aligned them with their respective treatments in the decision tree, you will be able to make some very robust calculations, clear concise presentations to your commissioners and council, and quick decisions on what to do with your new found sources of funding.

For example, I can use my friends and colleagues up in Piqua, Ohio. Their City Manager came back and said to them in public works, here's an extra half a million dollars, you can do more mill and inlays this year.

Because of the fact that they have a pavement management program in place, not only could they see which candidate selections of roads required mill and inlay, they could also budget for taking care of some of the more deteriorated roads down the curve into the red zone with things like full depth reclamation (FDR).

In a matter of a few short minutes, these decisions on where the additional funds should be allocated are computed by the software, in this case StreetSaver Pavement Management Software.

Since most cities in the US and Canada saw an extremely cold winter, a lot of the roads are now so far gone that they almost have to all be pulverized and rehabilitated with the FDR process. Because the deep freeze cycle has been extra bad this year, and with the amount of moisture in a lot of our roads, my advice would be to take whatever you've learned in the past about mill and inlay, and whatever state you're from, just have a look at the other options that are out there.

I would definitely encourage you to take a loaded dump truck out there on your candidate selections of roadways for mill and inlay, lift that rear mud flap up with a bungy cord, and watch carefully as you slowly drive the dump truck over your potholed and alligatored areas.

If you see any more than about 20% of areas that would required deep patching with hot mixed asphalt on the candidate roadway, I would urge you to consider doing an FDR treatment with some sort of wearing course on top in lieu of conventional mill and inlay or overlay treatment.

---

Want to read about FDR? You wonder why I seem so passionate about this stuff, well, I knew back in the 90s this in-place recycling method worked. Click here on your Kindle Reader **http://thebarnhardtgroup.com/wp-content/uploads/2010/06/Asphalt-Contractor-1999.pdf** or check out the resources tab at **www.thebarnhardtgroup.com** for The Road to Savings Gets Recycled by Asphalt Contractor. Here is a 2005 magazine article on the FDR process that I wrote for FHWA Public Roads Magazine. Just go ahead and click here **http://thebarnhardtgroup.com/wp-content/uploads/2010/06/The-Way-to-a-Better-Road-Public-Roads-FHWA.pdf** on your Kindle Reader or go to **www.thebarnhardtgroup.com** and look in the Resources Section for **One Way for a Better Road, FHWA Public Roads Magazine**. By the way there are a bunch of articles not only on the TBG website, but just spend a few hours on a Google search when you get a chance. You may be amazed at the abundance of success stories out there. Kind of makes you wonder why the naysayers are still muttering? For an article that I wrote in April 2011 on the hot in-place with Re-HEAT process, click here on your favorite reader **http://www.roadsbridges.com/sites/default/files/60_PE%20Market_0411RB.pdf** .

---

Again, while you are taking the time to learn by reading this book, take a few notes along the way, but know that all I am talking about works across the globe successfully. Even if some states are hold out states, and there are naysayers on your left and naysayers on your right, consider the source.

If you're not familiar with some of the treatments in the book, do a little research on your own on this great thing we call the internet! For example, you might hear locally in your neighborhood that the microsurfacing is "snake oil," but in Tennessee for example, you know they are doing millions and millions of dollars for local agencies and the Tennessee DOT.

I'm not sure about Kentucky. I can't remember reading too many articles about their pavement preservation program recently, but if you do what I do, for you guys that want to follow what is going on across the nation, just set up some Google Alerts.

If you're pretty savvy on the computer, just type in Google Alert on things like hot-in-place recycling, microsurfacing, cold-in-place recycling, high density mineral bond and the likes of that. You will start to see these articles come up as the press releases are sent out by the cities, counties and the companies that provide the materials and services.

Sometimes you'll hear about cities and counties in North Dakota doing 2.5 million dollars with these treatments on one job alone. So that's some good advice that I'd like to share with you guys.

---

Set up some Google Alerts. Just go to www.google.com and make some alerts and then every day you'll get notified by email what is going on in other parts of the country and the world with any of the treatments that we mention in this book. This way you will be better prepared to deal with the naysayers when they start going over your head trying to talk to your elected officials. And I can assure you with some degree of certainty that depending on where you live, this IS going to happen.

---

So, for two cents a square yard, whether you do it yourself or you hire a consulting firm to do it, you can save yourself about 10 dollars a square yard by picking the right treatment, on the right road, at the right time, with the right contractor and for the right reason.

And I've known about this since about 1996. This is how long I've been doing this, and it's 2014 now, so that's almost 20 years, right? Every day I've tried to spread this message, and some days, I felt like I was doing it alone. But now I know that there is a lot of help out there; a lot of agencies are pulling together. We're going to make this work. Once and for all.

This is my crew in the photograph below, with the full depth reclamation pulverizer passing the cold in-place crew back in the mid 90s. And I thought at this time, this was the biggest no-brainer of all time.

The other shot on the next page is from the same time frame and is quite a unique shot. One day, one job, alone we had this operation going on in Middlesex County in Canada, Ontario—if you've ever been there. This is cold in-place recycling with emulsion. We're loading up and taking it to another midland mix paver around the corner. Two cold in-place jobs were going on the same time as my full depth reclamation crew was right around the corner working for the Township. With full depth reclamation and making foamed asphalt, like you see in the cores I show quite often at live events.

A rare and vintage shot of my crew in Canada at work, mid 90s

1996 folks. How many people were in their jobs in 1996 taking care of the roads? So let me just ask you, how many people remember 8 track tapes? Yeah, I know some of you readers get that, and some of you younger engineers will have to ask your mentors what we are talking about. It's been a long journey, hasn't it? We've gotten a lot better at technology along the way, I have to admit.

So, some people might say, "Blair, what the heck do you know about me? I'm a local agency person, I'm a city engineer, I'm a county engineer." Guess what? In 2005 we got the call from CH2MHill and someone on

Three in-place recycling jobs going on at the same time, mid 90s

the other line said, "Do you think that your Blount Construction can take care of all the public works for City of Sandy Springs? We are putting a bid together to run the largest privatized city in America." And how did we answer that? "Hell, yeah!" Right? So for a year, I worked on putting this bid together for our firm to provide CH2MHill with all of the City of Sandy Springs Public Works Department people and equipment.

And then, all of a sudden one morning, I woke up, and I had 21 guys working for the City of Sandy Springs. Things at Blount Construction got a little exciting for a while as I had to rush to set up a yard, get anti-icing chemicals, salt and sand ordered in advance of the winter, and the Public Works thing set up. Everything you guys have to worry about. There was one significant difference, however, between Sandy Springs and your agency. Sandy Springs had no income for the first year as a newly incorporated City. They had no tax revenue collected on the night of Incorporation.

We had to go out and basically make everything work for little or no money in the first year. That was really the very first year when I started thinking about building out the concept of **The Three Legged Stool System of Pavement Management**.

So, again, I can't stress this enough: Every city engineer, every county engineer, every pavement manager, every road superintendent, everywhere in this world, you are all set up for failure. You're screwed. You guys know that, right? There's nothing you can do to please the county or the city because they are not giving you enough money to do what you need to do to maintain or increase your current PCI (Pavement Condition Index). It's not the county's fault. It's not the city's fault. Maybe the County Commissioner doesn't know there's not enough money.

I remember being in one county doing the final presentation, and no sooner had I sat down after telling them they needed another 2 million dollars, that the guys came up from the EMC. They just crashed their ambulance and needed another $300,000 to get another one.

Everybody needs money, right? Look, if the road isn't drivable folks, the new ambulance can't drive down it to get to the patient. So, I really do

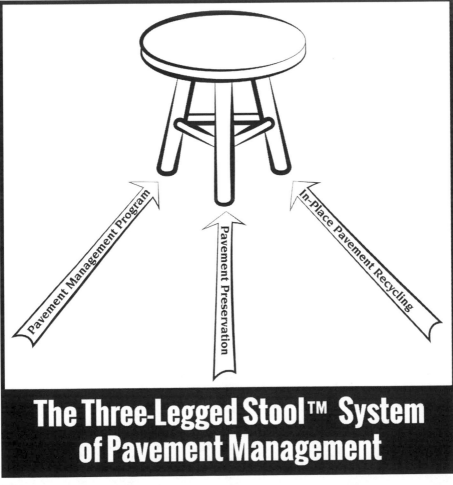

# The Three-Legged Stool™ System of Pavement Management

feel for you pavement managers. If you thought you were screwed now? What I'm about to show you is even worse.

So here's a guy, Hans Larson, P.E., who has been doing pavement management, StreetSaver for the last two decades. He's doing in-place recycling, and he's doing pavement preservation. And he's winning awards, like from **IPMA** and from the Green Roads Foundation.

Just like you may have read in Part One, but well worth reiterating, Hans has 20% of the money he needs to spend on roads in the City of San Jose. So, in a city where we have Google self driving cars taking us places, and the smartest people working in high tech industries, we haven't figured out a way to generate enough tax dollars to keep the roads in good working repair.

Hans and his team has a 400 million dollar backlog deficit of bad roads he's basically never getting to. And to make matters worse, they've divided it into 900 high priority center lane miles. And to make that even worse, they only have enough money to fix 450 of those high priority lane miles of roads. And, again, I'm not pointing a finger at Hans, and saying their team is bad, or The City Fathers are bad; they're actually really good. They are really smart people. They just don't have enough money to go around.

---

So, they're looking at getting a quarter percent sales tax, and you can listen into all of the details here at the **www.betterroadsradio. com podcast show Episode 5**. Better Roads Radio is the only podcast in the world dedicated to saving America's crumbling roads.

---

If things continue without getting more revenue, check this out. In 2020, he'll have an 870 million dollar backlog deficit. This is why the three legged stool system will work. The paving contractors have nothing to fear. This is never going away. They will never get to it unless we can figure out how to get more money.

So, no longer do we have to have crumbling roads like this. Page 84 shows a typical StreetSaver graph I use when we go do our final report. And I make the announcement to the City Councilors, the Mayors, the County Commissioners. I say, "Ma'am, you have a 2.63 million dollar backlog right now. It's on its way up to 6 million dollars, if we don't get more money."

In this situation you would hear me typically say to the Council or Commission, "The Pavement Condition Index (PCI) at present is a 71. You have a really good system of roadways. It's a pavement condition index many

---

* HYPHEN CAUTION: If a link includes a hyphen as it goes to the next line of text, when you retype the link into your computer **do not include the hyphen.**

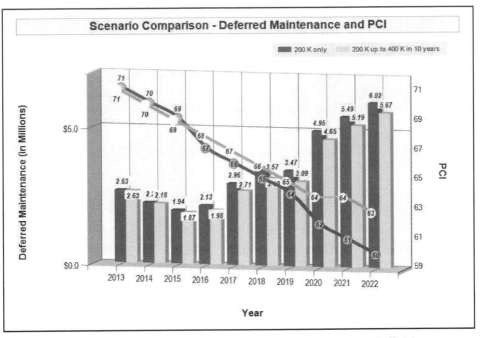

Typical downward spiral PCI vs funding plot we present to elected officials

would be very happy with. It is also pretty darn good when you consider you can really only get to an 84 or an 86 at best with your Network Level Average PCI. You can never get to 100."

I would go on to say, "That PCI of 71 is going to go down to a 60 if we don't get more funding for your agency." Ya'll get this?

---

If you haven't done so already, go ahead and register your book here at **www.thebookonbetterroads.com/register** and we will be sure to get the video of this presentation sent out to your inbox. This way you will see the pain and anguish in my facial expressions as I go through this rant with a live audience.

---

You readers, do you get this graph? You figure it out? Yeah? I bet those listening to the Audio CD Box Set for **The Book on Better Roads** understand what I am talking about. Now, here's where things get a little tricky. And this is kind of why we put this session together as an **IPMA Academy LIVE** event in Georgia and California, along with some special Road Schools like Purdue and Utah LTAP. We wanted to get this vital information out to you ASAP so you could tell others in your **Circle of Pavement**

**Management RockSTARs.**

The US Department of Justice recently made a clarification of what is pavement preservation and what is an alteration. And it's not really congruent with what we've heard from our Federal Highway folks in the past. And Federal Highways has done an amazing job getting sustainability into the MAP-21 (US Transportation Bill) and promoting in-place recycling and pavement preservation.

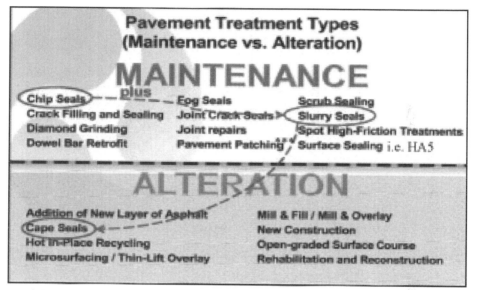

It is imperative that the practical pavement manager understands this definition

You know, they paid to publish the BARM: ***The Basic Asphalt Recycling Manual***. You know they paid to upgrade the NHI class I've been teaching across America over the last decade. The National Highway Institute class. They really have been very big advocates for pavement preservation and in-place recycling. In the past hot in-place and cold in-place were considered pavement preservation, but here is what has happened:

It seems like the US Department of Justice has come in and trumped Federal Highways. They're serious people. They're saying if you do a fog seal that's okay, but if you do pavement patching, which means just the throw-and-go pothole stuff, don't cut it out, don't zip it out, don't dig it out and make it a really good patch work, otherwise it's going to be an alteration.

If you use scrub seal, if you do slurry seal, if you do like high density mineral bonding, often called the HA5 treatment, that's okay. You don't have to do all of your ADA upgrades as these techniques are considered "Maintenance," based on the informational slides presented in a recent DOJ/FHWA Webinar and depicted on page 85. (The circles and lines are my own.)

But as soon as you do micro surfacing, or a cape seal, or if you were to do a chip seal and put a slurry seal on top at a later date, it's now called a cape seal, and it now becomes an "alteration." Now you might say, "Blair, what does this have to do with me?" It means if you are in a city anywhere in USA, and you have a 3 foot sidewalk in a subdivision that needs some kind of rehabilitation treatment, the whole project is now catagorized as an "Alteration" and every intersection has to be brought up to current ADA standards.

We all benefit from the new ADA accessibility standards, but, if I'm going to go in and recommend as part of our pavement management program, that we do 3 miles of roadway with microsurfacing or, say, cold in-place recycling, and let's say it's for Converse, Texas, where all the roads are heaved because of the Houston clay, the bad news is depicted in the photo below.

I check in with Carl, and he's planning chip seals. I said, "Carl, you keep doing chip seals and maybe throw in a little bit of pothole patch in the big deep depressions, but, buddy, if you go in there and do hot in-place, which Federal Highways considers a pavement preservation technique, or

This new 3 foot wide walkway would need to be upgraded per DOJ Alterations - ADA standards.

cold in-place, which Federal Highways considers preservation, Department of Justice is going to make you do all the ADA upgrades on this 3 mile section that we need to fix.

And here's a slide below from the Utah DOT folks who were saying chip seals are 2 bucks a square yard, and the smoother microsurfacing is $2.15 a square yard. The thought arose: maybe we could consider doing microsurfacing on everything and not do chip seal anymore. And I said, "If you start doing everything with microsurfacing, then you're also going to have to add in all the ADA transitions and upgrades as well. Today, you've got to know the difference between alterations and maintenance."

If you thought we were already screwed, well, now we've got this on our hands. You know the stuff that we talked about with Hans Larson, PE, at the City of San Jose—the budget shortfalls. His scenarios we discussed in the podcast episode for **Better Roads Radio** didn't even include the most recent DOJ ADA clarifications.

Slide from UAPA 2014 conference by Howard Anderson, UDOT

So, it's really bad what's going on right now. You might say, "What if I get caught, Blair?" Who's going to catch me? Right? Were you guys thinking that? Who's going to catch me? Well, the same fancy lawyers that sued the pants off big box retail stores, I suspect they are going to come to your cities and your counties, because lawyers need income for their offices, and, if they find out you're doing something that is not in compliance with Department of Justice, they may try to sue your city or county.

If you have been found guilty, what I'm hearing from my friends and colleagues, you could be forced to do all of your ADA Transition Plan in one single calendar year.

I hope this never happens to you but a good friend of mine is a County Engineer in Washington State. She said that one of her bucket truck drivers accidentally left the bucket truck boom and bucket up in the extended position and drove off. As he drown away the raised bucket hit and bent one of the uprights, ever so slightly. It cost her county $1.6 million in upgrades to the signalized intersection and to also to bring that intersection up to current standards for DOJ and ADA compliance.

So, in wrapping this up for this chapter, if you only remember one thing, you guys can take a picture of this if you want while it is sitting on your screen or in your book.

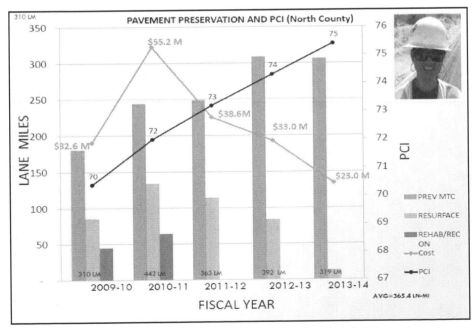

Imelda Diaz, PE, APM, IPMA Advisory Board Chair and LA County graph

On your iPhone, Android or your Blackberry, go ahead and take a snap shot of this photo above. If you leave here and only remember one thing, this is the one graphic I'd like you to remember. So, our Chair of the **IPMA Advisory Board** is Imelda Diaz who works for LA County, California.

This is a slide from LA County. It is from the northern part of the county. And what's happened over a 5 year period, this is **the Three Legged Stool System of Pavement Management** at its best, right there, larger than life. I think about the few short years ago when Imelda and I sat down in a sushi restaurant in Pasadena, CA. I asked her if she would be willing to accept the position of Chair of **The International Pavement Management Association (IPMA)**.

It was here at this restaurant that she wrote on a napkin with me, this mission statement for **IPMA**:

---

The **International Pavement Management Association** will revolutionize the practice of pavement management through expert education, comprehensive technical training programs and professional certification for the world.

---

And here's how we follow through with our **IPMA** Mission Statement: You get money, you spend it wisely, you raise the condition of the roadways from 70 up to 75, and you eliminate the backlog deficit of bad roads. You'll notice above in the graphic of LA County Pavement Management Program that there is no red there anymore. The backlog deficit of bad roads are completely gone. And now Imelda is managing her network for an average cost of $3.41 a square yard.

If this cost a hundred bucks to get all these layers of asphalt on the 10" core I presented earlier in this book, and it costs 25 bucks per square yard to put a new FDR with HMA overlay together for a longer life service life, you may start to put the puzzle together about how LA County's backlog deficit of bad roads was totally eliminated. Does everyone reading this book understand that? And now Imelda simply has to go out and perform pavement preservation techniques to keep their good roads good to make them last longer.

You get that, folks? Yeah, it's pretty good if you are getting this now. For those of you who haven't gotten this whole **Three Legged Stool System System of Pavement Management** down yet, go back and re-read the last few chapters, then catch up with us later. Because if you can't grasp the simple concepts outlined here to date, it will be even harder to follow us deeper into the next chapters as I outline the framework for you.

I'm going to end with this. Now, let me tell you guys a little story here. Hockey pucks are hard, right? So I'm up in Canada, skating around the ice rinks playing a little hockey, and I shattered my kneecap one day, last game of the season, last ten seconds of the game. My wife had us booked for a trip to Cancun, Mexico. She had to be the one to unpack the suitcases because the surgeon said, "Don't leave the country."

And we were going to surprise the kids, so she hated me for three years after that for shattering my kneecap. I was lying on the ice; I went knee first into the boards. And ice is hard, you know what I'm saying? Knee first into the boards. I was lying there, and I was in pain. Man, I'm telling you right now, I was in pain.

But, what was even more painful was that it was now time for the public skate. At 2 o'clock all those kids wanted to get on the ice and skate. So, they let my ass lie on the ice. The arena attendants came out and put orange cones around me. The Zamboni went around me as he cleaned the ice. At 2, those damn kids began using me as target practice, putting ice in my face, you know how they stop on the ice and squirt out the snow?

So what did I learn from that along the way? I learned that ice is hard. My knee still hurts now, the doctor told me he was going to leave my kneecap out if it was broken in more than 3 places. It was. The doctor said, in the driest doctor dialogue you could imagine, "You'll look like a gimp when you wear shorts." I grabbed his arm and said, "Doc, you tie that puppy back up and wire it up. I'll quit playing hockey for life."

The one thing that sticks out in my mind is I always remember being in the rink and looking down in the penalty box. I spent a lot of time in the penalty box just for stuff I said.

They kept the game pucks in a bucket of ice, It'd be full of ice, and as a puck went up in the crowd, the ref would come along and would reach down in the bucket of ice pull out another ice cold hockey puck. In real hockey you have real pucks, and in practice hockey you have sponge pucks.

This job that you have, being a real pavement manager, this is real hockey, we are using hard, cold pucks, and you could get hurt by making the wrong decision.

So, please listen to me when I tell you, if you listen to folks like us talk about how great this pavement management stuff is, and someone comes into your office from the DOT, maybe it's a high ranking US DOT official, maybe even from Federal Highways, or a concerned citizen, or an industry trade association member, and that person starts telling you that whatever Blair is talking about in his little book, whatever the guests on his **Better Roads Radio Podcast** are talking about, whatever the folks in all those Video Case Studies are talking about, whatever the **IPMA Academy LIVE DVDs** from other speakers say, if that naysayer starts telling you crap that only thin overlays, medium overlays and thick overlays will work, just put your **IPMA** filters on, okay?

If the naysayers start saying you can have your motor grader operator evaluate your roads and do the pavement distress evaluation, put on your **IPMA** ears, and say, "Hey, you know what? I'm not really buying this, Charlie. You might want to just pack up your stuff and get on out of my office because I've already made 7 or 8 calls to other cities and counties in America who are doing this. I called Richmond, Virginia, and they did 240 thousand square yards of hot-in-place recycling, and they love it."

These guys have been doing HA5 (High Density Mineral Bond) for the last 12 or 13 years in Utah and for customers in three states. They love it. It's working well.

Then there are guys supplying rejuvenating fog seals, scrub seals, many other tools in the proverbial toolbox. I guess my advice to you is realize that there's fake stuff and there's real stuff, and what we're talking about is real. That's all I'm going to say for now.

---

As a quick reminder, if you haven't already signed up with **IPMA** as a local agency, please consider doing so now at **www.ipma.co**. For all agency folks it is no charge, so this is the biggest no brainer in life. When doing so you get the one hour **IPMA PDH Power Hour** each month directly to your inbox along with some very special benefits. As a private sector representative, **IPMA** is 5 bucks a day to be part of all this excitement, so please consider JOINING US!

---

# Chapter 5 —

# The Three Legged Stool System of

# Pavement Management — Part 2

Welcome back, everyone! Before we get started, I want to take you all out and watch a little movie from one of our **IPMA Academy** Alumni, Mr. Jonathon Heese, APM, from Araphaoe County, Colorado, USA. In the next 10 minutes you will see and hear the effects of someone who has gone through 70 hours of online training with **IPMA Academy**. Even if you haven't registered your book yet, you can still click to watch or type http://youtu.be/_D4_kx-7nPg into your favorite browser to check this out! Thanks, Jon, for sharing your story with us! And I received a special request from Jon to include this statement from him: "Thanks to the guys back in the office for their willingness to take a critical look at what we are doing to see if improvements can be made going forward."

I love the fact that no longer am I alone in this effort, in fact, each and every day when I wake up, breath, exercise and look at my e-mail and listen to voice mail, I realize that there is an entire army of **Three Legged Stool** soldiers out there marching to a common goal of common sense pavement management.

I would like to share a link http://on.ted.com/h08eK here from a TED Talk delivered by Derek Sivers on how to start a movement. Here is the transcript for the TED Talk by Derek Sivers for those of you reading the printed book with no internet access:

## Transcript begins

Derek Sivers: So, ladies and gentlemen, at TED we talk a lot about leadership and how to make a movement. Let's watch a movement happen, start to finish, in under three minutes and dissect some lessons from it.

First, of course, you know, a leader needs the guts to stand out and be ridiculed. But what he's doing is easy to follow. So, here's his first follower with a crucial role; he's going to show everyone else how to follow.

Now, notice that the leader embraces him as an equal. So, now it's not about the leader anymore; it's about them, plural. Now, there he is calling to his friends. Now, if you notice that the first follower is actually an underestimated form of leadership in itself. It takes guts to stand out like that. The first follower is what transforms a lone nut into a leader. (Laughter) (Applause)

And here comes a second follower. Now it's not a lone nut, it's not two nuts — three is a crowd, and a crowd is news. So, a movement must be public. It's important to show not just to the leader, but the followers, because you find that new followers emulate the followers, not the leader.

Now, here come two more people, and immediately after, three more people. Now we've got momentum. This is the tipping point. Now we've got a movement. So, notice that, as more people join in, it's less risky. So, those that were sitting on the fence before, now have no reason not to. They won't stand out, they won't be ridiculed, but they will be part of the in-crowd if they hurry. (Laughter) So, over the next minute, you'll see all of those that prefer to stick with the crowd because eventually they would be ridiculed for not joining in. And that's how you make a movement.

But let's recap some lessons from this. So, first, if you are the type, like the shirtless dancing guy that is standing alone, remember the importance of nurturing your first few followers as equals, so it's clearly about the movement, not you. Okay, but we might have missed the real lesson here.

The biggest lesson, if you noticed — did you catch it? — is that leadership is over-glorified. That, yes, it was the shirtless guy who was first, and he'll get all the credit, but it was really the first follower that transformed the lone nut into a leader. So, as we're told that we should all be leaders, that would be really ineffective.

If you really care about starting a movement, have the courage to follow and show others how to follow. And when you find a lone nut doing something great, have the guts to be the first one to stand up and join in. And what a perfect place to do that, at TED.

**Sivers transcript ends**

When Imelda and I sat down and wrote the mission statement, I felt like there were only a handful or two of us at the time who were crazy enough to think we could actually make an impact on our economy in this country by doing things slightly different than we had been historically doing. Here's what we wrote:

---

The mission of **IPMA, the International Pavement Management Association,** is to revolutionize the practice of pavement management through expert education, comprehensive technical training programs and professional certification for the world.

---

When Jon sent me the presentation I mentioned above, it reminded me of all of the **IPMA Academy Alumni** who had gone through the online training, received their **APM** or **Accredited Pavement Manager Certification,** and have now gone on to change how things are done at their agency.

Moreover, they have not only changed their agency for the better, they have told their friends and colleagues in the industry for the better. (It has been said by one of my mentors that each and everyone of us have a close circle of about 300 friends and colleagues whom we can influence.) So, much like the vivid description that Derek Sivers makes above in his TED talk, it is because of our first round of learners that went through **IPMA Academy** from all walks of life and backgrounds. They are the ones whom I would like to personally thank for starting our movement, for igniting the fire under their agencies. To stand up and say, we don't need to just mill and inlay any longer. We don't need to wait 20 years to do something with our roads. We can preserve them for a few dollars instead of wasting ten dollars a square yard on them for no reason.

Here is a BIG SHOUT OUT to all of our **IPMA Academy Alumni,** those who are in the program, and to those of you who are spreading the message of **The Three Legged Stool System of Pavement Management** across the planet. Without you, we would be nothing.

I just want to take a moment to remind everyone that we talk about MicroPAVER and Street Saver Pavement Management Software in the book as these are the two most popular software programs out there for doing pavement management. I do, however, encourage you to use whatever software you are most comfortable using, and further ask that you do a thorough and exhaustive search as to what programs are available at the time you are reading this book.

MicroPAVER and StreetSaver are the two that we teach when I do the UC Berkley ITS Webinar Series. In fact UC Berkeley asked me why I was only talking about StreetSaver and MicroPAVER, and I had to do my research and find out that MicroPAVER and StreetSaver are the two most popular software systems out there. Again, on the consulting side of our business at TBG, we use these two programs exclusively at the time of writing this book.

On the teaching side, we use these two programs at **IPMA Academy** extensively, but do mention in passing other types of programs that are available publicly. As with Berkeley ITS Department, they said it was okay for me to talk about those two software programs based on their popularity, but they made it clear to their learners, as I am making it clear to you, in no way shape or form am I trying to endorse any one product, service or vendor by their mention in this book. So, I just want to make sure that everyone understands that these are some of my own personal views as I write the book and not **IPMA** or the **IPMA Advisory Board Members**, or any of the Universities that we teach for or Auburn University.

Sometimes I just put on my own hat, and I come up with a few things I feel I must say. Remember, you can never feel bad about something you didn't say, right? But here's what I learned from my mentors, if someone in this audience of readers we have grown doesn't get a little irritated because of something I say, then we are not doing America justice, then we are not really doing anything to change our current economic situation.

That's why we say **get the right treatment, on the right road, at the right time, for the right reason and with the right contractor.** And not just because it is an election year. Again, 215 years is how long it will take our hot-mixed-asphalt paving contractors to clear up our backlog deficit of bad roads based on the simple calculations I made one night in a few short minutes on an airplane trip.

Go ahead and let your local pavement contractor in town know how you feel after reading this book. You don't have to worry if a hot in-place train comes from out of state and into your county because you, as an asphalt contractor, are still going to get all the tonnage you got last year, and then some. The only difference is now you will actually be helping your local agency customer with a solution to our economic problem.

So, you readers can go ahead, and your local paving and concrete contractors and suppliers will know right out of the gate, hand them a copy of the book and say, "Here you go, man. You are going to get twice as much tonnage this year if we just follow this **Three Legged Stool System of Pavement Management** plan that is laid out in this book."

At what point does the pavement section become too thick?

So, have a look at this photo and tell me, folks, what do you think? That's a collector road for sure. It's gotta be, right? Damn thick asphalt isn't it? It must be an arterial somewhere out there in a busy county somewhere!

Well, no, it is not. It's actually a trailer park. There are three cars a day likely driving down this road but, "Gosh darn, it ain't never going to rut!"

Okay? You get what I am saying here, folks? Did we have to put all that money up there in this photo for a road with three cars a day in a trailer park? Probably not. I mean look at that photo again. That paint can is over 9 inches high, clearly thousands of dollars were spent putting the sequential overlays on in the example depicted here.

Could that money have been spent somewhere else in this county or city? This could have been anyone in the America because I see that this same dilemma has taken place across this country. Remember, I drove over 83,000 miles last year across the country. I have seen this first hand, and it sickens me.

"What is the answer?" you ask.

Take the money that we are spending on this unnecessary stuff. Invest some of it on a pavement preservation. And take the rest of the money and spend it on roads that really need it — like the one pictured on page 98.

I went in there with the full-depth reclamation crew in this medium sized city, back in the days when I was a contractor. We spent three weeks there, doing FDR with Portland cement in this case, lowering all the manhole frames and grates with steel plates on top, fixing all of the broken concrete curbs, adjusting the driveway aprons to match the new (which was actually the original) grade and doing all of the ADA upgrades.

Paving crew placing HMA binder course on top of FDR base

The local contractor came in to pave it, not mentioning any names, and they were very excited because they were in there for just one day. We spent three weeks getting it ready for them and they spent one day paving it. Hell, I've been in the pavement business knee deep half of my life. I used to bid 50 million dollars worth of paving and reclamation projects a year. You know what is good in the paving business? Profit. Let me hear you guys say "hell, yeah! Hell, yeah, profit is a good thing. You see profit is not a swear word. Without it we wouldn't have anyone left in business to take care of our roads.

Poor workmanship is never a good thing, right? But profit is a good thing. Here's another example: sometimes the local paving contractors get nervous about their milling (cold-planing) machines. In fact one of the folks in Utah said to me that their owner has these cold in-place trains, and he also likes the idea of going out and recycling in-place, but he also owns 50 milling machines. He said, "We've got to be careful what we say."

I told him we don't have to be careful what we say because as we do the three-legged stool system, he'll need to purchase even more machines. He will find ways to use the milling machines on pretty much every in-place pavement recycling and base stabilization project that we do with **The Three Legged Stool System of Pavement Management**. This was the case in the photo on page 99 taken at the McCollum Airport in Kennesaw, Georgia.

I think it might be one of Georgia's busiest, if not the busiest, regional airport. So, we get this rather large runway widening job as a subcontractor to a earthwork prime contractor who owns like 6 big pans, earth movers,

Innovative usage of cold planing machines adds profit to milling firms

you know, like CAT 621 scrapers, pans or earth movers, whatever you want to call them.

I ran the numbers to use the milling machine in lieu of his pans with the owner of the prime contracting firm in his office. I said, "Sir, with all due respect, we can bring in a milling machine and load that top soil on dump trucks for less money than you can put it on a pan and move it around. Better yet, it will be fluffed up like screened top soil. So, when it comes time to close the job out, do your punch list, and perform all the grassing work, you will have this really nice screened top soil to use, and it will go down very quick."

I remember the owner of the prime contracting firm pondering that for a few minutes with his calculator and green felt tip marker. In minutes, he made up his mind to leave his pans sitting in their yard. And there were like all six of his pans sitting right outside his door collecting dust and rust in his yard— CAT 621 scrapers. He never moved them.

He asked, "How soon can you get those milling machines over to my job site and start to mill off that top soil?" You see that milling machine in the photo will load that dump truck in 45 seconds with onboard electronics that cut precisely to the desired grade. We also took out the sub-base material with the same milling machine, and cut it to final grade. You know the thing I really like about cutting to grade with a milling machine? It doesn't affect the sub-base.

You know, you get in there with a bulldozer and you start squashing the dirt around. You start spinning the metal tracks, and twisting up the sub-base, then before you know it, you've got to go down a little bit deeper and replace it with suitable compacted fill. This method can turn into a vicious circle. In the job example above, we had to do a 9 inch deep, cement treated base, with imported aggregate that was at a precise grade control. So, we needed to make a void space for the runway widening.

We cut the top soil off, and we cut the sub-soil off to grade with the milling machine very quickly. All night-time work, with some very costly user delay penalties if we weren't off the runway each day before the specified time in the contract. I urge you contractors, as you read this book, to think outside the box with your equipment. See what other ways you can get them to work. Embrace the **Three Legged Stool System**, and open your arms up to any and all opportunities to be part of a project with an existing in-place recycling or preservation contractor, or go out and purchase the equipment to do it yourself.

Cold in-place recycling multi-unit train, Middlesex County, CA, mid 90s

Next up, in-place recycling. In the photograph above you see one of our cold in-place recycling projects back up in Canada from the mid 90s. While this book is not meant to cover all things in-place pavement recycling in detail, I will point out that there are three subdisciplines to the cold in-place asphalt recycling process.

BTW, if you would like to learn in detail about anything that we discuss here in the book, please visit our Marketplace for all additional training products and services that we offer over here at **http://ipma.co/marketplace/**. And be sure to register your book at **www.thebookonbetterroads.com/register.**

So, back to in place recycling with the cold in-place method. You've got a single unit train, dual unit trains. This is a multi-unit, cold in-place train which literally brings the crushing and screening operation from a local quarry, puts it on wheels, and brings it to your job site.

Now you may have been thinking as you read the book or listen to the audio version, well, Blair, what is the big deal with this cold in-place recycling, the hot in-place recycling and the full-depth reclamation with bitumen. Well, here's the deal. That three or four inch layer of cold in-place recycling or eight inch layer of stabilized base is a highly rut-resistant mat with a high Marshall Stability. If you put a chip on top of that or microsurfacing, or paved surface on top of that, now you've got structure.

---

"Why I love in-place recycling so much; and what does chocolate soy milk and cereal have to do with pavement design?" It's a video I made for **IPMA Academy:**  http://youtu.be/jBTEwwtt6Fl.  Check it out.

---

A flexible pavement with high Marshall Stability and rut resistance is a pavement designer's dream structure. So, local agencies, realize that this is going to provide for some very long lasting pavement sections in your city or county for many years to come: a layer coefficient of 0.40 for every one inch, with bituminous in-place recycling, but, more importantly, twice the crack mitigation from the underlying cracks coming back up.

I remember when we used to teach these pavement recycling workshops across USA, back when the Asphalt Institute was contracted to FHWA's National Highway Institute, to deliver the curriculum. Wayne Jones and I would say, if you put an inch of new asphalt down, you get one year of crack mitigation.

If you do hot in-place recycling, cold in-place recycling or full-depth reclamation with the bituminous stabilization process, you get two times the crack mitigation compared to conventional rehabilitation techniques.

This is a huge factor in the long term longevity of these projects and again **The Three Legged Stool System of Pavement Management** is designed to marry all things pavement management, pavement preservation, and in-place pavement recycling together.

On the consulting side of the business with **The Barnhardt Group (TBG),** we like to go out on each job we do and perform the network level diamond coring. So, we can verify which rehabilitation and preservation

**Three three legged stool system of pavement management marriage**

treatments will work most effectively at the project level. We also like to follow the Department of Justice recommendations in terms of the ADA upgrades and what they deem is maintenance and alteration.

We use StreetSaver or MicroPAVER pavement management software exclusively at the time of writing this book. One unique thing that we do on the consulting side with TBG is, unlike most consulting firms who only collect 7 distresses for StreetSaver, we collect all 20 asphalt pavement distress types per ASTM 6433 (American Society for Testing and Materials) with the PAVER Distress Identification Manual, while preparing to input the data into StreetSaver.

In other words, whether we use StreetSaver or MicroPAVER as the pavement management software, we always collect the data with the same ASTM 6433 methodology. Thanks to MTC StreetSaver for allowing the collection of data with 7 distresses per Dr. Roger Smith, or the 20 distresses per Dr. Moe Shahin and the US Army Corp. of Engineers.

For those of you who are not familiar with the StreetSaver pavement management software, I can get you contact information for about 15 local agencies in Georgia that have used it to date. (This same software has been used for over 25 years in The Bay Area of San Francisco by 109 local agencies.)

Here is a video of Jason Spencer, APM talking about his pavement management system at the City of Oakland, Georgia http://youtu.be/Vl8Y92-Ab68. For those of you listening in or reading simply visit our YouTube Channel, **www.youtube.com/barnhardtgroup** and scroll for Jason Spencer video.

The City of Oakwood was the very first city to do StreetSaver, and that was about eight years ago. Now Jason actually comes out with TBG and helps us do some of the pavement management distress evaluation as well. So, whether you are using StreetSaver or MicroPAVER. They are both computer-based software programs. Both programs are based on the ASTM 6433 standard. I want to point that out since I believe they may be the only or one of the handful of programs that are ASTM approved.

We, on the consulting side of the business, follow this ASTM 6433 standard, but we have also added a few things along the way like the network level coring and collection of key drainage data along with the Top Ten List of Liabilities. Below is a shot that I took in Heard County, Georgia. I don't make this stuff up, folks, and it isn't always easy to get the Better Roads Bus turned around on these narrow county roads!

Can you guys read the sign in the photo? If not, or if you are listening to the audio version of the book, it says "Learn to fly here" with a crunched airplane crashed next to the upright sign. That tells me that whenever I'm trying to learn something new, like when I had to learn how to make videos,

Learn to fly here! – Learn from those who have crashed.

I actually had to take myself back to do some online training and teach myself how to make videos. I always want to learn from the person who not only talks the talk, but who also walks the walk.

If you guys want to learn how to become **Pavement Management RockSTARS**, I think the most comprehensive learning program out there is **IPMA Academy**. I believe there are other methods you can learn from, but, by the time you attend every seminar and spend thousands travelling, you might as well have done it all in a few months online with us. You may also consider the purchase of some of the DVD sets that we did for Auburn University. Maybe I will go ahead and put a link to these products on the **Marketplace at IPMA**. So, you will have some options as you read the book. Here is that link again **http://ipma. co/marketplace/**.

Here is what one **IPMA Academy** Alumni wrote about **IPMA Academy**:

Jon Heese:  Blair will admit that he's not for everyone.  Personally, I like what they are doing over at **The International Pavement Management Association (IPMA)**. I enjoyed going through the **Accredited Pavement Manager** (**APM**) program and learned some good practical things—usable things—even though I've been around the industry for a quite a while.  As a long-time practicing Pavement Manager, this was right down my alley.  Blair is a good presenter, and the subject matter does a good job bringing newer folks up to speed, shortening the learning curve, while filling in the blanks, connecting dots and tying things up nicely for those of us that have been around for a while.

I think emphasizing and elevating the Pavement Manager role is a very good thing that can benefit many agencies. I highly recommend the **APM** accreditation, or other similar programs, if you can find one. Thing is, I don't know of anything even remotely similar out there. I've attended quality seminars for years without coming away with nearly as much gain. I found the **APM** program invigorating and it amped-up my game.

— Jon Heese, APM, Arapahoe County, Colorado

You can go online and purchase our programs, DVD and Audio Box Sets this afternoon right from your smartphone if you want when you visit the **IPMA Marketplace**. We've also got the ITS UC Berkley webinar series available. That's another good way to get some short online webinar training in for your agency each year.

We are living in a time and place when desperate measures are taking place.  For example, county and city engineers are doing things now that were never done in the past in sheer desperation. Many local agencies are pulverizing their in situ paved roads, and, literally, turning them back into dirt roads to be motor graded and shaped instead of repaired with pothole patching (I won't do any video links here because I know this is a sensitive subject, and I have spoken to many of you in person and promised not to divulge your situation publicly).

Even stranger things are happening such as this city cited in this article http://www.wksu.org/news/story/38604?utm_content=buffere74ff&utm_medium=social&utm_source=linkedin.com&utm_campaign=buffer where they are actually milling the severely potholed, in situ asphalt pavement up and off of the underlying bricks from decades ago. The city engineers have no idea how the road will hold up going forward with only the bricks now carrying the full traffic loading, but they are left with little choice but to take desperate measures.

---

If you would like to download the mp3 for this article click here http://www.wksu.org/news/daily/2014/03/18/40601.mp3.

---

When you get to be an **Accredited Pavement Management Rock-STAR,** you are going to have a lot of people coming up to you, and they are going to be really looking to you to provide them with guidance on their network of roads. With that comes a huge responsibility and a great deal of trust. You know what I mean?

The ratepayers and the elected officials will be looking for accurate answers on your tens of millions of dollars worth of infrastructure, and, I can assure you, all the learners that have gone through our **APM** Online Certification Program are really, really changing the way they manage their pavements for their local agency. They are going out and buying the exact equipment

People will have a lot of trust in you as a
pavement management ROCKSTAR

* HYPHEN CAUTION: If a link includes a hyphen as it goes to the next line of text, when you retype the link into your computer **do not include the hyphen**.

105

that we recommend, whether they get it on eBay, or whether they get it from the local stores.

We have taught consulting firms how to grow their businesses with pavement management as an add on, and we have connected contractors and service providers to folks across North America who will help them create more ROI and more business opportunities.

We teach them everything: how to set up a system, how to do it themselves, and how to hire out what they need to hire out. They get this **Accredited Pavement Manager Certification** hanging on their wall and put their **APM** Designation on their business cards. In fact Jon just sent me a copy of his new business card in an e-mail. Jon Heese, APM. He's pretty proud of it. And so he should be!

So, it really makes me feel that the **Stringbenders** (you will learn about them later in the book) are fighting a good fight with the naysayers, and I am mighty proud of you folks for doing so. Finally, I feel that we are a sizable group of warriors now, not just a few explorers.

I want to share with you some of Jon's presentation on pavement management.

Jon: What do you guys think when you see this in the photo of the donkey-pulled asphalt train? I feel for the little donkey there. They are probably putting out a third of a ton per day, but they all seem to be happy and smiling, and they know that the hot-mixed-asphalt they are making is going to provide a lot better road than the old dirt road they are paving over. Let's face it, I love driving down a

One ton at a time, we will get this road paved sometime this year!

smooth hot-mix road as much as the next guy, but, right now, in China, for example, they are building billions of dollars worth of new Interstate type highways. I think these countries get so wound up in building all this infrastructure that they don't think about how the heck are they going to preserve it in the future.

Just as Jon stated, it is feasible that we built 4 million miles of roads beginning in 1956 with Ike, and the whole regime with the Interstate System, and no one ever really thought, "Hey, how we are going to preserve it?"

So, listen up, as mentioned in Part One, www.smartgrowthamerica.org states that we (USA) now spend 57% of our GDP (Gross Domestic Product) on 1.3% of our roadways in America building new roadways, building new lane miles and building new bridges. That doesn't leave much money to take care of the other 97.7% of our roads, does it?

Last year as I drove down an interstate highway somewhere in USA, and I won't mention any states in particular. Let's just say I was on the I-40 somewhere, and I stopped at a truck stop. I interviewed one of the truck drivers as we were refueling.

So, I said, "Hey, dude, what is it like out there, man? How's it like bouncing around in those trucks? Those big $200,000 rigs?"

He said, "Man, have you been down the so-in-so lately?" (I won't print the name of it.)

I said, "No, I really haven't."

He stated emphatically with a firm overtone, "Dude, when you go through there, it is going to kick your ass right out of the seat of that RV!"

And you know what? I didn't have to call him up and ask him what he meant, because when I came up on that road, I knew exactly when I got there and what he was talking about.

I'm talking about an interstate with 5 inches of raveling and rutting. When I got into the raveled areas with the RV, the Sprinter Van, I could hardly get out! I couldn't let the steering wheel go on its own, because it would have followed those deep rut tracks. So, I did the right thing. I got myself pulled over to the side of the road, and I recorded a video right from there about how bad a shape we are in here in America.

I hope you guys really understand the ramifications of where we are going if we don't soon change what is going to go on here.

---

When I pull that video on one of our LaCie 4 TB external hard drives I will be sure to get that out to all who register their book with us at **www.thebookonbetterroads.com/register.**

---

Now my pavement guru colleagues and I usually swear that we won't talk about asphalt all the time, and never mention anything to do with the white stuff. Okay, but I will say this, hot-mixed asphalt pavement makes up about 95% of our 4 million miles of roads in America. But with all due respect to the PCC road builders out there, there is an entire box full of tools for preservation and rehabilitation of concrete roads, and I always encourage the use of these techniques in lieu of conventional rehabilitation methods.

So if upwards of 95% of our roadways in America are made up of hot-mixed asphalt pavement, and the other guys, the white guys over there, have the remaining 5%, then we need to have this conversation. You see, I'm not here to bash the PCC guys, but I sent this message to the Utah Asphalt Pavement Association (UAPA) while doing a presentation for them a while back.

This was a strong message that went something like this,

> To all you asphalt paving contractors in the room: All the while you guys have been worried about some slurry contractor coming into your back yard and taking business away from you, you let 23

miles of concrete interstate roadway get busted up, hauled over to a local stockpile, and all new, ready mixed concrete roadway go back out there to the job site.

A net savings of 23 million dollars could have been made if they simply would have rubblized this road and put a thick asphalt overlay on it. After all, this is a successful technique that has been used since the 90s. Did you guys hear what I just said? $23 million dollars! One job!

So, I sent a little video out on the internet, and I started getting calls from friends and colleagues at the Federal Highways Administration. I asked my friend with the one of the rubblizing firms to verify the results of what I estimated in our little **IPMA Tip of the Week**. He said that it was actually $28 million dollars that could have been saved on this project. But, worse than that, you know what happens when they close an interstate for months to reconstruct it?

They send me, driving the RV, into oncoming traffic. They put up a bunch of barrels to protect me from a brand new Peterbilt tractor coming this way at 85 mph, okay? Yes, that is right, a tiny reflective barrel is all that separates me from death. So, we could rip up an interstate and rebuild it from the bottom up; it could have been rubblized in-place for a third of the cost in a third of the time.

Can you think of a bigger waste of money than what you see here?

By the way, here is a link to the **IPMA Tip of the Week Video** on this project I am talking about. So, if you have a decent internet connection you can watch it here http://youtu.be/HZmfaEO6yqU. If you are listening to this book on an Audio CD, simply check out our YouTube Channel www.youtube.com/ipmatv and look for a Tip of the Week that is 9:42 minutes when you get a chance. We will send you the follow up video to the **IPMA Tip of the Week** on the potential savings that could have been had with rubblization for those that register your **Book on Better Roads.**

And all the while I am stuck in these crazy construction zones, I'm trying to type on my computer, and drive at the same time. Now what happens if I'm not paying attention? (That was a joke.)

I do, however, sometimes look at instructional DVDs while I drive 1,000 miles a day in the **Better Roads Bus,** but in any case I don't like when the mirrors of the dump trucks are brushing my RV mirrors on the way through on an interstate, So, it is an awfully unsafe situation, and a big waste of money, if you ask me. So, let's talk about the three steps here that make up **The Three Legged Stool System of Pavement Management**.

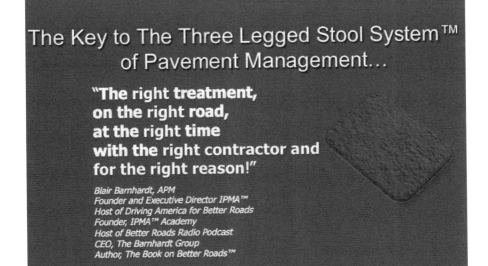

The key to the three legged stool system of pavement management

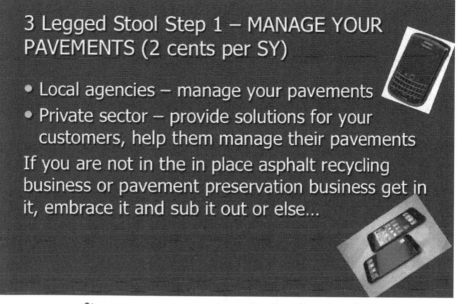

3 Legged Stool Step 1 – MANAGE YOUR PAVEMENTS (2 cents per SY)

- Local agencies – manage your pavements
- Private sector – provide solutions for your customers, help them manage their pavements

If you are not in the in place asphalt recycling business or pavement preservation business get in it, embrace it and sub it out or else...

Step one – manage your pavements – three legged stool system

Before we go to the framework, however, let's first recall the basic premise behind everything we talk about here, the Key to **the Three Legged Stool System of Pavement Management**:

Step One in the **Three Legged-Stool System of Pavement Management**. Manage your pavements. If you are a local agency, you simply have to manage your pavements. If you are doing so, kudos to you. If you are not, we need to get you started ASAP!

Private sectors have to learn how to provide solutions for your customers and help them manage their pavements. That means if you are not in the in-place recycling business, like my friend and colleague Dr. Mike Hetizman said when we did the NHI class for him so many years ago, he called up the local asphalt contractors and the local Asphalt Paving Association Executive Director and said, "You folks better come on down here and listen to what these guys have to say about in-place asphalt recycling because, if you don't, someone else is going to come into this State of Iowa and do it because we ARE GOING TO BE DOING IT!"

Mike actually did some amazing things up there as the Chief Bituminous Engineer for IOWA DOT at the time. You want to talk about FDR innovation, Mike was involved in some very, very amazing recycling jobs. For example Mike tried to do the 1.5% fly ash supplemental addition to the foamed asphalt stabilized base for added tensile strength.

Step Two: Preserve It!  We've got to take care of our infrastructure. Local agencies should be on the lookout for different solutions that don't involve the same old same old  rehabilitation method from 1956.

I would like to add that it takes me a long time before I feel comfortable  recommending something to you pavement managers.  Everything

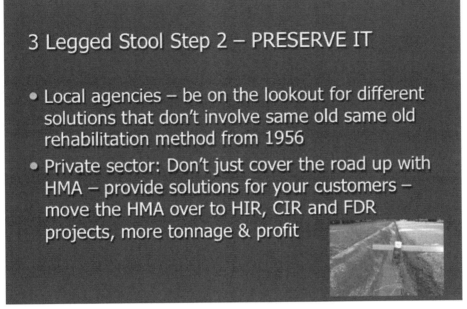

## 3 Legged Stool Step 2 – PRESERVE IT

- Local agencies – be on the lookout for different solutions that don't involve same old same old rehabilitation method from 1956
- Private sector: Don't just cover the road up with HMA – provide solutions for your customers – move the HMA over to HIR, CIR and FDR projects, more tonnage & profit

Step two – preserve it – three legged stool system

that we talk about in this book I have seen firsthand. I have interviewed other county and city engineers, just like you, to make sure before I do a pavement management job and before I start trying to put things into the decision tree to help you all out, that no viable options are left out.  So, I promised myself when I sat down to write **The Book on Better Roads** that I would  give you all a road map to save money for your local agencies. I hope you are going to go and walk out and start implementing some of this information today.

Always be on the lookout for different solutions.  If someone comes to you, or one of the guys comes into your office to talk to you tomorrow about something that you haven't heard of, don't think it is like yesterday's news. These tools in the toolbox have been used for decades.

These are tried and proven methods.  Remember when I mentioned that my prize for travelling across the country in the **Better Roads Bus** for days on end, weeks on end, and months on end, was to find out what worked out there and what didn't.

Here is an example of a product I discovered while teaching Utah Road School one year. Listen up, I know you will appreciate it! The owners of the company that make this high density mineral bond stuff, or HA5, waited for 5 years to make sure the material they put down on the roadways was going to last as they projected it would. It was only then that they started to market to the 2 or 3 states they work in. Now, after 14 years, they are moving around to offer HA5 in other areas of the country.

---

Check out this video on HA5 here http://youtu.be/2rRGxAAz-I0.

---

Slurry was invented in the 50s, microsurfacing in the 70s. Ultra Thin Bonded Wearing Course, my guess is that it has been going down for like 20 years. Granted it went through a whole patent thing, and it was proprietary for the longest while, but the point I'm trying to make here is we have brought nothing to this book today that is new. Nothing. The newest thing in this book is the paper that it's printed it on and the way it was done. All these paving techniques have been around for decades. Just trust that it is going to work for you readers. Private sector companies don't just cover up the road with the same old, same old.

## 3 Legged Stool Step 3 – RECYCLE IT IN PLACE

- Local agencies – recycle, recycle, recycle
- Private sector – provide solutions for your customers – repurpose it, reuse it

If you are not in the in place asphalt recycling business get in it yourself or open your arms to subcontractors who can subcontract to you if you want your business to survive

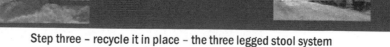

Step three – recycle it in place – the three legged stool system

Finally, recycle in-place. You've got to get out there and start recycling in-place. I can give you guys case study after case study of local agencies that have literally saved 5, 8, 10, 12 million dollars on a single project by doing in-place recycling. They get the same life cycle, the same asphalt road on top, strong bases, wider, safer and stronger roads.

Remember about safety, edge drop-offs and such? A great way to go out and widen your platform at the same time is to recycle those roads in place, local agencies. Private sector, why in the earth are we milling up asphalt in the middle of the desert, dumping it in a ditch and pushing it over with a D6 dozer and then hauling asphalt from a plant 70 miles away?

Hello! It frustrates me to heck. Why can't you start providing solutions for your customers as contractors and take care of our environment? You can still make the same or more profit by implementation of the material covered in this book.

Now that we have the three steps out of the way for The **Three Legged Stool System**, let's talk about the key elements involved in our journey together as pavement management **RockSTARS**.

As long as you are willing to manage your pavements, preserve your pavements and recycle your pavements in-place, you are 90% of the way to a long successful career as a pavement manager!

For the private sector folks, it may be a little harder to grasp the concept, but know that I have sat in your seat. I have bid those complicated jobs, I've had the sleepless nights, I have watched the equipment sit in the yard as I try to estimate the right numbers to get it moving, while still turn-

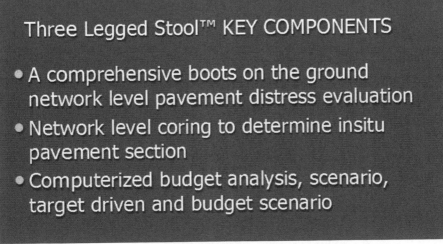

Three Legged Stool™ KEY COMPONENTS

- A comprehensive boots on the ground network level pavement distress evaluation
- Network level coring to determine insitu pavement section
- Computerized budget analysis, scenario, target driven and budget scenario

The three legged stool system - key components

ing a little profit. I can assure you that, based on my decades in the business, there is a brave new world out there in the land of the **Three Legged Stool System** that can bring you more profit and more tonnage.

A comprehensive, boots-on-the-ground, pavement distress evaluation is a key element in setting all this up for your local agency. If you have not done so already, consider that it will cost only about 2 cents per square yard to manage your pavements. Yes, I know that we covered this earlier in the book, but this simple calculation is worth repeating again to drive home the point. It doesn't cost money to have good roads, it actually costs you more when you are not managing your pavements.

If you take your center lane miles of road, let's just say you have 485 center-lane miles of road. So, do this right now with your calculator just for an exercise. Go ahead, I will wait here for you to get your iPhone out. Let's take 485 center-lane miles of road x 13,000 square yards.

I usually figure a county road with two lanes to be about 22 feet wide. If you take that, times 5280 feet long for a mile of road, it figures out to be about 13,000 SY rounded up.

---

22' x 5280' = 116,160 square ft.

116,160 sf / 9 = 12,906.66 square yards.

13,000 sy X 485 CL miles = 6,305,000 square yards

6,300,000 sy X $50 = $315,000,000 (Total Asset Value)

315,000,000 X 3% = $9,450,000 (Annual Maintenance Cost)

---

So you should get approximately 6.3 million, right?

So that's 6.3 million square yards times a replacement value of 50 bucks per square yard or so depending on which region you are in, because that's what it is going to cost you in network level replacement. And then usually if you have an iPhone you have to turn it sideways to get this big number to show across the screen in scientific mode.

Most readers and listeners should get about 315 million dollars.

So, this hypothetical county, let's call it Good Roads County, they have 315 million dollars of replacement value for their entire network of roadways. Now take that number and multiply it by 3%. So, if I am your Pavement Manager and I'm going to go to the Good Roads County Commission, I'm going to recommend this is how much we have each year.

315 million dollars x 0.03. So, that is about 9.45 million dollars a year to maintain your roadway network. That is before ADA clarifications came along. Are we close to that yet?

So to set up and implement your network level inventory and comprehensive pavement management plan while following **The Three Legged Stool System of Pavement Management,** you can figure it would be about $270 per mile for a typical county situation starting from absolute scratch. So, whether your crews do this or you hire a consulting firm either locally or one that is willing to travel nationwide like the consulting side of our business, you can figure about $270 dollars per center lane mile turn-key.

I will add this caveat, however. If you are planning on hiring a consultant to do this pavement evaluation and pavement management work for you, I urge you to consider putting an RFP out using qualifications based selection. You can find out more about how to purchase the ultimate guide to this topic, namely "The Red Book" from the APWA Bookstore at www. apwa.net.

In the case of the example above, a lot of the other agencies are just tagging on to this one particular bid because it was indeed a qualifications based selection decision. However, as a bonus to the agencies we work for, we were $50,000 less than the next higher ranked consultant. Again, this is not an endorsement for the Barnhardt Group, I am merely using real life figures. So, you can plan out the budget for this type of work to be done for your agency with reasonable accuracy.

So, for estimate's sake, let's say it will cost Good Roads County a mere $126,000 to set up their entire network level pavement distress inventory and pavement management system with **The Three Legged Stool System of Pavement Management.**

And then you take that ($126,000) and divide that into the square yards we talked about, and, I think you will find it is nominal. So, if you pay 2 cents per square yard to manage your pavements, and you save 10 bucks per square yard, correct me if I'm wrong, but that is like a $9.98 net gain every time you bid out a project.

Again, you can talk to the counties and cities across North America that we set up doing this. They do this all day long. Some local agencies in their first letting will bid upwards of 3 million dollars worth of work using FDR alone. It takes little or no time at all for their Commissioner or Council to understand the cost savings in using the system.

116

So, readers, what did you get when you did the math? Did you get a bigger number than 2 cents per square yard? So, it was 485 miles x 13,000 square yards, that was like that big number, right? A whole bunch if million square yards, like 6.3 million or so. And remember the overall network level replacement value of the system in Good Roads County was about 315 million dollars.

Think about it like this: as an estimator, I always used to think about sprinkling money into a carpet because after a long week at work when you are estimating, it is easy to forget what you are dividing, what you are using, and what the numbers all really mean, and what gets divided by what. So, I think, okay, I've got this much money, I spread it over these many square yards and it all comes out to pennies.

$126,000 divided by that big number in the square yards of 6.3 million square yards and you get like two pennies per square yard. I am not really good with math, so I hope you readers and listeners to the Audio Book are checking on me here. So, 2 pennies per square yard to have your crew, or our crew, to go out and do the set up of your ASTM 6433 pavement management distress evaluation survey, inventory, and robust budgeting machine so that you can start treating the right roads at the right time with

"This Three Legged Stool™ System of Pavement Management is the Biggest NO BRAINER EVER, even an eight year old kid could figure this one out!"

the right treatment and the right contractor all for the right reason. You spend 2 cents and save upwards of ten bucks per square yard?

Yes, this is actually the BIGGEST NO BRAINER OF ALL TIME, FOLKS!

Next in the list of Key Elements for **The Three Legged Stool System** to work is a fully computerized budget. Here's what happens. So, there's three scenarios we like to run. The first scenario is, for example, one of the readers comes up to me and says, "Blair, we've got $700,000 to spend this year, that's it. Now, we ask the software, 'What do you do with $700,000 per year?' It gives us a generated list of all the roads, all the different treatments we are going to do. That is, assuming we have all of the requisite data in the software from the pavement distress survey."

At the end of that calendar year of work you would put all the work history into your pavement management system. Know that you can enter this data each month, each week, or you can wait until Christmas, and do it between Christmas and New Year; but the bottom line is, it gives us real time, PCI updates the moment you update your work history. The pavement condition index changes every time you fix a road or treat a road. That's a **Budget Scenario**.

The second way to generate a budget report is with an **Unconstrained Budget Scenario**, and I always say that is like winning the lottery for your roadway network repairs. Think of this as you walk into your Good Roads County Commissioners and say, "Blair ran the pavement management algorithms out here for us, got our network level PCI rating up to 84 over the next 10 years on the computer, but, gosh, we need to have 72 million to do it." So, that's like winning the lottery scenario.

Very few local agencies ever have the funds to do this budget, but it is worth knowing that it exists. Sometimes I am tempted to staple all those Unconstrained Budget reports all together in the three ring binder full of reports, knowing that the City Engineer will never in this lifetime be able to implement that strategy.

Then the third way to run your budget forecast is with the Target Driven Scenario, and I will give you an example. So, let's say your next door neighboring county goes out and does their pavement management calculations, and they started going to their local newspaper bragging on how they got an average PCI of 72.

The next thing you know, your Good Roads County Commissioners get a hold of that newspaper article and asks, "What are we with our pavement management system and ratings?"

And you say, "Well, Ma'am, we are actually at a network level PCI of 61."

He or she from the Good Roads County Commissioners says, "Well, darn, I want us to be a 72. Better yet, I want us to be a 74. I want to beat that Tommy's butt over there with his PCI rating."

In the **Target Driven Budget Scenario** we actually tell the computer to get us to a 75, 79, and 86 over the next 10 years (or whatever PCI rating number you ask for). It will tell us how much money to spend and where to spend it, which roads to preserve, which roads to recycle.

So, three different ways to run your budget scenarios. These computerized budget calculations are really fast, and best of all, if you as the Pavement Manager of Good Roads County came into an unexpected short fall of money (maybe you spent the whole budget on deicing salt) you can change everything on the fly.

Conversely, if you were to get a windfall of money like the guys in Ohio did, they actually, with a click of the button, figured how to spend an extra half million, or 1 million dollars, literally, with a click of the button. It will change all three of the budget scenarios. Very powerful tools. It is easy for me to underestimate just how powerful these are. Let me give you an example.

You and I, in the course of 5 minutes in 2014 with this software available today, can run a budget scenario for our entire county. In comparison, when the City of LA was starting off with MicroPAVER so many years ago, they would set the computer up on a Friday to run the calculations and by the following Wednesday they would have all of their computations done. So, that is how far we have come. We have computers in our pocket now.

Again, we are discussing what the key components are in **The Three Legged Stool System of Pavement Management**. You have to have accurate unit prices from estimators, or other professionals who understand what is going on in your marketplace. For example, how much does FDR cost? How much is hot in-place recycling historically? How much is the cold in-place recycling? How much does slurry or microsurfacing cost when compared to HA5?

So, then we go out and set up the decision tree. Here each functional class code is aligned with a specific treatment in a specific PCI range. So, think about that. You have collector roads, arterial roads and residential roads. You have asphalt roads, concrete roads, and you have asphalt overlay roads. Plus you all have some chip seal roads, if you are a county.

It's worth noting that one small adjustment in how we take care of a specific functional class code, or surface type, can mean hundreds of thousands in savings for your agency in a single calendar year. You may say, for example, that from now on, we will only overlay PCC roads with hot-mixed asphalt, but the surface-treated roads are going to get a different treatment than a paved road.

One of the fastest things we do with a lot of our counties is we just say, right out of the gate, that there will be no more asphalt overlays on chip seal roads in the future. That saves an agency tens of millions of dollars a year. Next, take that same money you would have spent on the chip seal roads, and move it over to the FDR roads. Many of our county engineer and city engineer clients own or rent an asphalt zipper (you can rent to own these, as well), and do a lot of their pulverizing in-house. So, a common sense approach to sectioning is a key element in the three-legged stool system.

We don't section every block or every quarter mile. We actually run out maybe two miles in the county, and we think of it as if it were an asphalt or preservation contract. Do it as if you were going to let a contract for the work. That's how we think about sectioning the roadways when we set it up. As a former Vice President of a paving and reclamation firm, I know just how fast the bid price would run up for those lettings that had multiple lowboy moves in it.

As you may have already imagined, a strong reliance on the in-place asphalt recycling techniques, and eco-efficient pavement preservation wher-

## Three Legged Stool™ KEY COMPONENTS

- Accurate unit prices and decision tree set up
- Common sense approach to sectioning during evaluation and contracting (i.e. TIB)
- Strong reliance on in place asphalt recycling and pavement preservation wherever possible

The three legged stool key components

ever possible, is one of the Key Elements for successful implementation. You might have read about that earlier in this book.

Heed the warning signs quickly. Over the next 18 months to 3 years, 3 billion people will come online for the very first time ever and use a smart phone and the internet. You guys heard of the internet? Maybe you readers have heard of this thing they call the Google LOL?

All the rate payers like to get onto Facebook and let the county or city know how they like to complain about everything. And there's Twitter, and all that stuff. But there is also, now, a great opportunity for everybody in our industry to learn online; to get some new education. Remember, the number one search engine for 25-30 year olds is YouTube, right? Maybe you found **The Book of Better Roads** on Amazon because you searched for "how to manage pavements?"

Great things are happening with social media spreading the great word of the pavement management circle of **RockSTARS** that we are growing with the **Accredited Pavement Managers**.

Let's read the comments of Miquel Valentin, PE, APM, as he discusses their pavement management success in Rockdale County, Georgia. Miguel not only went through **IPMA Academy**, he also had TBG perform their pavement distress evaluation and set up Rockdale's StreetSaver Pavement Management System.

## HEED THE WARNING SIGNS

- Over the next three years, 3 billion people will for the first time ever come on line with the internet and start searching for the best way to do things like manage their pavements
- Number one search engine for 25 – 35 year olds is _____!!!!
- The number one search phrase on AMAZON is _____!!!!!

Social media will either reward you for being a hero or punish you severely for not acting as a steward for your agency. In the private sector your business will simply dissolve if you insist on doing things like it is 1956

The practical pavement manger must heed the warning signs

You will be able to purchase this **IPMA Academy** LIVE training event as part of a Greatest Hits BOX Set at the **IPMA Marketplace http://ipma.co/marketplace/** but for now I want to go ahead and share the transcript with you.

## Transcript begins

Miguel:  Well, as Blair mentioned, we had some discussions a few years back about how to manage our pavements. One of those things we were doing at the time, and I would imagine I'm speaking particularly to agency personnel, I would imagine you have found yourself either in similar circumstances or you are still there. We were trying to figure out how we were going to manage our pavements with the funding we have available. Every year the funding would go down. So, we had to come up with a strategy to be able to continue to address, to manage the pavements, and be able to stretch the dollars as much as we could.

One of the things we were doing at the time, and, again you may still be doing this, is we would have information on our pavements. We would rate the condition of the roads using typical Pacer or Paces, depending on the state that you are in or from the methodology you use, where you look for deficiencies, and that sort of thing, and you rate and compare one road to another. We were doing a little bit of forensics, but we were doing it sort of like just getting started on a spread sheet. We realized that there is so much information that you have to obtain and to monitor and to track that the spreadsheet just was not doing it for us any more. So, we were looking for another way to be able to gather the information onto a database and have it all available.

Going back to the 1990s, they were doing this, and putting the condition and the rating at that time in the spreadsheet. So, we did have, and we still do have, a lot of historical information on the roads, but it was difficult to manage and difficult to access. So, we were looking for a way to migrate into something that made it much easier to access and compare.

We understood then, and we understand today, and probably many of you as well, that it is just not feasible to continue to manage pavements the old fashioned way, which was the mill and inlay, or just straight overlay on the pavements. The funding is just not available, so, we looked for techniques that would facilitate preserving the roads until we could get to them and do a more exten- sive rehabilitation process.

We had to go through an education process ourselves. Having civil engineering backgrounds, we were familiar with some of the techniques, but certainly not all of the techniques, and not the latest techniques out there. So, we had to go wherever there were seminars — the **IPMA Academy** or GDOT training sessions — to try and get as much information as possible to allow us to learn about the techniques that are available out there, and then learn how to implement the techniques.

That is part of the key, and after a while of doing this particu- larly with Blair and **The Three-Legged Stool System (of Pavement Management)**, that is when we learned it had a name. Before, we were just doing what typical Pavement Managers do, and Public Works Directors do, and, that is, find a way to manage and main- tain your roads in the most cost efficient way possible.

So, we began to get a little more structure and began to get into the software where we could input the data. Brian spent quite a bit of time getting the information in there. He is our resident Pavement Management Expert in Rockdale County (Brian Frix, APM, also **IPMA Advisory Board Member**).

He (Brian) is very familiar with both the technical side and the contracting and field operation side. We found that there are tech- niques out there today, and many of you represent this industry, that provides subcontractors who provide those services that can help manage a pavement, preserve the life and extend it to where you would have the ability to get funding whether it be through a SPLOST (special local option sales tax), through a general fund, or perhaps through some Federal funding for overlays and mainte- nance projects and the like.

It is a strategy where, if you have a road that is in very poor condition, you might be able to apply one of these techniques and preserve it until you can address it. So, that is what we found our- selves doing, getting into a more structured management program for the pavements. We found out the different techniques we had done historically in Rockdale, well before my time: Foamed asphalt base stabilization, and certainly the milling and inlay.

We had not done, I don't believe, any full-depth reclamation with Portland cement. We didn't even know about the High Density Mineral Bond (HA5) and the like. We have more recently gone through those treatments. There are treatments out there that will help in specific situations. So, part of the exercise that we found ourselves going through, was to try and determine what type of treatment fits what type of situation. With the information we had about our pavements and some knowledge and education about the techniques that are available, then we would try to marry the two because we found, obviously, that if you try to do full-depth reclamation on a pavement that's got 10 inches of asphalt already, that is going to be kind of tough. There are applications for the various techniques, and part of the exercise as agency personnel is to get ourselves to a comfort level with what techniques are out there and where they apply.

It is sort of like somebody is sick, and you go to the doctor. The doctor is going to try to make an assessment as to what your condition is before he prescribes the remedy. It's the same with pavement management. **The technique that you use to address the road has to be tailored to the condition of the road.** The structure of the road is one of the components, but there are new techniques out there, and, I say new, perhaps new to our area.

Some of these techniques have been around for quite a long time. They have been utilized elsewhere satisfactorily, but we just have not had the experience locally with them. We did not have the comfort level. I imagine many of you are perhaps in the same predicament. You want to maximize your investment with pavement management and preservation. You have limited funding, but you want to be able to apply techniques that work. You have not done it before. You want to learn from others who have done it successfully, then get yourself to that comfort level to take the plunge and go ahead.

I believe one of the messages in the **IPMA Academy** videos is to follow the plan. Stick to the plan. You have to have a plan and you have to stick to it because it is very easy to say, well, that didn't quite work out. So, therefore I'm going to abandon the whole thing. But you would be not getting the full benefit of what the plan could offer.

So, our experience was first getting the education. We had a lot of data, and then finding where the techniques are applicable, and then putting them into practice, getting the contracts out there, and we had the same issues that were discussed earlier. You have to have enough square yards of a particular treatment to attract a contractor from Illinois or Florida or wherever they might be. Our goal is to be able to make these techniques so common place in this area that it does not need a contractor coming from Illinois or Florida. There would be local contractors who would do the same thing.

That would be beneficial to everybody because, well, you know, it costs to transport things. The longer the distance, the higher the cost. That is sort of our goal in sharing this with you because we understand what it takes getting to a comfort level. We've been through enough of it to have a comfort level and have tried different things. We understand that each of your agencies have to go through the same thing, and you don't have to take anyone else's word for it, but you have to try in my estimation something —a different approach.

You just can't keep doing the same thing the old fashioned way because the funding is just not there. It is not going to be feasible. So, that would be my suggestion to you. Get a comfort level. Learn about the techniques—whether you do it through **IPMA Academy**, seminars, the recycling associations or wherever it might be—get a comfort level because there are techniques out there that will help you maximize your investment. It is going to take more agencies making that decision to move forward to get us to where it is common place to have full-depth reclamation, cold in-place and hot in-place recycling and HA5 or High Density Mineral Bond, whatever it might be.

It has saved significantly in our budget, and Blair was mentioning earlier about how are we going to make the shift from the old fashioned way to a new way, whatever that is going to be, which we weren't 100% exactly sure.

I had a concern that it was going to take some time. It didn't take nearly as long as I thought it would, and the key to doing it, and I think you can understand that because you probably have a similar reaction, is if you can tell your agency, the Board of Commissioners, or the City Council, or the Transportation Committee; if you can tell them I can save the organization 20%, 30% by employing these different techniques, then you get their attention, and you can do even better if you go ahead and do it and have positive results.

Once you get over that, or overcome that inertia, and you see the results, and you are able to say we tried this technique in this area, or this road, or this subdivision, and you can go out there and take a look at it, and you see it looks beautiful. In fact some of the Committee Members went out because I told them we are going to do full-depth reclamation in this particular subdivision, and you are welcome to go out there and have a look.

One of them at the following meeting reported back and said, you know the paving on a couple of those roads was not up to par. It looked like was substandard, so I'm really concerned about the technique. I said, well, what roads are you referring to? Well, it turns out what they thought was the pavement was actually the FDR full-depth reclamation road (with Portland cement stabilization) before it got paved. It looked too much like a finished product. They thought it was paved.

They could ride on it and it looked like a road. When I told them those roads have not been paved yet, it was like, yeah, I drove it. So, you can see, when you are able to make a decision whether you piggyback with somebody else, consolidate between counties and agencies and be able to employ some of these techniques within your jurisdiction, and show good results, people will come around faster than you would have ever imagined. That was our experience.

In fact, now they think that this is the way to do it and wonder why weren't we doing it this way before. Well, again, it took us a little while to get the education, the comfort level, and to learn about all of these techniques and the contractors who offer them. There is a lot of demand for addressing pavement that is not being fulfilled today, and that is what Blair was referring to as latent demand.

What happens is, as an agency person, if you are given 2 million dollars per year to do pavement management and preservation, you are not going to employ techniques and say, well, we only spent 1.5 million so here's half a million back. No, you're not going to do that. Don't give half a million back. What you are going to do is, you are going to spend the 2 million, and you are going to get more roads done.

It is not that having and employing techniques that are less expensive is going to lessen the demand. The demand is there. What is going to happen is, as the agencies get comfortable dealing with these different techniques, there is going to be the ability for them to plan if I can get 50,000 square yards of this particular treatment, or 100,000 of FDR, whatever it might be, then we are going to put out a contract for that amount because we all understand contractors are in the business of making money.

We get that, and we want you to make money, but we also have to address the needs of the community more efficiently. The funding is just not there. So, we are going to spend the money. We are just going to be able to improve the condition of the roads, hold them together longer until we can get to them, and do the full treatment that we intend to do.

For example, if we do HA5 on a particular road, that does not mean that the road is now going to last 50 years, but it is going to last longer, and going to stay together longer, until we can get to it. We monitor the condition and, as it deteriorates, either we employ another treatment, or repeat the treatment, or decide okay it is time to go in and do FDR on that particular road or some other treatment.

So, that would be my advice to the agency personnel. Get yourself a comfort level with the techniques that are available. Get some information on your infrastructure so you know how to marry those two, and then, to the extent that you don't have a lot of one particular technique, or square yards, or tonnage of one particular technique, you can piggyback off of another agency's contract as I mentioned before.

We've had several local counties and municipalities contact us about piggybacking off of one of our contracts, and they've done that. I don't know what the limitations are for each agency. I imagine there is a State regulation and an upper threshold that you cannot exceed, but perhaps different agencies can set a lower threshold for themselves. For us, most anytime we do a contract, we gotta go to the Board, which is fine because they now under-stand that we are doing different techniques, and they are okay with that.

As long as we save them money, that is the way they look at it. If they give us 2 million dollars, and, with the old fashioned way, we did 10 miles of road. Now we can do 13 or 50, they get that. In fact, before we were putting out contracts that were monolithic, more of the same type of treatment, whether it was mill and inlay or just straight overlay, and now when we get a list of roads identi-fied, we will break up the contract.

We will put a piece together for a particular treatment, a piece together for this other treatment, and we may have three, I think we've done up to three different, or perhaps four different treatments, for one list of projects. It is a little more work for the agency personnel, but it really stretches your dollars in being able to address your pavement infrastructure.

I would be happy to answer any questions quickly, but I would like for Bryan to get in a little more detail of some of the experience we had here. If you have any questions, we can either take them now or defer to after he is done.

Phil: (Inaudible question).

Miguel: We do have a paving crew but it is not a long line crew. We don't have the equipment with the controls that would yield a smooth enough cross section on the road for us to engage in that, but we can pave. We do patching and smaller areas generally with our own crew. So, most everything else we contract out.

. . . We periodically need to do a recap, sort of a more com-prehensive assessment of where we are, and for something like that, we would bring in a consultant to do it; however, we do have in-house staff that is familiar with the techniques of the pavement assessment. If you are asking about between those major com-prehensive studies, then we would do that in-house. . . . We get to the more major comprehensive studies point, which are typically perhaps every three years or four years. That is when we would bring in a consultant.

Audience Member: (Inaudible)

Miguel: I don't know how you get yourself there if you are not already there. Recognize that we, as an industry, we, as a public agency, cannot continue to do things the old fashioned way. The funding is not available. It just isn't there, and, frankly, as an agency it is easier to understand that if you can say to your Councilman or Commissioner this year we did 20 miles of road versus last year we did 15 because we are employing (new) techniques, that is definitely a plus. And then you bring them over to—not like bringing them over to your side. It's not like Star Wars; it is not the dark side versus the Jedis—but get them to understand.

They have to get themselves at a comfort level, too, but they understand the financial implication. On the contracting side, if that is what you are looking at, we used to do overlays, and that is what we did. So, we want to keep it that way. I would just remind you of one thing, one word. Kodak. Kodak.

What does that mean? The Kodak Company was doing very well for a long time, but when the industry changed, as the world evolved from a film based to the digital age, if Kodak stuck to film they'd go extinct. They had to migrate and understand that the future was in digital. So, what did they do?

They started manufacturing digital cameras, pretty good ones, too, but as a contracting industry recognizes that, if we had the funds to do it the old fashioned way, we would all still be doing it. We can't do that anymore, and as we are pressed to come up with a different way of doing things, you either understand that, and go with it, and benefit from it, or you go extinct. Does that answer your question?

Audience Member: (Inaudible).

Miguel: Yes. Yes. Well, if there are some techniques... if the typical, the average—there's no average—if contractors in the area can do different techniques, then that is fine. If we need somebody that can do FDR, well, not all contractors in the area are capable of FDR, so, we will package a project that has the FDR component.

Certainly FDR is going to take the top (wearing course), so you still have some of the same players in the mix, but, if we have, for example, a High Density Mineral Bond application, then we will not mix that in with an overlay project because it is going to take two different techniques, and two different contractors. So, we will break that up. Does that answer your question?

Audience Member: (Inaudible).

Miguel: As it relates to the data management component, we still have a lot of the information on a spreadsheet. The intent over time is to migrate that, but our resident expert is hard to catch up with because he is so busy doing other things. Because of me mostly. So, we still have a lot of the information. but we've migrated to StreetSaver using MicroPAVER techniques of analysis, but we were using Street Saver before.

Again, it would work just as well if you developed your own, but went with a different type of program. You can do it in Excel, in fact I was doing pavement management, well, I'm going to date myself, probably about 25 to 30 years ago, and I was using Lotus 1-2-3. You guys remember that? Yeah. So, you use what you have available until you can upgrade, and that is what we did. We were using Excel, and it works well. So, we keep a copy of that spreadsheet around. We are using the StreetSaver.

Audience Member: (Inaudible).

Miguel: I'm sorry. It's the MicroPAVER analysis methodology. It is actually ASTM 6433 and it is a structured way of doing a pavement assessment that tries to weed out the bias for agency personnel and even the contractors as well and consultants. You know that when you are making a visual assessment of the condition of a road, there are several factors that come into play.

One of them you look for is cracking. The road is cracked, but there are different types of cracks and different reasons why the pavement cracks. You need to be able to distinguish that, but also one component that we found was that, if not the ruling factor, is it the street that you live on? If it is your road, the condition looks horrible, and you just need to get it done quickly.

But if it is somebody else's street, well why are you doing their street? It is not as half as bad as mine. So, you try to weed out the subjectivity and make a structured decision so that at least you have half a chance of having, and, I refer to that as the "theory of relativity," and, we are not going to get too philosophical here, but to me the "theory of relativity" in pavement management is you have many different roads, and you want to be able to gauge the condition of one relative to the other.

The reason for that is, you want to come up with a list you are going to be addressing as part of your limited budget, and you want to have some rationale for why you chose those roads. So, you want to have some relativity in there; some relative condition, and it can't be it's cracked, and this one is more cracked than that one, because it could be just that.

Let's say a road that is cracked has 12 inches of asphalt versus one that is just as cracked and has 1-1/2 inches of asphalt on dirt. You need to be able to gauge that and make your decision as to which one you address soon versus later.

Brian Frix, APM: About the MicroPAVER ASTM 6433, that does provide what they consider random, systematic sampling. So, it is supposed to be as unbiased as possible. If you use the GDOT system, the Paces system, to me, it creates a biased sampling of your roadway because you are at what you consider to be relative to what is out there.

You are going to look at a pavement section, within the 100 foot sample section. This is the sample section they need to take, whereas the ASTM 6433 uses an equation. Basically you go out and measure the roadway, and it gives you a specific number of sample sections that you take at specific distances. You can take more sample sections than that, but essentially there is a minimum number of sample sections you would take, and you would evaluate your pavement based on 20 or 23 different distresses. Then you would calculate your PCI based on that. So, I'm going to talk a little bit about that this afternoon as part of my presentation.

## Transcript ends

Okay, I hope you had a chance to really pay attention to that conversation from a real **Pavement Management RockSTAR**. Miquel walks the walk and he talks the talk. Yes, it is really happening, folks. There is no reason for you to fear doing something different than you are used to.

This marriage of pavement management, in-place asphalt recycling and pavement preservation is the real deal. And you know, I may be the first person on earth who put those three things together in the same sentence. You see, all the while each little company, and each little association was growing their businesses and promoting their message, I was up thinking, wait a second, if we just combined this with this, and with this thing over here, we could really make a difference.

Then I started looking where to learn how to do all of this, and realized that there was no one place where a person could do all of this. And then, it occurred to me, we have to build this. So, we made **IPMA** and then a few months later **IPMA Academy**.

It certainly helps that we have a consulting business out there in the trenches each and every day across America actually doing the pavement management. So, we can use the real life scenarios in our online class room. Then I met Imelda Diaz, PE at LA County, and we sat down and wrote the Mission Statement, and well as trite as it may sound, the rest is history!

Speaking of Imelda, let's go out again and review the graphic of her pavement management plan for the northern part of her county. So, let's start at the top left-hand corner that's Imelda's graph, right. That's just a reminder for us all to marry the in-place recycling and preservation treatments so you can realize that average price of about $3.41/SY range that Imelda is getting at LA County, CA.

Top right-hand corner of the slide on the next page, that's cement treated base. The pulverizer is going down about 10 inches there, and actually doing patches for a local agency as opposed to the entire roadway width. If you all want to write this down, this is another nice little note for you guys. Seven pounds per inch, per square yard. So, I would recommend that you aim for that number of seven pounds of Portland cement per inch per square yard. Take a note from Darold Wiggins from Heard County, GA, when you are out there pulverizing with an Asphalt Zipper or a Bobcat milling head or even harrows with the motor grader, which I would not recommend but if that's what you've got, we've mixed cement in with a backhoe bucket before if we had to set it up in an emergency.

If you can get your hands on Type III Portland cement, it will set up in a few short hours, almost instantaneously. The pulverizer is capable of going down about 22 inches but, if you go down 10 inches and use 7 pounds per inch, per square yard, it will get you 70 pounds per square yard, and take care of almost every problem with unstable sub base you can think of. Call the ready mix producer and ask, "Can you bring me dry cement out here in the ready mix truck?"

What I'm saying here is, if you go do this on your own with an Asphalt Zipper, you can actually hire the ready mix concrete mixer like Darold does, and have them deliver dry Portland cement to your FDR jobsite. Great idea.

I don't know why I didn't think of it. So, the ready-mixed concrete mixers have augers inside them.

They are meant to mix the cement on the way to the job site. So, instead of putting the water, the rock, the aggregate and sand they just put the dry Portland cement inside the barrel, take it Darold's site, they turn the augers backwards, they let it roll down the chute. He just measures the 70 pounds per square yard and his crew mixes it in with the Asphalt Zipper. He adds a little bit of water to the mix to hydrate it. So, that is going to give you the Portland cement-treated base there 10 to 12 inches thick.

We did this in truck terminals and roadways all over America 10 to 12 inches thick with the big pulverizers. So, if you are using cement 10 to 12 inches and, if you are using Bitumen, it is 6 or 8 inches for the foamed asphalt or the engineered emulsion.

Bottom right-hand corner in the graphic presented is cold in-place recycling—partial depth reclamation, anywhere between 3 and 6 inches. If you go more than 6 inches, it is really hard to compact a cold in-place recycled mat even with a 25 ton rubber roller. What you've got here on the bottom right-hand corner is a partial depth reclamation. So, they are going to go down partially into the asphalt or all the way down but not into the underlying rock.

133

The picture up there with the pulverizer is full-depth reclamation and they are going through the asphalt, through the rock, and into the underlying base.

Now on the lower left-hand side is the hot in-place train which in this case is about 2 inches in thickness period. I took this shot in Vegas during a Con Expo demonstration project. That train is picking up about 2 inches of old asphalt and running it through an onboard mixing drum on that hot in-place Re-HEATtrain coming out the back end, putting it down at 320 degrees, compacting it, opening it to traffic and it is finished.

I would like to see that you have 3 inches of asphalt before we recommend a hot in-place job because you don't want the machines picking down through into the rock and bringing up deleterious materials into the mat. One more thing, now that you've mentioned it, if you do go out and do some patches ahead of time for the hot in-place train, use 9.5 mm asphalt, that's the F mix, right? The 9.5 mm HMA; use that for your patching, otherwise it comes up a little bit coarse when they do the hot in-place train.

---

Remember, readers, don't ever feel bad about asking a question, fire away. E-mail me at blair@ipma.co if you have anything that is keeping you up at night.

---

I go out and look at distressed roads every single day, and we think it is going to be good for a certain treatment, and the next thing you know there's not enough quantity for that county to bring in the train to that project we selected. So, it's like we go out and find the perfect candidate on the perfect road to do cold in-place but there's only 8000 square yards of work, if you know what I mean.

Well, in that case then, I'm going to leave it up to you guys to put together some cooperative type bids where Tony's got 8000 square yards, Audrey has 10,000 square yards and maybe Mickey comes up with another 20,000 square yards. Then it is something we can put out for bid and get the contractors to come in and do that work. So, whether it is micro, HA5, hot in-place or cold in-place, they are going to be looking for a sizable amount of quantity like 5 or 6 miles of work to do and put it all together.

Yeah, what happens a lot of times is say the hot in-place train will come in from another state. Let's say they are working in Tennessee. They will put everything on a low boy and get it down here. Once it is here locally for him to go over to the next county they will just use heavy wreckers to pick them up and pull them over. So, I will give you a perfect example. This spring the hot in-place train is coming back to Cobb County, GA, to do a couple hundred thousand square yards. This is the best time for a local agency to be bolting on to the larger contract with the county. Because your 40-50 square yard job just got added to the big job with Cobb County, their agency has already 'paid' to have them come into Georgia.

# Chapter 6 – The Stringbenders vs. The Naysayers

In some states there is a specification for hot in-place recycling, but only with one of the three subdisciplines. It is based on the remixing spec, which, I think, there is only one remixing train in all of America. So, they've recognized that hot in-place recycling is a viable option, but they don't have an actual specification in the green book for the Re-HEAT, Surface Recycling, or the Re-paving hot in-place subdisciplines.

Some states do have a supplemental specification for cement treated base, but they don't really recognize FDR with bitumen yet. Many a consultant or contractor has tried in vain for decades to get some of these states to add specifications for in-place recycling and pavement preservation treatments to their state specification books. Finally, most local agencies, who often look up to the state DOTs, have said, "Forget it. Our local agency has given up on waiting for specifications and funding from the state."

A lot of times the local agencies just take their SPLOST (Special Local Option Sales Tax) money and spend it how they see fit. They say, "I'm not waiting for the DOT to write a specification. I can use my LMIG (Local Maintenance and Improvement Grant) funding. I'll just take the LMIG funding and do what I can with it." The local agencies must wonder sometimes why certain state DOTs are so reluctant to change their policies and open up their arms to acccpt in-place asphalt recycling and pavement preservation treatments that most all other state DOTs are doing.

So, let's talk about that for a second. In the business of training, all we can do is come in and say here's what's going on. Here's what you can do. I certainly can't make water run uphill. I can't control if I leave today, and someone from an association comes into your office next week and says whatever Blair said is a bunch of bull.

I can't control that, and, if they have some fixed views, and they want to continue to do things the way they always have been, we really can't control that. I sure am perplexed at the resistance level of some of our state DOT folks and their elected officials. A perfect example here is that while we are here putting on our own seminars in some states, other state DOTs are calling us and asking us come to their state. They say, "We've got room for you. We want you to do some training for our DOT." This is crazy isn't it?

Some state DOTs love to chip seal a lot, and I'm all for the chip seal. I mean, look at my friend Jason Sorenson at Montana DOT. Every mile of road that Montana DOT owns seems like it is covered with chip seal! I've got newfound respect for the chip seals. It makes me wonder sometimes why I'm driving through some of these states and it is all concrete interstate. Could it not be asphalt with chip seal on top, for that matter, like MDOT? Are the trucks different in Montana than they are in other states? Probably not, but I guess it depends on how much money they've got to spend, right?

I think it is a crying shame that some state Departments of Transportation feel the need to change the tried and true specifications, for whatever reason, before they give the processes a chance in their neck of the woods. And, again it is worth reiterating once more, with **The Three Legged Stool System of Pavement Management,** we all win.

You, as a local agency, win by stretching your dollars, just like Miguel said in the last chapter. The local contractors win because they get more tonnage down, in less time, with more profit, and the rate payers win because they don't see their hard surfaces being turned back into dirt because their city or county is going bankrupt. Don't laugh. It is happening right now somewhere in America.

It is obvious to anyone who is willing to invest about an hour on the good old Google search, that there internet thing, that there are plenty of in-place recycling and pavement preservation contractors who have done hundreds of millions of dollars worth of work with hot in-place, cold in-place and full depth reclamation all over America. They have done it with some very simple specifications that have worked for decades. But, for whatever reason, some state DOTs, I'm not mentioning any names here, they want to change the specifications or write their own specifications. I'm thinking, hell, if they saved hundreds of millions of dollars in Virginia on the I-81 project with these processes—and that's an interstate, right? — why couldn't they just use the same specification, and let some work already?

In fact, right now, some trade associations are busy working on refining specification guidelines for all of these treatments, across the board. There is NO NEED TO RECREATE THE WHEEL, FOLKS!

If you are wondering how to put your hands on these guideline specifications, e-mail me, and I will be happy to share just how easy this is. You see, it has been about two decades since I sat down in the office at FHWA and helped write a specification for FDR on the Natchez Trace Parkway for the National Park Service.

I cannot stress this enough: there is simply no excuse for your local state DOT, or local agency personnel, if they are NOT doing what is right in

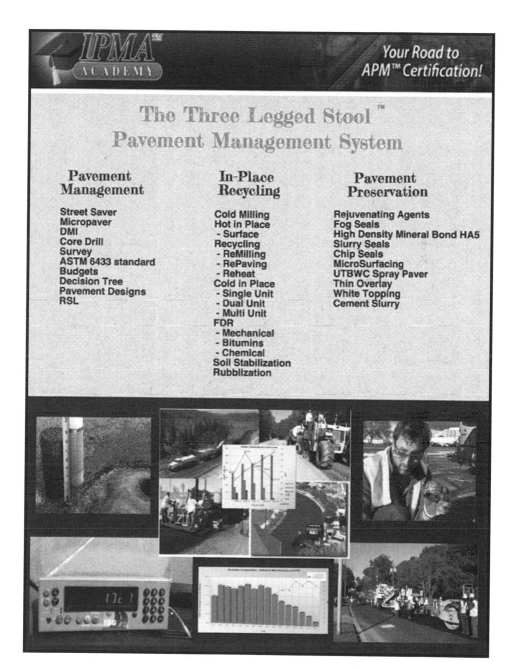

With the Three Legged Stool System of Pavement Management we all win!

139

your area of the country. The time has come for the **Stringbenders** to call out the Naysayers. We need your help, please.

The only way for us to save our economy is to band together, to form a movement, to stand up and say, once and for all, "Enough is enough of this bull\*\*\*\*!" It is time for all of those so called pavement engineers with their heads buried in the sand to either catch up with the rest of the world, or go get a job greeting customers at their local you know where.

There, I said it. I drew the line in the sand between the **Stringbenders** and the Naysayers. I want to keep on the high road here as promised. Again, I'm not here to bash anyone, but at the same time I can't spend too much time trying to convince people who simply don't want to listen. I want to invest time with those who do want to listen.

I appreciate it when the phone rings, or I get an e-mail from a local agency, or a state agency, and they say: "Can you come to California and do something for District 8? We set up a room for you, Blair. We haven't advertised the seminar yet but we know we would like you to be a part of it." (In California we already have 17 Caltran people signed up because they want to learn how to do things differently and for the better.)

I ask, why? Why are we still doing things like it is 1956, and mining out aggregate 400 feet deep? Two hundred million year-old rocks. The photo on page 141 is what the inside of a quarry looks like. Maybe a lot of you have never driven into a quarry to see what it actually looks like.

We throw that quarry slide up during all of our live training sessions, and, we think, "Man, that's a lot of aggregate that has been blasted up and

Why are we still doing things like it is 1956 with our pavements?

Why do we keep mining more and more 200 million year old rocks?

out of this place," right? We keep mining and blasting, and dynamiting, and trucking, and hauling all of that 200 million year old rock and burning diesel fuel. We are wearing out all of the local agency roads to get back to the job site, and I don't know why. Hopefully things will change here shortly. You know what I mean? You feel my pain? **Stringbenders,** let me hear you say, "Hell yeah, Blair!"

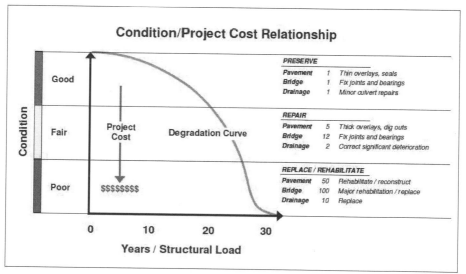

### Condition/Project Cost Relationship

| PRESERVE | | |
|---|---|---|
| Pavement | 1 | Thin overlays, seals |
| Bridge | 1 | Fix joints and bearings |
| Drainage | 1 | Minor culvert repairs |

| REPAIR | | |
|---|---|---|
| Pavement | 5 | Thick overlays, dig outs |
| Bridge | 12 | Fix joints and bearings |
| Drainage | 2 | Correct significant deterioration |

| REPLACE / REHABILITATE | | |
|---|---|---|
| Pavement | 50 | Rehabilitate / reconstruct |
| Bridge | 100 | Major rehabilitation / replace |
| Drainage | 10 | Replace |

A Typical Degradation Curve for Roads and Bridges

141

Note the typical degradation curve for roads and bridges on the previous page. That graph actually comes from a presentation that Federal Highways Administration put on for one of the Northwest Pavement Management Association conferences. Notice the recurring theme here in the entire book, whether it is me talking, one of our **IPMA Academy** Learners, one of our **IPMA Academy** LIVE seminar speakers, or whether it is our US DOT graphs. For every 1 (one) dollar you spend to preserve a road or a bridge, you will save 50 to 100 dollars by not having to deal with it in its deteriorated state.

I mean, how many readers and listeners here would let their windows break and not fix them? Would you let the roof leak and not fix it? You could just wait until the building needed to be replaced. That's how we have fixed our roads. Would you buy a new car and never change your oil? You could wait until you need a new engine, but you don't. Nobody does.

When not teaching I am doing – the teacher is always a student first

Yet, we watch our most valuable resource, our roadways, crumble before our very eyes due to mismanagement of funding in certain states and municipalities. What is wrong with this picture?

Here's a photo of me out in the field coring. Just in case you guys think I didn't actually work, I really do get my hands dirty. I get out there and get stuff done! Anything to help out our **Circle of Pavement Management RockSTARS!**

This is a core from a private sector job in Chicago, and I found out that their in situ, hot-mixed asphalt was a little bit on the fine side. The mix was unstable and appeared to have some plastic flow to it which caused a lot of rutting and heaving. Plus, the drainage was not all that good. So, I recommended to the owner that they do full-depth reclamation (FDR).

Even though it was a private sector project, I brought my little PAVER Distress Identification Manual along with me. We followed Dr. Shahin and the US Army Corp's ASTM 6433. This is scientific evidence to back up our decisions as pavement managers.

William Robertson, former Director of Public Works from the City of LA, said to me on the phone one day, "When the Council Districts in our City (LA) start complaining about who is getting more money and who has better roads, I rely on my PAVER data, and report to back up their decisions as if they were 'pavement managers.'"

Mr. Robertson actually went one step further with his PAVER system, which would normally be set to provide an average network level average across the entire City. He actually set up each Council District with its own separate network level PCI rating. He maintained the roads so each District would have the same network level PCI rating.

He could then stand in front of the Mayor of the city and state that no one got preferential treatment. With scientific evidence he knew exactly what was going on in every single Council District. Moreover — how about this one — one of the first cities to purchase a pulverizer for their own in-house crews was the City of LA.

The Mayor of LA and a group of city officials flew to Toronto and looked at some of the work that was being done up there. The convoy of LA officials came back to LA, contacted Wirtgen American, a milling machine manufacturer, got an RFQ together, and ended up purchasing a cold-in place train shortly thereafter.

It was a million-dollar, cold in-place train. In one year, according to Mr. Robertson, they saved 6 million dollars! The City did it themselves! Mr. Robertson went on to say that when all of the layoffs occurred in the City of LA Public Works Department, theirs was the only division that did not get laid off because they were looked at as leaders, and were actually "making the city money" by doing eco-efficient, in-place recycling. Crazy, isn't it?

Typical cold in-place recycling project
in Southern California

So, there you have it, cold in-place recycling is a typical job site illustrated in the photo below. In this case, the crew went down three or four inches with the cold-in place train. (Thanks to Kevin at Western Emulsions for supplying this photo for us to use in the book and **IPMA Academy**.) As a side note, I highly encourage you pavement managers to go out and proof roll these type of roads with a loaded dump truck,

That is something we've really recommended because not every road needs FDR. Again, not every road has to have full-depth reclamation. I have been tricked more times than I would like to say here. It is easy to look at the pavement distress and think the worse. But once you get out there, roll up the mudflap on the loaded dumptruck, and walk along side watching carefully for deflection in the base, you may be pleasantly surprised to find out that the pavement section is not as bad as you thought. And certainly the underlying rock may be more than adequate to support a new cold-in place recycled mat.

If you can get by with a cold in-place recycled layer, then with maybe a slurry, or an HA5, on top, that's the way to do it. After all, you've already got the structure there. Furthermore, the cold-in place contractors also do a great job of "following the rock" on job sites where the layer of asphalt on top and the underlying rock grades are consistent. In other words, they can "skim" over the top of the base rock, pick up all the in situ asphalt, recycle it with the engineered emulsion (or foamed asphalt) and put it right back down for compaction and leveling.

Now, take that money that you were going to spend on hot-mixed asphalt on all the projects that have historically been done that could be preserved and rehabilitated with **The Three Legged Stool System of Pavement Management** criteria and move it over to the FDR projects. This way your local agency or state DOT will start making a dent in your backlog

**The in-place recycling equipment has efficient mobility**

deficit of bad roads. You know the ones that we all agreed are never going to get fixed due to budget constraints.

When you do proof roll your roads, and find out that there is considerable deflection, consider using the FDR process. Typically, if there is more than 20% of the project level selection of roadway that requires deep patching with a milling machine and hot-mixed asphalt pavement, the project by default (because of costs) becomes an FDR candidate.

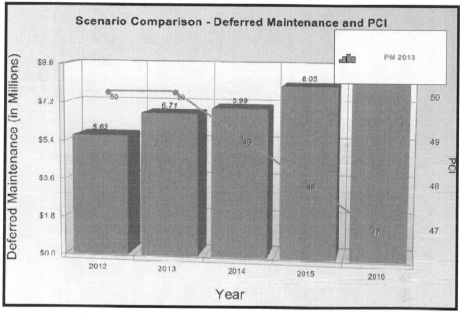

One of TBG's typical pavement management budget scenarios

In the photo on page 144 we are at Emory University, Georgia. I wanted to give you an idea of the mobility of these big, in-place recycling machines. This is at the Center for Disease Control (CDC) in Decatur and what Ashley did there. I don't know if you can see him up there, but he actually took a wrench and undid the U-clamp on the upright exhaust stack and rolled the entire assembly down on its side so he and his machine could crawl underneath the catwalk.

Pictured above is a graph that we typically see once we run the pavement management program budget analysis. In this case, this is one of our local agency clients who used StreetSaver software. Now, keep in mind, this could be any county or city in North America. If we went out there and did the pavement management for your local agency, don't be surprised if you see a similar situation happening when we run your budget scenarios.

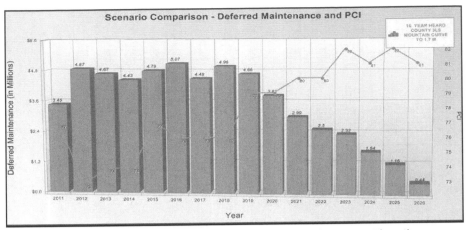

The Three Legged Stool System of Practical Pavement Management in action

In this example, the average network level PCI was 50, and it is on its way down to a 47. The backlog deficit value will go from 5 million to 8 million over the next five years! Clearly there is not enough money to go around, and, by now, this should be a recurring theme that you have heard throughout the book. This is analogous to us owning a nice sailboat that has a hole below the waterline. We set out for sail, and you or I would have to keep bailing the water out of the hull. Even though we poured money into fixing the sails, rebuilt the engine, filled up the diesel fuel, whatever, bottom line is, in this example, the local agency is spending many man-hours and constantly paying out their annual allotment for paving repairs to fix "leaks" in their network. They add up significantly.

Conversely, this graph above on the other hand follows **The Three Legged Stool System** approach. Little tweaks go a long way. In the example above we made some sound, practical pavement management decisions. We all agreed we are not going to place asphalt overlays on chip sealed (surface treated/tar & chip) roads anymore. Rather, we are going to move the pavement funds that would have typically paid for those overlays to paying for the full-depth reclamation work. That way we start to chip away our backlog deficit of bad roads in the county.

This is what you can do, too. Make practical pavement management decisions, little tweaks in judgment go a long way when you have very few dollars to go around your entire network of roads.

You can raise the PCI rating and eliminate the backlog deficit of bad roads. Does everybody understand that?

You are a bunch of readers. Remember to leave this book prominently displayed on your desk at all times, because, one day, I may stop into your office unannounced. Now, I am not saying this is like winning a radio contest or the likes of that, but your **IPMA Academy** Learners and Alumni will be the first to tell you that I have stopped by in the **Better Roads Bus** and completely shocked the heck out of them on occasion!

So, back to the graphic above, you are likely saying to yourself, "Wow, the cost of deferred maintenance is substantial!" And you are right. Remember the **Better Roads Radio Podcast** with Hans talking about how his backlog would go from 400 million up to 870 million by 2020?

In the example above, we started to chip away at the backlog deficit of bad roads by implementing the **Three-Legged Stool System** and making the little tweaks in our thought process: such as, no more overlays on chip sealed roads. Sure, we decided we might put some microsurfacing down on the surface treated roads if there was a need. There may be a church, or a school, or something on the road that raised the AADT (average annual daily traffic).

Note that the network level PCI rating is going up in the graph above. Now, you readers are pretty sharp, I know. Some of you being Auburn grads and all: the "War Eagles." Let's look here for a second. Why do you think the first little dip went down to a 73? What caused that? Why do you think that was? It kind of stalled a little bit before it started going up. Can you figure out why that might have been? I will go grab a coffee and give you pavement managers a minute to check out the graph again. . . .

What happened was the last round of SPLOST (Special Local Option Sales Tax) money dried up because they built some really amazing ballparks with it. The economy trailed off, so they weren't collecting as much as they were in past years.

Then the new influx of money came back in 2013-2014, and they got more money: 1 million per year. So, before we got in to do the pavement management, they were in a lull with tax income. Remember the economy had tanked, so even the SPLOST money they were supposed to be collecting (that they thought they were going to be getting) wasn't as much as they thought. Just because of commerce, right? We are all relying on that.

So, let's take a show of hands here. Do you have a SPLOST in place? If so, is it one percent? Two percent perhaps? If you just answered no, are you going to try to get one in place to help offset the cost of your pavement management program implementation? Okay. If you need any help writing a magazine article or a newspaper article to promote the SPLOST type election, I did this little magazine article when someone requested it for Cobb County.

You can read it here by clicking on this link http://mdjonline.com/bookmark/11695185-Blair-Barnhardt-Support-%E2%80%98SPLOST%E2%80%99-or-%E2%80%98Simple-Plan-Leverages-Opportunity-Saves-Taxpayers%E2%80%99 on your Kindle. And for you book readers, you can read it here below:

# Marietta Daily Journal article —

### Blair Barnhardt Supports 'SPLOST'
### Simple Plan Leverages Opportunity and Saves Taxpayers:

— **$700,000,000:** the amount that Nevada DOT has saved over the last 20 years by using pavement management, pavement preservation and in-place asphalt recycling.

— **$6,000,000:** the amount that the City of Los Angeles saved in the first year that the mayor allowed the bureau to purchase a $1.2 million in-place asphalt recycling machine to rejuvenate their worn out pavements.

— **$7,760,000:** the amount that Grady County saved by using in-place recycling on Old State Route 179.

— **33%:** the amount that one homeowners' association in Paulding County will save by using in-place recycling over conventional mill and inlay projects.

While we all deliberate about whether a SPLOST should be passed or not, our Cobb County infrastructure continues to crumble. We all worry about saving 13 cents a day by switching light bulbs in our office to more "green" illumination, yet we go ahead and potentially waste hundreds of millions of dollars by worrying about whether or not we should pass a simple SPLOST vote to allow Cobb to spend much-needed funds on repairing our aging infrastructure.

We are indeed fortunate to live in one of the most fiscally conservative and responsible county in the South. But we are light years behind the rest of the nation when it comes to spending our money wisely in terms of our road rehabilitation. Granted, we do have local asphalt producers that need to continue to prosper. These employers are going to great expense to produce eco-efficient products like warm asphalt mix, yet the county stumbles when it is time to implement this innovative green technology on an actual job site.

While privatized clients such as the City of Sandy Springs, gated communities like St. Ives Country Club Home Owners Association and Cottage Cove Home Owners Association jump at the opportunity to save 30 to 40 percent over conventional methods of rehabilitation for their own roads, our local governments continue to trip over local politics to justify spending millions more for their road reconstruction.

Note to Cobb County: if we don't vote in favor of the SPLOST, our roads will crumble beyond the point of a simple repair and fall into the much dreaded red zone of a Pavement Condition Index rating of 54 or less (pavement condition index of 0-100 where 100 is new and 0 is impassible).

When this happens, the $1 per square yard SPLOST funding that we would have spent to preserve our infrastructure with pavement preservation and in-place asphalt recycling will quickly become an $8 to $10 per square yard repair based on Federal Highways Administration research.

I have been involved with construction for over 30 years and have taught civil engineering classes for the past 17 years. It frustrates me to see our Cobb County citizens waste time arguing about the SPLOST funding vote.

If the roof of your half a million-dollar house was leaking, would you call someone to repair it immediately? Of course you would, and such is the case in Cobb County with our roads. In fact, 82 percent of the SPLOST funding is dedicated to resurrecting our crumbling roads, preserving our existing infrastructure, parks and facilities. We just need to pass the SPLOST and learn how to repair our roads most cost effectively by implementing techniques that other counties and states are using.

* **HYPHEN CAUTION**: If a link includes a hyphen as it goes to the next line of text, when you retype the link into your computer **do not include the hyphen**.

149

If we all vote "No" to the SPLOST, here is what will happen: At a rate of about 3 PCI points per year, our aging roads will fall from a network level average of about 63 to an average of 54 over the next three years. When this happens the cost to repair the same infrastructure will increase about 60 percent. In other words, the roads that we may have saved, such as Barrett Parkway, with a $9/SY in-place recycling and warm asphalt overlay will cost upward of $22/SY to repair, if we delay the SPLOST implementation. In addition, the length of the project duration will increase four-fold, thus causing more and more traffic delay for our ratepayers.

I have travelled from Alaska to California, from Maine to Florida, and everywhere in-between, teaching governments how to save money by using in-place asphalt recycling, pavement preservation and pavement management. Fortunately, most all of them get it. However, once Delta brings me back home, and I am in my driveway, I continue to be distraught by the fact that we are all wound up like a top over the SPLOST vote. Moreover, we continue to overlook the fact that our roads are wearing out faster than we can imagine, but we still have not learned how to repair them most cost effectively.

Kudos to Cobb DOT for implementing a Peach Roads Program. If this program becomes a success, our GDOT will replicate it state wide. As part of this program, our Cobb DOT emphasizes the importance of implementation of cost saving eco-efficient techniques, such as hot in-place recycling and micro surfacing for our roads in Cobb County. These techniques coupled with a solid pavement preservation program spell success for SPLOST.

I say vote "Yes" for the SPLOST, and hold our politicians and DOT engineers accountable for rehabilitation of our roads county wide with cost-effective asphalt recycling and pavement preservation techniques, such as those used by forward thinking and responsible agency engineers nationwide.

**Blair Barnhardt**, of Kennesaw, is a National Highways Institute Certified Instructor for Federal Highways Administration and a course designer and instructor (pavement preservation, recycling and management) for a prominent university. He is also a proud member of Citizens for Cobb's Future.

# End of *Marietta Daily Journal* article

Now, the vote didn't pass by a windfall in Cobb County. In fact it passed at 51% to 49%. It was a very slim margin. One percent margin? Yeah. The way to get the SPLOST passed each and every time is to prove to the residents that your agency is going to be fiscally responsible. Take a few quotes right out of the article above if you want if you think it will help your city or county get more money for pavement management.

Afterwards, you say we've got the SPLOST (or whatever acronym your agency comes up with), and thank you so much because, over the last six years, the PCI went up six points, and the deficit backlog went down. Now, let's talk about this for a second. I will share this with you because we did the pavement management for Lee County in Georgia under a Federal Highways Administration grant of some sort.

---

An MPO (Metropolitan Planning Organization) grant paid for 80% of their pavement management system set up and evaluation there. So, if you are in an MPO, you may do well to apply for your own similar FHWA grant, and get money to pay for the pavement management system implementation.

---

This one tip likely just paid for your book and a handful of seats to **IPMA Academy**.

The effects of multiple sequential overlays in urban environment

So, if you are the recipient of the FHWA MPO grant to help you with the implementation of **The Three Legged Stool System,** you are only putting out 20% of your own money from your local agency. You think about that for a minute. And, if you need any help with that let me know.

---

Shoot me an e-mail at blair@ipma.co.

---

So, any more questions on this slide? So, this is the good news, this example that I have just shown is replicating Imelda's slide right from LA County that I showed earlier.

I put the photo on the previous page in to show you what I see on a regular basis as we perform the pavement distress evaluation surveys. The residents hate these roll over curbs. I hate them too because they are so bumpy getting in and out of their driveways. They act as a small moat in between the road and their castles. When you start raising the pavement's elevation, people start putting pipes in for drainage.

In a little bit, I will also let you know how and why a perfectly good PCI 92 pavement may actually end up getting the FDR treatment as a result of multiple sequential overlays.

Now, in 1999 I wrote my first magazine article. It went to **Asphalt Contractor Magazine**. The topic we (Brian Mountjoy and I) discussed was full-depth reclamation and cold in-place recycling. Please note, folks, this was 1999. I thought for sure the industry and the world would soon learn what

The evolution of the Stringbenders versus the Naysayers

we knew about in-place recycling, and how eco-efficient and cost effective it was. It, however, seemed to stall for decades, and still stalls to this date in some states, much to my amazement.

So, I want to take a minute again to talk about the **Stringbenders** and the Naysayers. I mean you may be wanting me to tell me you a little bit more about the in-place recycling and preservation so you can get your arms around the idea if it is all new to you. Perhaps you haven't the time or the energy to GOOGLE the results of what other agencies are doing in terms of **The Three Legged Stool**.

Let's look at this photo on page 152 and talk about it.

---

In the left hand corner, in the red trunks, weighing in at . . .

---

No, let's be serious. Some may think that there is not enough information out there and not enough people talking about these tried and proven methods of recycling and preservation. I would call those people **the uninformed**. They simply need to spend a day on Google or set up some Google alerts on the types of treatments that we talk about in this book.

Now when someone does ignore Google, and ignores all the success stories out there, and they stick their head in the sand, and they spew venom about all the other treatments—those snake oil things—they are **the Naysayers.**

And the Naysayers will never change, I am certain. Unfortunately for all of us, many of the Naysayers hold very high level state and federal roles, and the local agencies look up to them. We wait for them to tell us how we should take care of our roads. And many of the small local agencies with little or no funding, hang on the words of those experts, the Naysayers. So, when the Naysayers tell them that the "snake oil" treatments don't work, and that is why those treatments are not in the state DOT specifications, and, as such, that is why the state DOT can't fund those treatments with their local agency allocations, well, that is really something between a lie and a distortion of the truth, to say the least.

So, by that little rant, I am asking the **Stringbenders** to unite, grab your torch, shed light on the uninformed, and bring them over to our side before the Naysayers get to them. For the sake of this country, for the sake our economy, for the sake of mankind, while you are reading this book, send out a strong message to the Naysayers for you are a **Stringbender,** and we must raise a generation of **Pavement Management RockSTARS** who will no longer dig up everything in sight and haul it away to a local landfill site, who will no longer allow the Naysayers to taint their fresh engineering minds.

---

It is evident that too many people are bashing pavement preservation for the wrong reason. Look at this project using the link to the **Asphalt Contractor** magazine article: http://www.forconstructionpros.com/article/10316741/lanford-brothers-uses-in-place-pavement-recycling-on-i-81-project. (At the risk of boring you one day, if we meet in person, remind me to tell you the backstory of when I met a representative from Landford Brothers in our NHI Workshop in Baton Rouge, LA, years before this project ever got out of the dirt.)

---

You see, I knew back in the 90s, that all of this worked. So, the next time when some uninformed pavement manager comes up to you and says, "I am not really sure that this Blair guy and this Three Legged Thing really work. I am not sure I really believe what he is talking about. I need some more evidence."

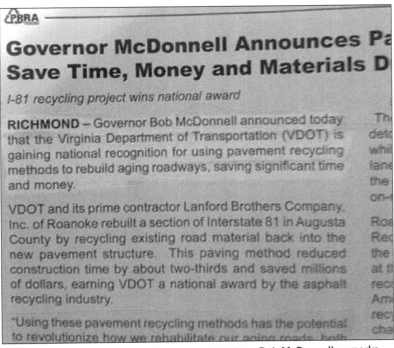

# Governor McDonnell Announces Pa
# Save Time, Money and Materials D

*I-81 recycling project wins national award*

**RICHMOND** – Governor Bob McDonnell announced today that the Virginia Department of Transportation (VDOT) is gaining national recognition for using pavement recycling methods to rebuild aging roadways, saving significant time and money.

VDOT and its prime contractor Lanford Brothers Company, Inc. of Roanoke rebuilt a section of Interstate 81 in Augusta County by recycling existing road material back into the new pavement structure. This paving method reduced construction time by about two-thirds and saved millions of dollars, earning VDOT a national award by the asphalt recycling industry.

"Using these pavement recycling methods has the potential to revolutionize how we rehabilitate our aging roads. Both

From the ARRA Newsletter – Governor at the time, Bob McDonnell, remarks

I would ask that you inform this person about this award-winning project with **Roads and Bridges Magazine**. The now, very popular Interstate 81 project from VDOT. They did cold in-place recycling, cold-central plant recycling, and full-depth stabilization all on one single project.

They let the truck traffic run on the cold in-place recycled lane long before it ever got the asphalt pavement wearing course. Brian Diefenderfer said there were more ESALs (Equivalent Single Axle Loads) in a couple of short weeks on that cold-in place recycled roadway than most cities and counties get in a entire year.

Furthermore, the VDOT engineers went out and did core depths, rut-resistance testing and falling weight deflectometer testing. The cold recycled mat passed with flying colors. As always who got the credit for this amazing job? . . . The Governor! (There is actually a new Governor now.)

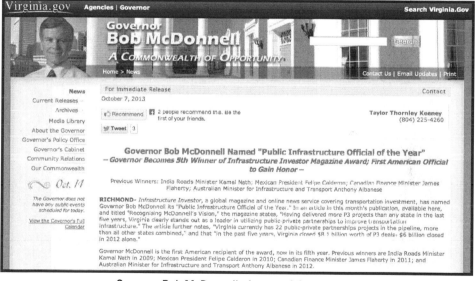

Governor Bob McDonnell wins prestigious award

But you can read more about what he said by doing a little Google search on that particular job. He said in an article that I read that using these pavement recycling methods has the potential to revolutionize how we rehabilitate aging roads both in Virginia and nationally. I would go one step further and say it has the potential to revolutionize how we rehabilitate our aging roads everywhere in the world.

There he is again in the photo below. He was honored as the public infrastructure official of the year, the first US citizen to ever win this cov-

* Hʏᴘʜᴇɴ Cᴀᴜᴛɪᴏɴ: If a link includes a hyphen as it goes to the next line of text, when you retype the link into your computer **do not include the hyphen**.

155

eted award. You don't get that by doing things wrong. So, again, I want to reiterate, at the risk of sounding like I am battering you guys, when you are finished reading, and you go back to your office, and someone knocks on your door from a local association, or a DOT, or a concerned citizen, or any combination of that, and they start bashing recycling and preservation, and calling it "snake oil," just know that that person is the Naysayer and you are the **Stringbender**!

You can actually have a little fun with the Naysayers. Let them go on and on, and pretend you don't know squat about pavement management, in-place recycling and preservation. Then, when they say to you that these methods are like "snake oil," you can simply excuse them from your office, and follow up with a few facts and articles you found in this book or doing your own research. In fact, let's all take a pledge that, as part of being a **Stringbender,** we promise to always take the high road together; the Naysayers will get what they deserve.

After all, how can a state DOT person walk into the County of Good Roads Office and say microsurfacing is "snake oil" when that same state DOT did 600,000 SY of it during a prestigious international event, and their own staff members went on to write a TRB report talking about how impressed they were with the technique?

Award winning cold in-place recycling - foamed asphalt cement VDOT I-81

156

Some of the DOT folks I talked to said microsurfacing—I am talking about in this example—stayed around for years. Years! And provided a great wearing surface. I'm just saying consider the source. There you go.

Here is a photo of the cold in-place train working away on the I-81 project for VDOT. That's a single-unit train. He's pushing the asphalt tanker. This is PG graded asphalt, 300°F plus asphalt. In this case, the project was using the foamed asphalt process in lieu of using engineered emulsion, although both have been used with a great deal of success. Foamed asphalt (also called expanded asphalt or CIREAM in Canada) was invented in 1956 at Iowa State University. It is the real deal, folks. I don't know what else to tell you.

---

Next up, hot in-place recycling.

---

Millions and millions in square yardage are recycled in-place every year in this country using hot in-place recycling. Again, beware of the Naysayers out there. Sometimes you may find your local trade association out coring roads in Good Roads County trying to find fault in the mix that was just laid. Just saying. Well, for what it is worth, I have gone out and cored these hot in-place recycled projects as well. And I have boxed up the samples and

Hot in-place pavement recycling — Re-HEAT — no wearing course required

HA5, High Density Mineral Bond – pavement preservation maintenance

sent the cores that I took to the lab. And the laboratory has performed Hamburg wheel load tests on the hot in-place cores that I took.

You know what? Everything passed perfectly fine. In my neck of the woods, we've done over 75 miles of hot in-place recycling alone. I some-times tire of the Naysay-ers when they start tell-ing you it doesn't work, but on a positive note, if it weren't for the Nay-sayers, I may never have had the commitment and impetus to write this book, hence you may never have read it. For that I guess we should be thankful

Boots on the ground pavement distress evaluation.

There's your HA5 going down in Heard County, Georgia (page 156).

Andrew, my son,  and Drew are doing pavement management assessment in the photo on page 158. The Yamaha Rhino 660 is what you see beside Andrew. It goes 43 mph. Street tires. It has signal and warning lights. It is legal in most of states. It's a great tool for managing pavement.

We break the roads up into simple categories: good, bad and ugly. We determine the "at risk" category.

PCI 50 is the critical break point in terms of HIR/CIR versus FDR with one caveat that I will mention next. Once things start going below PCI 50 then you and I would want to go out and start looking at stuff with a loaded dump truck and identifying where deep patching is required.

HIR surface recycling prior to HMA overlay – proof rolling done in advance

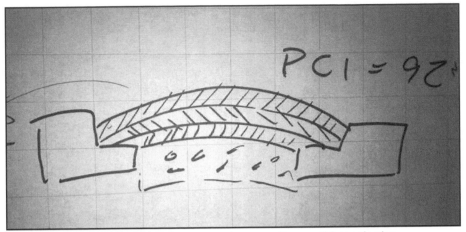

**When a PCI 92 is not a pavement preservation candidate selection**

Let's say you and I do a loaded dump truck proof roll. We start painting up over 20-30% for deep patching with our white spray paint. We might just want to go out and do the full-depth reclamation either with the big machines, or we might just rent an Asphalt Zipper type apparatus like a lot of county and city engineers do.

For comparison sake the photo below is a good example of the hot in-place surface recycling prior to a hot mix top of this section with a one inch layer. In this case, the local agency did a comprehensive, loaded, dump truck proof roll on all of the candidate selections at the project level where HIR was proposed. Very little deep patching was required, and most of it in the cul-de-sacs. Hence, the city proceeded with the HIR process.

Now a lot of times in urban environments, we are going to come across a situation like this sketch where the PCI (pavement condition index) is going to be in the very good range, or say for example a PCI 92. The road is going to be in decent shape, but the dreaded parabolic curve of the cross section of pavement is such that the buses driving down the roadway now are on such a sideways lean that they are almost in danger of clipping the utility poles at the edge of the curb line. You know what I'm saying?

So, it is unfortunate that on a road that has been built up like this, even with plenty of structure, and even though the PCI is hypothetically a 92, the software is going to tell Dave and I that it is okay. It may be necessary in 3 years to put a preservation treatment such as microsurfacing, or HA5, on it. But, when you and I go out in our pickup truck and drive it, we see the buses clipping the utility poles. We go, "Damn, we've got to take this, and do something other than a preservation treatment."

So, more likely than not, you are going to take this road and do a complete overhaul with the cold planing operation to take away the overburden of multiple sequential overlays, and get back down to its original grade with FDR and inlay.

In this example above, look for potential problems with hydrology and sheet flow once your curb and gutter section is filled in. It becomes a problem, and a liability, when ratepayers call up and say their garage is getting flooded because the water that is supposed to be draining from the county or city road is not getting into the inlets.

From my contracting experience, we are going to typically mill this up, get down to the old sub-base, do FDR, and build it back up with asphalt to the original gutter condition. That way it is going to come right back to the top of the gutter where it belongs. The amazing thing is when you do that FDR right, the 50 or 60 year-old curb gets bleached with all the Portland cement during the couple of weeks of work (assuming you are doing chemical stabilization as opposed to bituminous).

When preserving your roadways – think safety – think about Johnny and her glasses.

It is almost like bleaching your teeth white. Now you have this brand new asphalt, brand new truncated dome detectable warning panels (assuming you have complied with DOJ), and I've literally been tricked when I've driven up on the job site and I thought to myself, "I don't remember bidding new concrete curb and sidewalks," but it actually gets bleached along the way.

It rains, you run the water truck on it for two weeks, the crew sweeps in it, the power broom comes along, and before you know it, you've got a curb as white as the paper this book is written on. That's what the curb looks like. So, it is really cool to get out and do this. It is unfortunate we have to do a PCI 92 with this invasive process, but we can't control the misguided spending of money that went on over the last 50 years. I hope you guys understand.

Now I want to introduce you to Johnny who is in this photo on the previous page. I regretfully must say that Johnny has since passed. When I took this picture she was about 92, partially blind, and had been struggling with a severe bout of cancer.

Now, she's on a Heard County, Georgia, road. You are looking at a coarse, chip sealed road, that is in perfectly good condition, from the 1976 era. When we met out there at her mailbox while we were doing the pavement distress evaluation, Johnny said to me, "I used to be able to go drive this thing down the road and visit my friends. I'd follow the yellow stripe in the middle of the road with my little Yamaha Mule. Now the road is so faded I can't see the yellow stripe."

At the time of this photo, all she could do is go to her mailbox and back to her house. She couldn't go down and see her friends because she wasn't able to see well enough. So, I said to Darold, the County Engineer, we ought to think about getting some fog seal, some of the HA5, a rejuvenating seal, or something, just to make the surface treated road black again. Because I'm starting to think if Johnny can't see in the daytime, and I go down there on a rainy night, I probably can't see either because I can't see that well at night now.

It is a very dangerous situation, and I see a lot of county roads in the Southeast like this one. The surface treatment is still holding up incredibly well for their age, but the surface of the road has faded so badly you can't see any signs of the painted stripe. So, think about putting $1/SY $2/SY yard treatment just so that people, like Johnny, can see where they are going. My thoughts on this are, if Johnny can't see, most of your travelling public may also have the same problem at night when they are behind the wheel of their vehicle.

And really consider proper project rehabilitation techniques whether you are preserving or are doing rehabilitation. Look at what is happening. Look at the forensics. Look at your pavement structures at the project level.

Long after your crews and I have done the network level pavement management for your county or city, we still have to be able to go out to each individual road that the software is selecting and apply the common sense approach to what needs to be done at the project level.

So, the next photo is a City of Marietta, GA, road, basically in my backyard. Remember, I showed the Re-HEAT hot-in-place train photo on page 157? This particular sub-discipline of the HIR process has the in situ asphalt heated upwards of 2 inches in depth, picks it up, mixes in rejuvenating oil, and puts it right back down with no wearing surface overlay required. This particular project saw about $950,000 worth of work done in the City of Marietta a couple of years back. We had some folks out recently from the City at one of our **IPMA Academy** LIVE training events. The road is still holding up great as a result of this treatment.

Great candidate selection for Re-HEAT HIR recycling – BEFORE photo

The Re-HEAT train came in here, heated up both sides of the road, put it back down again and compacted it. They striped it, and that was it. At that time the cost was like $9/SY. No milling. No dust. Nothing. ReHEAT, stripe it, done. The photo on the previous page is the old road before it got Re-HEATed. Notice the abundance of trench repair from the new water main installation. Do you have roads like this in your city?

Now as a side note for those of you who do trench repairs and use the old class B concrete trick. This will come back to haunt you if you later decide to do HIR. If you put class B concrete back in these trenches, and just put 1 inch of asphalt on top (the hot in-place train is capable of heating to a depth of 2 inches), that would prohibit the use of HIR because the asphalt would not ne thick enough.

---

Also, what I will do for those of you who register your book at www.thebookonbetterroads.com/register, I will go back out when I get the opportunity and try to find this same location a few years after the fact and get some video of how the Re-HEAT is holding up. If I can get someone from the City to interview on film or do a **Better Roads Radio** Podcast session I will do that as well and you will receive the link directly in your inbox when it is available.

---

Small areas of rutting lend themselves to Zipper type FDR repair

Zipper type attachments for FDR small to medium sized projects

So, the photo on page 164 is a shot I took it in Augusta, Georgia. I was over there doing some LTAP training, and the folks in the classroom said you better go out to this roadway and have a look at it. It looks a little rutted there doesn't it? So, the folks who are reading this and already own an Asphalt Zipper, or some sort of pulverizer attachment, your pavement managers already know what you'd be doing with that, right? The old zip-er-roo job with some Type III Portland cement, right? I'd bet by lunchtime you'd have that zipped up by now with cement in it and get it all set up again.

Then you could call Dr. Mike over at NCAT. He would send you an awesome job mix formula for some SMA (Stone Matrix/Mastic Asphalt), some really highly rut-resistant, hot-mixed asphalt to put back on top of the FDR. There's a little shot of the Zipper type attachment I am talking about.

On the way to becoming a **Pavement Management RockSTAR**, I'd also like to see you do the manhole adjustments, water valve adjustments and any other type of utility adjustments professionally as well. It drives me crazy when I drive through a fancy subdivision, and I get that ba-bump, ba-bump, right? No need for that. Change order #1. Get some riser rings, and make the contractors use them. (Many agencies simply put a line item in the bid for water valve and manhole riser ring adjustments.) Even if that means it would involve some ready-mixed concrete around the frames and

One of my personal pet peeves —
poor workmanship

Top ten list of liabilities —
Be on the lookout for situations like this

grates, you know, setting that up, and putting the concrete around it.

Get some riser rings, and make the contractors use them.

What we like to see is we go in and we drop these during full-depth reclamation projects (CIR and HIR if possible), put steel plates on them well underneath the depth of the proposed treatment and locate them with a GPS (you might just reference it on the curb and gutter). When we come back to raise them up to the binder grade and add concrete around them, we'll put the concrete level with the binder grade, but raise the actual structure up to final wearing course grade, then pave around them with the top course asphalt (or white topping). Ideally when you are finished, the top of the water valve or manhole cover is 1/4" to 1/2" below the new surface so our friends located in snowy parts of the country don't hit them with their snow plows.

Another example of practical pavement management with **The Three Legged Stool System** is what we call a **Top Ten List of Liabilities** on the job deliverable list. This Top Ten Item below would be a huge liability to a county or a city.

In this example on page 166, Brian Frix, APM, one of your **IPMA** Advisory Board Members, is standing underneath the basketball net in Rockdale County, GA. This basketball net pole is embedded in concrete and sitting in the county right-of-way. So, you see a problem with that?

If I'm a resident, and I rent a Hertz rental truck, and I drive around that cul-de-sac tonight in the dark, and I scrape up the Hertz rental van, I'm not going to pay for it out of pocket am I? Hell no, I'm going to sue the coun-

Resist the urge to block off your paved HMA surfaces if possible

ty. Isn't that what we are supposed to do? Sue the people with the most amount of money, right? So, what we do is we take pictures of this, put in the Top Ten List, put in the comment field on our paperwork, and notify the agency we are working for. I would highly encourage you all do exactly the same thing when you are doing your field surveys.

Now in the next two photos below, I would like to draw your attention to a situation we see from time to time in the field. We know as pavement managers, that you've got to put traffic on your asphalt.

---

After all, hot-mixed asphalt pavements are viscoelastic. It is never good to NOT run traffic on them, or they will deteriorate faster than the paved roads that people are actual driving on.

---

So, when we we're out doing the pavement evaluation, we are looking for this situation as well, and that's what you see in these photos.

The top photo on page 165 is a four-lane highway. It has been blocked off, but I resisted the urge to check how fast my SUV would go, and stuck with just doing the pavement evaluation. But, I can assure you, if I went back and looked at the PCI conditions of this roadway shown below, on the side that is blocked off, the PCI rating would be substantially lower than the side that is not blocked off.

**Good candidate for HIR surface recycling depending on section thickness**

Because we are not putting traffic on it, I made the suggestion to the county that they may want to consider opening up a day care center down there (in behind the blocked off area) and tear the fence down. Or give the property freely just to let traffic drive down there every day and keep that asphalt pavement flexible.

In the bottom photo on page 165, the local agency is deterring traffic flow on their hot-mixed asphalt pavement, and, therefore, this section, on the right hand side of the photo, will actually wear out prematurely. Wherever possible, resist the urge to deter traffic flow on your pavements. The pavement wants and needs traffic to keep them in good shape longer.

The road photographed on page 168 is a perfect example of a road we recommended to receive the hot in-place surface recycling out there. Now again this is the BEFORE picture. The contractor went in, did the hot in-place surface recycling technique and it got covered up with microsurfacing as the final wearing surface. In this case it could have also been covered up with High Density Mineral Bond (HA5) or similar treatment.

So, you may be thinking, well, if that is a good candidate for hot in-place, at what point should I be considering doing a cold-in-place or full

Example of a pavement section suited for CIR or FDR

depth reclamation instead? In the photo below, I would draw your attention to the severity of alligatoring and the apparent delamination of the asphaltic layers. This is a road I would definitely want to proof roll with a loaded dump truck after it has been selected for project level rehabilitation for that particular season.

A good **Pavement Management RockSTAR** is going to look up his reports, check the percentage of load related distress there is on this section pictured below, check the percentage of environmental distress there is, as well as "other," and then make a determination on CIR or FDR. Clearly it is too far gone to do a HIR treatment. Again, we go into this in detail during over 70 hours of online training at **IPMA Academy**, and I can't cover all of the specifics in this book for every occasion that might present itself.

---

If you would like more information on enrolling in the **IPMA Academy,** you can visit **www.ipmaacademy.com.**

---

At this point I want to reiterate the importance of not only network level coring per **The Three Legged Stool System of Pavement Management**, but also at the project level. This is where you will determine which treatment to use to rehabilitate your aging roadways.

The old 'quilt work' pattern - patch within a patch dilemma

For example, on a section of roadway that I investigated for Diane at Thurston County, WA, it was determined there were actually two layers of delamination in the 9 inch cores that were taken. We mutually agreed that we could let the project as a CIR project at a depth that would eliminate the two separate layers of delaminated asphalt .

If there had been 3 or more layers of delamination on this same section of County Road, we would have mutually determined that CIR would not effectively remove the delamination in its entirety and hence we by default would have reverted to FDR.

So, maybe now is a good time to also mention that, as consultants, contractors and material suppliers, providing solutions out there, getting ready to implement all that you are reading about, know you have the capability to separate your firm from the pack, so to speak, simply by following the guidelines in this book. We have seen many learners like yourself go through our **IPMA Academy,** and coming out on the other side with the knowledge to increase their value to their customers with their newfound pavement management knowledge. Not to mention that, along the way, you get to meet some really cool people who are managing pavements everyday just like you, all across the planet!

Do you see roads like on page 170? The old "quilt work" pattern road, you know, where there are patches within a patch. Guess which is wearing out faster? The new patch or the old road? The new patch!

The new patch is "tore up," as we say here in the Southeast! The old road is still holding up pretty good. If you follow the quick-cut saw marks you can tell which is the old patch and which is new patch. There you go: a little trick there for you readers to remember the next time you are out investigating pavement distress on patched roads (no extra charge for that tip).

**Drainage, Drainage, Drainage – The 3 most important things**

I get the feeling we are about to wrap this chapter up, folks. What time is it anyway? One thing before I end this chapter, just as Dr. John Emery told me, one of my main mentors from a way back in the days of hockey and freezing temperatures in Canada:

"Blair, the three most important things in building roads are drainage, drainage and drainage."

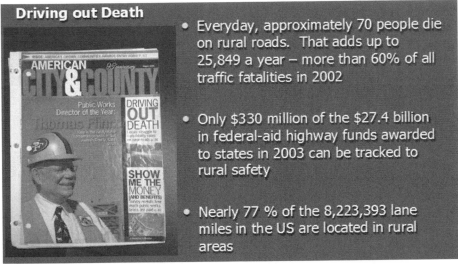

**Driving out Death**

- Everyday, approximately 70 people die on rural roads. That adds up to 25,849 a year – more than 60% of all traffic fatalities in 2002

- Only $330 million of the $27.4 billion in federal-aid highway funds awarded to states in 2003 can be tracked to rural safety

- Nearly 77 % of the 8,223,393 lane miles in the US are located in rural areas

Wider, safer, stronger roads should be our number one goal

Hard to imagine i have been doing this for two decades

Please remember as you are out there doing your pavement distress evaluations, look for drainage problems. A good amount of time the reason your roads are failing are because of drainage problems.

So, if it is in the middle of a drought, and there are cattails (you may call them bull rushes) growing up out of the bar ditches, you might want to consider some cross drains, and drainage improvements ahead of whatever rehabilitation techniques you are considering. Worth showing again, here is a photo below of what I typically see in most city and county ditches.

And in closing for this section of the book, I want to point out that while you are reading, seventy-five people will die today on unsafe rural roads because of that high severity edge drop off. I know we discussed that earlier in terms of pavement management, and how it can affect the PCI rating.

I would like to think that our number one goal in building better roads across this planet is to provide our travelling public with wider, safer and stronger roads. While we can't always do that with certain preservation techniques, we certainly have that ability in the pavement design of our recycled in-place pavement sections. There will be plenty of free BONUS content on this subject coming directly to your in-box after you register your copy of the book.

That's my FDR crew on the bottom of page 172, right in my back yard, at the City of Kennesaw, Georgia. You know the road was kind of buckled. You know we call them woopty-doos in the Southeast. Do you call them that in your township, city or county? Welcome to the South now. This is

30 Miles of FDR with Portland cement – Natchez Trace Parkway – NPS – FHWA

a woopty-doo. Right everyone? You get out there and you get a couple of woopty-doos, and you go out and fix it with a full-depth reclamation pulverizer. In this case foamed asphalt cement is being applied. This is the fastest way I know, bar none, to double or triple the strength of the in situ pavement section literally overnight for a fraction of the cost of conventional rehabilitation. And again, you won't hear this from the Naysayers because they don't quite understand **the Three Legged Stool Vision.**

In our vision, the **Stringbenders** will watch over the next decade as the shift in hot-mixed asphalt pavement goes over to the FDR roads, the CIR and the HIR roads. The preservation will help keep the good roads good longer, and the paving industry folks will take the next 215 years to clear up the backlog deficit of bad roads in this country, at 800 million tons of HMA a year up from the 600 million tons they are currently putting down.

As a bonus for you all for getting this far in the book, I will throw in a little info on soil stabilization. When my back has been up against the wall, nothing performs better, quicker and stronger than a little Portland cement or quicklime or whatever you have on hand to accomplish the task. Here are a couple of quick stories, and you know I have plenty of them!

Page 173 is a photo of a reclaimer. We did 30 miles of FDR with cement on the Natches Trace Parkway. Again people may ask, "Blair what the heck do you know?" I say, well, there are a few things I don't remember; but there's one that sticks out in my mind like it was yesterday. You see, this one job taught me about the capabilities of using FDR with Portland cement. Again, this is 30 miles of cement treated base on top of Mississippi mud.

FDR with foamed asphalt – private sector base stabilization work

That's a lot of woopty-doos out there because of the Yazoo Clay. We went out there (back when I was with Blount Construction in Georgia) and spent a couple of months doing this project for NPS (National Park Service and FHWA); Natchez Trace Parkway, Jackson, Mississippi. Cement treated base. They paved over our FDR with a shuttle buggy—that is an 80,000 lb. MTV (Material Transfer Vehicle)—and put a hot-mixed asphalt overlay on top of the FDR stabilized base course. A word of caution: Even though MTVs have high flotation tires, you don't put a big shuttle buggy just anywhere. You have to proceed with caution, even when doing an asphalt overlay.

Mississippi mud is a challenge, I tell you. We had blow counts of zero doing DCP (Dynamic Cone Penetrometer) testing, which means there was nothing in the soil to stop the weighted cone from penetrating the soil until it reached the 20' below the surface! Twenty feet! They dropped the hammer onto the cone and there was no resistance! Mississippi mud. We almost lost the pulverizer up against a bridge deck one night. It got hung up against a bridge deck and began sinking into the mud. The FHWA (Federal Highway Administration) inspector told the Vice President of Blount Construction, "I don't care if you've got to unbolt that machine bolt by bolt to get it out of here, don't scratch my bridge deck!" After some tribulation, they did get the machine out of the mud, and all was good.

Soil stabilization Hartsfield Jackson Airport – P301–P304 specifications

In fact, FDR works so darn good that the private sector folks, who are always concerned about their ROI (return on the dollar), started doing it early. They've known about this for decades. In some parts of the country you may see lime used mostly in new developments and other stabilization agents used in built-out areas.

Also, you can use lime to modify your soils and cements to modify and dry up wet mud. We've done plenty of that for local agencies and at the Kia Plant. We saved 30,000 cubic yards of wet fill from getting replaced with imported fill at the Kia Plant in Georgia by drying it out with quick lime! You contractors can appreciate the cost savings in that endeavour!

Below is a photo of one of our paving projects at the Hartsfield-Jackson Airport. This is back in the days when I was the Vice President of Atlanta Paving. We had this project that we could not get completed on time because of the high moisture content in the sub base. It was too wet and too muddy to be worked. I asked the consulting engineer on the project if we could use the same cement treated based that we did at McCollum Airport a few weeks prior. I showed them the P 301 and P 304 Specifications and some photos of what we had done at the last project at McCollum. They said, "Go ahead, Blair, let's get this thing done." After we added the Type III Portland cement, building a strong soil stabilized base, we were paving it the next day. Done. Problem solved.

Page 176 is a photo of a similar situation in Kennesaw, Georgia, back in my back yard again. This is a theater that was built up on the hill. Wet,

**Portland Cement Soil Stabilization**

unsuitable fill was used. The paving contractor asked, "Blair, what can we do? We can't get on here with our paving and the owner can't get their Certificate of Occupancy!"

They were saying to me, "We can't get the rock on. It's too wet. They won't let us get this thing opened up and paved. Everyone around here is getting a little crazy!"

I suggested, "Put some type III Portland Cement in it. Stabilize the base." The next day they got it paved! Unfortunately, the day after the road was successfully paved, the theater's foundation footings started sinking. Yes, they had to take every seat out of the theater and jack up the footings in the foundation wall, then put all the seats back in again. But the road going up to the theater was really good!

---

Thanks to all the folks in our **IPMA Academy** LIVE Training for giving us the feedback and comments for these past couple of chapters! Special thank you goes out to you folks for hanging out with us, spending your valuable time with us. I love talking about the three-legged stool and I'm blessed to know that the last 30 years of my life has been spent teaching people just like you and watching you save literally billions of dollars. Thank you for being *Stringbenders*!

---

# Chapter 7 — Meet the Stringbenders — Part 1

In a little bit I am going to take you to Boise, ID, for the IACERS Conference and introduce you to about 150 **Stringbenders,** and, yes, I will explain where I came up with that term as well, in case you have been perplexed all along.

But before I do that, I am going to introduce you to Brian Frix, APM, one of your **IPMA** Advisory Board Members.

---

Recall that, as an agency person, you are eligible to JOIN **IPMA, The International Pavement Management Association,** at absolutely no charge, and there's no hidden agenda, no strings attached. We set this thing up to serve our circle of pavement management **RockSTARS**. So, take a minute before we meet Brian, and head on over to www.ipma.co, and sign yourself up right now, ya' hear, (as he says with a Canadian/Georgian Southern drawl).

---

In this chapter I will introduce you to one man who, with a little help from his county public works director and road commission, took the **Three Legged Stool System of Pavement Management,** and, in a few short months, turned his county upside down, for the better.

Brian is a sharp dude. He understands all that we talk about, but, more importantly, he IMPLEMENTS IT. Yes, you heard me right, he actually took the knowledge, stood up for all of mankind, and said something like: "We can have a better planet. We don't have to keep doing things the way my grand diddy an' pah pah did it."

"Yes, join me down in Ge-or'-ja for a few weeks, and you will be talking just like that." ☺ . . . All joking aside, I am most proud of Brian for taking the initiative to stand up with Miquel, whom you heard earlier, go to their road commission, and tell them we have a system to change the way we do things for the better.

Both Brian and Miquel told me I would need to be patient as we set up their pavement management system. It may take up to three years or more to get the road commission to understand, to get the chairman and the county commission to fully understand.

. . . It actually took about 3 weeks!

That's right, it took all of about three short weeks for Brian and his crowd to say, enough is enough. If there is a better way to do this, a more eco-efficient, cost saving, time saving way, why the heck aren't we doing it?

And there it is. **The Three Legged Stool System** is adopted by another local agency, and now they do more roads with less money. This is happening every day, every week, every month. Not a day goes by when I don't see some success story of some local agency changing the way they manage their pavements. I get the news in my e-mail, my LinkedIn, my Facebook, my Twitter, and on and on. I LOVE IT. Because this is what our mission statement is at **IPMA**! This is what Imelda wrote on that napkin at the sushi restaurant in Pasadena:

---

The **International Pavement Management Association** will revolutionize the practice of pavement management through expert education, comprehensive technical training programs and professional certification for the world.

---

And so, enough about that already, let's listen in on an **IPMA** Academy LIVE Training Session where Brian talks about setting up his pavement management program with StreetSaver and TBG.

---

The video will be made available at the **IPMA** Marketplace as part of the DVD HD Box Set "**IPMA** Academy LIVE Greatest Hits Package. This Box Set will have upwards of 14 hours of HD DVD content on

it with amazing speakers from across the pavement management spectrum. For more details on this Box Set you can visit http:// www.ipmaacademy.com/live/.

---

Brian Frix, EIT, MSC, APM: All right, I don't think I've ever been welcomed that way before, especially by a government agency! Thank you!

Again, we'd like to welcome you here again. I know it has been a long day. I'm going to take this opportunity to dumb things down a little bit because I know we have discussed a lot of interesting topics — a lot of in depth information has been presented to you. I know everybody in here may not be an engineer, you may just be a worker bee, like me, you may be a worker bee engineer like me, you may be a PhD, you know, like our friend here in the back—Dr. Michael Heitzman—but I'm just going to dumb it all down a little bit, and just assume nobody knows anything about payment management.

Regarding our local program, I'll give you some information on StreetSaver, which is what we currently use for our pavement management. Then, I'll give you some information on some of the treatments we have done that most of these fellows have mentioned today. Then see if you have questions.

So, basically, I'm going to touch on pavement evaluation inspection, and some things we've done as far as resurfacing and maintenance. We've done FDR. We've done your patch mill overlay; micro-surfacing; heat scarification (hot in-place surface recycling); High Density Mineral Bond (HA5), we did a pilot project back in the summer. We are getting ready to do another relatively large project here this summer. We've also done crack sealing and patching. We've done that both in house, and we've contracted that out.

So, the first thing before you can do any type of roadway work is you've got to have some sort of pavement management program in place. It all starts with your pavement evaluation and inspection. Now, for most agencies, you may have some small program in place to where you may perform the surveys in-house.

You may have some staff that is capable of doing that. If not, you may have to obtain the services of professional consultants like **The Barnhardt Group**. There are several other firms out there that do pavement evaluation and inspection. There's the motor automated inspection as well, if that is something you're interested in. You know there are some differences between automated versus the on-the-ground inspection, but that is up to you to decide what you can afford, and what best suits your local needs.

We did a full network evaluation this past summer of our entire network. We have about 500 miles that we currently maintain. That includes paved roads and the gravel roads that we maintain as well. You can see all the different distresses we have dealt with here.

We have some high severe alligatoring on the top right corner, some concrete failure on top left, some edge drop off bottom left which looks like maybe some alligatoring, block cracking, all kinds of different failures.

I think Blair must have hacked into my slide presentation because it seems we've got a lot of the same pictures. But, again, this is what's been pressed the whole day, and reiterated time and time again.

It's pavement management. The graph on page 183 shows pavement condition versus time. The curve shows that the optimal timing to treat your pavements is at the top. As the pavement ages,

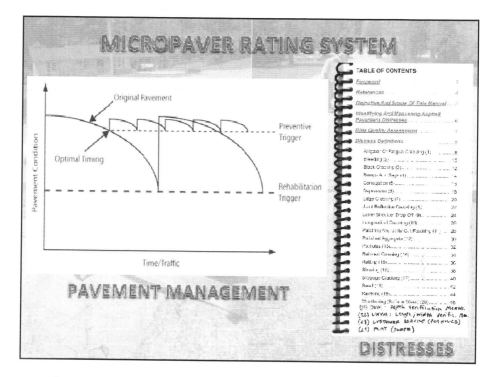

it starts to deteriorate, just like Mark went over this morning. Just like Blair has reiterated. It deteriorates, and every time you come do a treatment, it bumps your PCI back up.

Now, this curve is showing how a treatment at the bottom of the curve bumps the condition index back up to 100 PCI. That would be a reconstruction, or some thick overlay. But when you get down here to a reconstruct category, when you're at a failure, typically it is going to cost quite a bit of money to get you back up to a PCI 100. You are looking at $15 - $20/SY to get it back up. While a treatment near the top of the curve is about $2/SY. You should treat it sooner.

Here we're talking, as you know, pavement preservation. We are talking HA5 (High Density Mineral Bond). We are talking micro-surfacing, slurry seals; whereas down at the bottom of the curve you are looking at more of your overlays, thick overlays, FDR, full reconstruction, which has been reiterated all day to you.

This slide shows the MicroPAVER rating system. It includes the 20 different distresses. There are quite a few others that we've added over the last few years: 21 is depth verification measurement, 22 is length width verification measurement, 23 is customer service (potholes or anything that needs to be addressed immediately that may potentially be a hazard) and 24 is cross slope.

These are things that will be noted within reports. Many of you are probably familiar with most of these: alligatoring, bleeding, block cracking, depressions, lane shoulder drop-offs, patching potholes, shoving, raveling, weathering. All of these are asphaltic concrete distresses that you will find.

Now, there is another manual for concrete roads that you would use to rate your concrete roads as well, but we only have three concrete roads in our county. We've already repaired those. We are just dealing with straight asphalt now, but if you were dealing with concrete, you want to consult the concrete manual.

Here's the MicroPAVER rating system, all the way from zero, which is failed, up to 100 with the PCI. I won't get into that because Blair did go over that with you. This is what I wanted to touch on for a few minutes. This is this is StreetSaver.

The slide on this page is the interface, the dashboard for StreetSaver, which is what we use for our pavement management and analysis. So, once you go out and obtain all your pavement

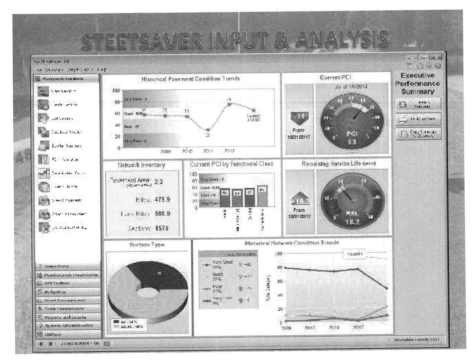

data, your distresses in the field, you will bring those back and input all that into your computer.

You will need your length, the width, so you can calculate your areas, and you would input all of your inventory data in these sections. This is very user-friendly software as well. I'm not promoting this particular software; this is just what we use here locally. There are several other software programs out there.

You would enter all your inventory data in here, and, once you obtain all your distress information from the field, you would enter that in. From there you can run . . . .

Well, let me step one step back. You have to plug-in a decision tree. Essentially that is your local unit costs and they clarify what you want to do to your pavement. The computer is not going to decide how to engineer your pavement; you've got to decide how to engineer your payment. In that sense you may have to consult with an engineer to decide how to best treat your pavements.

But once you've decided that, you may say okay for a specific local subdivision street with a PCI 80. We may consider applying HA5. You may say we want to have that road improve its PCI to 90. We may consider a single microsurface, too. But you, as the user, input your specific parameters into StreetSaver, telling it exactly what you want it to do. When you have the program run the budget scenarios, it will spit out that specific roadway with PCI of 92, and it's going to indicate a treatment using HA5, High Density Mineral Bond. You are going to know that it will cost you $2.25/SY including traffic control and mobilization.

It is going to run you a budget for that particular road with that particular area and tell you exactly how much you need to budget for that road. If you've got 2000 roadway segments when you run a budget scenario, you can run a total budget scenario. It will calculate your actual current network level PCI, which here we're at a PCI 63, and with some target driven scenarios, we have determined we could get to a PCI 70.

We would like to be in the 70s at some point in the next few years. You can run different budgets, and it will tell you how much money you need to achieve that targeted PCI level if you want to do it that way. Or you can say, "Hey, I've got $5,000,000, what do I need to do over the next few years to improve our PCI?"

You can tell it what you want to do over the next few years, and it will tell you how to spend your $5,000,000. I know a lot of you probably just don't get to take the dice, throw them and have a computer system tell you what roads to fix. We are in the same situation. Typically we have someone like a roads committee or maybe (county) commission staff member or maybe the public calls in and constantly complains about a series of roads or a sub-division or something like that.

Maybe you have had it on a list for a long time. You've already got a list of roads that you know you need to fix, so you are not just going to put in and say StreetSaver spit out $5,000,000 worth of work. You are going to say, "Hey, I know I've got a hundred roads I need to fix." You can also run an analysis through StreetSaver that way. It will tell you, here's the PCI for those roads and here's a budget scenario on how to fix the roads you listed with that amount of money.

There are different scenarios and ways you can do it, but again this is the performance dashboard. It shows the current PCI by functional class, your network inventory, how many lane miles you have in your in your network, the surface types. AC/AC is overlays. The straight AC would be a single course. Then you've got historical network condition trends which show over the past few years how you've eliminated some of your bad roads and increased some of your good roads. It shows a slight decline here, but that is what this is.

StreetSaver is a powerful tool. You can plug in your network information, your specific roads data and get just tremendous amounts of results back. It runs many different reports. You can export files into Excel. It has a GIS capability where you can link up all of your SHAPE files. If you have a GIS department that uses Ar-cMap, ArcView, ESRI, the SHAPE files could link up to your specific GIS map. You could actually go in and link up automatically to your roadways. You can print out maps that have the PCI information. If you've got a color map, it shows your good roads in green, your bad roads in red and what you said in between, you can specify how to set that up.

It will print out multiple reports, target driven scenarios, bud-get scenarios. It has endless possibilities and the other good thing about this software is again like Blair mentioned, it is a Metropolitan

Transportation Commission (MTC) so it's, in a sense, a government agency (MPO) that manages this. But they are, in fact, agency engineers that manage this software. They will actually take advice from you, if you have a specific need, or if you have a specific suggestion, on how you want a specific report that is not part of the software. You can request that they implement that into the system.

I just got an e-mail today from StreetSaver that wanted input on surface treatments and how that impacted the PCI. They wanted to know your comments on when you did a surface treatment to a road and how that impacts the PCI.

Let's say you go in and do a microsurfacing or High Density Mineral Bond (HA5) treatment. They are looking for your input to continually improve the software.

It is software that is on a database that you log into, so it's not software that you install on your computer. It's constantly updated. There's nothing you have to manage. You pay a subscription fee for the year and you have a user name and password. Multiple people can log in at one time, so it's not that you have to buy 1 seat or 10 seats. Again, it's pretty user friendly and they've got good support. You pay the yearly license fee and you get full access to it, unlimited access, so it is pretty good stuff.

Audience Member: Does it require traffic data or does it accept traffic ADT?

Brian Fix: It does accept traffic ADT.

Audience Member: Is it required?

Brian Frix: It is not required. The minimum data you would need to run an analysis on StreetSaver would be your inventory: the length and width of your roadways so it can figure the area of the roadway to know how much pavement you have in place, and then it would need to know the existing distresses that are out there. So, you go out and do a pavement evaluation and you come back and input that. You can run an analysis based on that, but it has multiple other parameters.

What we did was we surveyed only a portion of the network—20% of the network for some initial analysis that we needed to do—and ran all of that through StreetSaver. It says, "Hey, you've got a PCI of 80." Then we went out and surveyed all 500 miles and plugged that in, and it said, "Oh, you are not in as good a shape as you thought you were." So that's what you see right there. Again right here you'll see where the PCI was. This is a little lower here. We actually went in and did a ton of work in 2011 and 2012, so it shot it from poor to way up there.

Maintenance treatments. If you go in and do any maintenance treatments—and this is all the way from high density mineral bond to full reconstruction—you go in and plug all these maintenance treatments in, it will reconstruct your PCI based on the mainte-nance treatment. If it is a reconstruct, you are going to be reset to 100 for that road. If it is a maintenance treatment, like a surface treatment that is being applied to the asphalt, you are not going to be reset to 100. It is going to be based on what your current PCI is.

So, if you are microsurfacing a road that is a 55, it is going to reset your PCI to somewhere say in the 70s. Whereas if you are microsurfacing a road that is maybe an 86 you are going to be up in the high 90s somewhere. Now, if you are reconstructing a road that is 20, or an 18—say, you are doing FDR on that road—then it is going to reset you to 100 essentially. After that it will start depreci-ating that road every year.

If you ran our StreetSaver analysis today, it is going to give you a network PCI of 63. If we did absolutely nothing for the next year to our roadways, absolutely nothing, and we came back a year from now and ran another analysis, it is going to drop that PCI down pos-sibly 61, maybe 60, based on if we did absolutely nothing. So, a couple percentage points goes down annually.

Now if we do a lot of work, and we do have a lot of work planned, it is going to continually increase that PCI as we create these budget scenarios. If you have a pavement management program in place, that's key. You know you're not just going to go out and fix a pavement here, then fix a pavement there, and expect your network PCI to increase.

Audience Member: What's your goal for going forward? How often for a pavement distress evaluation? Every 5 years?

Brian Frix: That is a good question. Some agencies do it every two years. Some don't have the funds to do it every two years. They may do it every 3 or 4 years. Some agencies go out and do a full network analysis, so you'll go out and evaluate your entire county this year.

Some others do it in pieces. They may do 25%, because they only have 25% of the money each year to do it. They might do it in pieces so that by year four, you've evaluated 100% of your network and you start back over 25% again.

It is completely up to you how you do it, but you know essentially, it is obviously dependent on how much money you have and how much you maintain and manage. If it's going to be $40,000 for somebody to come in and evaluate your pavements, that might be manageable, but if you have 2000 miles of roadway, you know, and only a $250,000 budget, that may not be as manageable every year to have somebody come in and do that.

Depending on how many miles you have, you may decide to do it in-house. I do know of one agency in particular that does work with Blair, the City of Oakwood. The public works supervisor actually does all of his in-house. He is qualified to do it. He has the **APM** Designation. He was trained by Blair and his organization (**IPMA Academy,** www.ipmaacademy.com) and he does it in-house, but he has probably, what Blair, maybe 50 or 60 miles?

Blair Barnahrdt: Maybe about 30 center lane miles, Brian.

Brian Frix: So, not very much. For us, we've done it both ways as well. In-house we haven't done all 500 miles. We have typically used a consultant to do that for us.

---

Any other questions about Street Saver? So, if you are interested in StreetSaver at all. Again I'm not pushing the StreetSaver but it is a good program. If you just go to www.streetsaveronline.com they've got all the information there. If you just Google StreetSaver you can find all the information about that.

---

Audience Member: Can you give us an estimate on how many miles a day can be evaluated?

Brian Frix: Well, I guess that depends on how many guys you got working for you. Blair, how many miles per day can one of your guys do in one day?

Blair Barnhardt: Like Brian says, it really depends on city versus county, and how many folks you have, and how experienced they are.

Brian Frix: I've heard upwards of 10 miles. Yeah. Traffic has a big thing to do it. I've heard in upwards of 10 miles per one person, but that is a hard, miserable day. And you know you have to look at the number of sample sections, too, depending on what rating system you are looking at. If you've got a ton of sample sections, your efficiency is going to go down. If you are looking at just long mainline collectors, your efficiency is going to go up. Whereas if you are in subdivisions, and you are having to measure 30 roads out during that day, you are not going to be able to take as many sample sections. But if you are on a 10 mile long roadway, you know you can fly and go.

All right, so again, I'm going to dumb it down a little bit from here, and go over some of the projects we've done recently that maybe some of you other local counties or cities may be interested in, and see what we've done here locally.

So, again, we've done a lot of the FDR. We've probably done 300,000 to 400,000 square yards of FDR, a ton of FDR over the past several years. It's a pretty simple process to pulverize in

FULL DEPTH RECLAMATION

STEP 1: PULVERIZE

STEP 2: MIX CEMENT

STEP 3: COMPACT & CURE

STEP 4: PAVE

place structure, mix cement, compact, cure, and pave it. Now that sounds simple right? There's a little more involved. I would encourage you, if you are considering this, to do a couple of things.

I would encourage you to have the cement mix designs prepared by a geotechnical engineering firm so the proper cement and moisture content is determined for your mix. Depending on your pavement structure and the depth you are proposing to stabilize, the pounds per square yard of cement can be determined, plus the optimum moisture, which is controlled in the field.

There are several firms around the area, and all through Georgia. that do it. That would be the first thing I would do instead of guessing. I can hit it pretty well right on the head here in Rockdale, but in South Georgia or Northeast Georgia, your cement percentages might be different depending on the type of soil you are dealing with. If you are dealing with clay versus sand, your cement is going to change drastically. Around this area, the metro area, I've seen cement percentages go anywhere from 3% to 6% or 7%. If you are estimating for your project, I typically would use 6% as an estimate if you are trying to put a budget together.

About 40 to 45 pounds a square yard is a good estimation for FDR in this particular area. As far as when you go to construction, I would highly recommend that you hire that particular geotechnical engineering firm to come out and do your testing. I would encourage you to have them come out and do moisture testing, compaction testing and take the cylinders back and break them in the lab. They tell you what they are breaking at. If they are breaking anything other than at 300 psi, you ought to be proof rolling it regardless, but 300 psi is the target that we are looking for.

They will break them at 400 in the lab when they do the design. 300 is typically the target we look for (in the field). That is what you want to see, so with any reading below 300, you are going to want them to proof roll those roads and check them for soft spots. You'll need to fix those areas.

If it is below 200, our spec calls for the contractor to fix it at their expense because there is either poor workmanship or something is not right with what they are doing. We did run into a problem with that a while back where we did have some roads that were well under 200. We had to have them fix them at their expense. One of the main issues was compaction.

Compaction is key with this stuff because, if you're not getting a good compaction, this is worthless. One of the contractors that was doing the work for us was using a steel drum roller, and that is not the thing use for this type of work. Sheepsfoot (also called padfoot) is the way to go. They would argue with you till they were blue in the face that the steel drum roller was the roller to use, that they didn't even have a sheepsfoot roller. I won't say their name to protect them, but we argued with them otherwise.

We had our geotechnical out there and he said the same thing. They said to the contractor, "You know you guys are wasting your time with this." They put a small sheepsfoot roller out there the next week, and the problem was solved. A small sheepsfoot roller. So, we changed our specification to read that unless you have a 10 ton sheepsfoot roller, don't even show up to the job because we aren't going to approve you to start compacting. So, the sheeps-foot roller was used for initial compaction and the steel drum roller is used for final compaction purposes out there on these roadways.

Again, if you've got a consultant out there testing these roads for you, they can tell you what the optimum moisture is and what the current moisture should be. When the roads are curing, they can go out, cut a core, take it back to the lab, break the cylinder, and tell you what the break is at. If you are at 300 (PSI), you call your contractor up and tell them to pave.

On most of our FDR roads, our typical top layer is 2 inches of 9.5 mm SuperPave over an 8 inch pulverized base. On our local roads, it varies with traffic, but we are using about 8 to 10 inch treated base with the binder (chemical or bituminous stabilization) and then a surface course of asphalt. So, it is going to vary based on your traffic volumes and truck percentages.

You have to look at each project, you know, individually. When you get in subdivisions, however, a lot of them are the same. Again, when you get in subdivisions you are going to have to haul off material, more than likely. I don't know how many of you have had any experience with FDR, or total reconstruction of a subdivision, but, when you've got curb and gutter, you are going to have to haul off material. You are going to want to include in your specification to haul off a minimum of 2 inches. That way, when you pave it, you are flush with the gutter.

That may mean you have to mill some asphalt out of there if you have 6 or 7 inches of asphalt, but that is not likely in subdivisions. If you've got 4 or 5 inches of asphalt, and maybe it's got an additional 1 inch which has been overlaid once, you may have to mill a couple of inches off before you can actually start pulverizing. Then, when you get that 8 inch base, you're not pulverizing 5 inches of asphalt into 3 inches of dirt.

There may be a chance that you have to take some of that asphalt off, but, again, your geotechnical engineering consultant can determine that for you when they do the mix designs. As I highly recommend the mix designs from a firm, I also highly recommend that they come in and do the construction inspection as well, the field testing. If you don't, the contractor is going to get away with what they want to do, and you are not going to be getting what you paid for.

So, that's FDR. Here's some before and after pictures, and these are actually pictures I took over the past couple years of roads that we have reclaimed here locally. This is a before picture and after picture at a slightly different angle, but it's a brand-new road. Most of the roads we reclaimed are better than they were when they were first built. The problem a lot of the roads around here have, and you probably have the same issue, you've got 1 inch on dirt. You don't have any base. You don't have any GAB. You may have been lucky and had a contractor who used soil ce-

ment as their base. But typically you are dealing with 1 inch to 2 inches of asphalt on dirt in your subdivisions, plain and simple.

When we go in and reclaim a subdivision, like this one, these folks here have a better road than they had when their houses were built. They now have more asphalt than was there before we started. Now they've got 8 inches of treated base that's solid and stable.

We have a contractor that does FDR, and we've got a paving contractor. Now those go on one contract. We will do an FDR paving contract, and, typically, your big paving contractors will pick up the paving, and then they will sub out the FDR work.

These are typically anywhere from 15 to 20 year pavement designs. We will run them through. I don't know if any of you have used the GDOT pavement design software. I typically use it occasionally. You use it for what it's worth. It is a decent tool to estimate your pavement designs in-house while using some engineering knowledge and discretion as well as some common sense. Typically, most of our pavements that we are building are 15 to 20 year pavements. So, after that, it's patch and overlay.

PATCH & OVERLAY BEFORE

PATCH, HIR & OVERLAY AFTER

Depending on future funding, our current funding is sustainable. But, you know, the future may allow us to come back and treat some of these roads. We do have a lot of roads that are HA5 candidates right now. They are less than 10 years old.

This slide photo is probably what you don't want to do, right? Look at all the patching.

This was a lesson we learned a while back when we started to bring in HIR heat scarification. This was actually a road we did HIR on a couple of years back. We patched this road more than it needed to be patched, needless to say. The heat scarifier could have treated more of this road than what we patched, but we patched probably upwards of 20 to 25% of this roadway. It wasn't needed after the heater scarifier treated this road. This is a treatment patch and overlay before slide. And the after photo is a different shot, but it looks like a brand new road now.

This roadway had about 10 inches of asphalt on it in some areas. The section you just saw had about 6 inches. It does not look like it but that's about 6 inches of asphalt right there.

The next page shows microsurfacing. We've done quite a bit of this as well. We've probably done a little over 300,000 square yards of microsurfacing recently. We actually do our crack sealing and patching in-house, so essentially most of your roads, and you'll decide where that PCI peaks, and where you are comfortable with that. We've microsurfaced roads as low as the middle PCI= 50s before. Again, a lot of those roads may get double microsurfaced.

This was a single microsurface roadway that we did. Our crews came in, crack sealed, patched, and then the contractor came in and applied the micro. There's the finished product. So there is the before shot, and there's the finished product.

These roads had 2.5 to 3 inches of asphalt, and this was a single microsurface. Type 2, single microsurface is what we used here. Again, some more before and after pictures. Roads look brand new.

You may be wondering about how long we let the crack seal set up. With some jobs the sealant is several years old. Some we did apply probably 1 month before we microsurfaced. Some of the patching was done in the springtime, and then we came back in the summer and did the microsurfacing.

MICROSURFACING

STEP 1: PATCH

STEP 2: CRACK SEAL

STEP 3: APPLY MICRO

STEP 4: FINISH

MICROSURFACING BEFORE

MICROSURFACING AFTER

Audience Member: When do you do the crack sealing and filling?

Brian Frix: They can do it year round. We have the crew doing other things during the spring and summer months, but in the cooler months, we will have them crack sealing, patching, and getting ready. So, in the fall, the early spring, through the winter when they can, they will be crack sealing, patching and getting ready for the spring and summer contracts. So, we will patch what we can in-house. In the really large patching projects, the long line patching that's on higher volume roadways and higher speed roadways, we will typically get a contractor to do that. You had a question.

Audience Member: How deep do you deep patch?

Brian Frix: Anything about 4 inches or deeper.

So you've seen the microsurfacing. All right, so, here we are. So, regarding heat scarification, which is what Pat talked about, you have to have a pavement that is not structurally deficient to do heat scarification or the actual Re-HEAT process.

Two separate things here now; there's the hot in-place recycling repaving and ReHEAT, there's the heater scarification and then there's the remixing (subdisciplines).

Georgia DOT does have a specification for HIR remixing. It's actually a more glorified remixing specification. It's not even the Re-HEAT Process that Gallagher performs, and I don't know why GDOT has it. It just doesn't make sense because it is not like you can use that specification; it's too specific. So, you would have to use more of a generic industry specification for the HIR heater scarification. But it's a great technique to use on pavements that have 3 inches or more asphalt structure on.

We've used it on local collector roads. We haven't used it in a subdivision because of the length of the train, and because of the small cul-de-sacs. That's not to say you couldn't. We just had enough collector roads and local roads to utilize it there.

The other issue we have in subdivisions is you've got less than 2 inches of asphalt. So, there's nothing to Re-HEAT in the subdivisions. We've used it on local collector roads and it's worked out great. Now, you have to go in and patch those areas that are structurally deficient. Anything that is environmental related—non-load related, longitudinal cracking, block cracking, transverse—you know you can leave all those cracks. Don't crack seal it either, especially if you are going to heat scarify. But it's got to be patched beforehand (Blair recommends 9.5 mm SP, not 12.5 mm or 19 mm, for aesthetics). Then the heat scarify train comes through and heats it up and makes it look like it was brand-new.

We specified a 1.5" depth. I noticed Pat was saying earlier that I guess Chicago, or somewhere, specified three quarters of an inch. We specified 1.5 inches. Why not get all you can get if they are coming? You know, you may even want to go up to 2 inches. I think they can go up to 2 or 2.5 inches with a heat scarifier. That what I was told by a couple of the foremen who were out there when they were down here working.

Now, with the scarification, once it is patched and heat scarified, you have to come back and top it, just like Pat said. This photo is not the final surface. It may be your final surface for a month. You will want to include some temporary striping in your contract just so you will provide constant traffic control on these streets. But this is not your final road, and you have several options.

We've done hot mix overlays, 9.5 mm Superpave or 12.5 mm Superpave, depending on your volumes. We've micro surfaced. We did that this past summer on roads that had sufficient structure and lower traffic volumes. We actually did a HIR mat with a test section of HA5 (as the wearing surface) this past summer on this as well as a relatively short segment. That's another option as well.

If you are dealing with friction, you may want to consider something other than a High Density Mineral Bond (HA5), but the microsurfacing is certainly an option. Here's a slide on the High Density Mineral Bond (HA5). This is a road we did up in North Rockdale County. We went in. We had our guys crack seal it. There was no patching on this road. HA5 was applied, and, you can see, it's nice and black like the residents like it.

This slide was a sample section we did. The HA5 is to the left. That was in September 2013. Hot mix was done in July 2013. You can already see the color difference just how quickly this (HMA) was oxidizing just in a few months' time. Obviously this was a little newer. I think this picture was taken in late October so you can obviously see that this (HMA) is oxidizing pretty quickly, but again for the High Density Mineral Bond (HA5) there is APWA specification, and Blount Construction does provide that here (locally) in the metro area.

Again something we do in-house—crack sealing and patching—which most of you guys probably have the means of doing that. That's all I've got. Questions?

Audience Member: What is the cost of the StreetSaver Software?

Brian Frix: I think it is about $1200 a year for the licensing fee and the user fee and all that. But it is again, $1200 for the year, and 10 people can be on it at one time. As a matter of fact, when we were doing some of our input, there were two or three of us on it at one time doing inputting of data.

Audience Member: How many people can access the data?

Brian Frix: It's one user name and password. So, if you're from Jackson, your user name might be "City of Jackson," and your password might be "jacksongeorgia." (NOTE from Blair, there can be different levels of password access in your agency.)

Audience Member: But 10 different people could be on.

Brian Frix: You can be on it, Glenn can be on it, your supervisor can be on it, you can give the password out to whomever. You basically have unlimited access to it. That is the key.

Blair Barnhardt: (Blair explains the different levels of password protection available to your agency.)

Brian Frix: You can run scenarios with just the click of a button. We can run our entire network within 5 minutes. I run budget scenarios within 5 minutes of clicking the button. We maintain over 500 miles. I know down to a percent what it takes, what the cost break down is locally, and where one treatment is triggered versus another.

I know when it becomes cost effective to reclaim a road versus hot in-place and overlay it. Or, depending on the traffic volumes, whether I should microsurface it, overlay it or whatnot. You obviously have to look at your local unit prices, what you are paying for asphalt patching, and what you are going to pay for this and that. But, obviously there is a break, and you are going to find it is somewhere between 30 to 40% patching, that the road is going to kick into that reclaim (FDR) category.

Blair Barnhardt: When Dr. Shahin built this software to do US Airforce bases, a rut for a jumbo jet or a fighter plane is a serious, serious problem, FOD (Foreign Object Debris) can cause $5,000,000 in damage to a jet engine. These are the things that we have inherited. We have inherited US Army Corps Airforce base pavement evaluation in the ASTM 6433. Then Dr. Roger Smith took all of those procedures, because they used to work together, and he said, "Okay, what is important for us as pavement managers?"

The thickness of the pavement takes care of itself, in a way, because when we went to you guys, Bill, we determined what's arterial, what's collector, and what's residential. So, almost by default, you have set up three subcategories. Within those you've got an asphalt pavement that reacts a lot differently than an asphalt on asphalt. The asphalt on asphalt wears out sooner than the original asphalt pavement (virgin pavement). So, there are about 12 to 18 different subcategories already before you even talk about the coring depth or traffic count. Dr. Shahin said it was never the intent of the US Army Corp to involve traffic count, with the exception of functional class codes.

Now, your local busy road is very different than Georgia DOT's busy roads, and even more different than a congested city's busy road. Well, there's obviously local presence there. What we deem as a collector, can be different than someone else's. The point is that the ASTM was written to do methods and means that are based on scientific evidence (and visual inspection). The largest city in America, the City of LA, uses MicroPAVER. They go to the council meeting with scientific evidence that every single district has the exact same network level PCI.

There's never any talk about my thickness of pavement or my amount of cars on the pavement. Now that being said, at the state level, ride smoothness is a huge factor, right Brian? If I'm going 85 mph on a Texas Interstate, ride is an important factor and that is where the state gets involved with profilometer readings, IRI (International Roughness Index), all of that stuff.

Fayette County, you are all set to go to the races. When we did the 5% QC/QQ for you guys (TBG did QC/QA correlation with their PACES database), I don't know if you are aware of this, but we got you set up in the StreetSaver to do the 5% comparison. You already have it in your computer right now just waiting to put the rest of your network level distress evaluation into it.

It (StreetSaver) has run 109 Bay area agencies for the last 25 years. There's no need to question it. Brian, I, and along the way, Miquel, all had input. We've provided input and gotten better changes to the software by contacting the folks who write and update the software.

Brian Frix: Right, that's where the engineering judgment comes in as well.

Blair Barnhardt: At project level. Brian, you and I can determine a road is a cold-in-place recycling candidate, but, if Miquel says he wants to add some super elevation and curves down here, and some turnouts along the way, then all of the sudden, just by default, it just became an FDR job. We know we can fool around all day long with FDR, add a little RAP (Recycled Asphalt Pavement) here, add a little rock there, add a little super elevation here, and it's a brand new palette.

Brian Frix: Right, and that is where it comes into play also. If the program is spitting out information, and you set your decision tree to do local roads with heat scarifier in a subdivision, which may be your choice, you may have more of those than collector roads. But, you know you have a core that shows only a 2 inch thickness of HMA, and StreetSaver spits out to put a hot in-place train on that street. Then you have to sit down and scratch your head and look at that report and say, I can't do this, and here's why.

Cores are going to come into play when you start making those project level decisions. That's not necessarily information you have to input into the software to obtain results or to run scenarios. It's just a user input parameter that you can plug in and say, "save this for inventory purposes." Essentially that is what it's used for.

When you start making project level decisions, and start using engineering judgment, that is when you are going to want to know what the core thickness is, the type of mix you have, if you know if it was Superpave, or whatever. That is when you are going to have to start making decisions on the project level.

Blair Barnhardt: I just want to throw this out, for the sake of talking and just hearing myself, if you listen to the local experts in the state and the association people around here, they are going to tell you to get your motor grader operator out there to evaluate your pavements.

They will get you to question your decisions by asking, "Why did you hire Ralph to come in? Why do you want to hire Ralph to come in and evaluate the pavement when you can get the motor grader operator to do it? The software we invented in the 80s will tell you if you need a thick overlay, medium overlay or thin overlay."

That's all I'm going to say. Now if I had $200,000,000 worth of infrastructure, and it costs me 2 cents per square yard to have an expert come in and do it like Ralph, I would be getting somebody to come in and do the pavement management with the most robust software and technical experience that I could find. That's all I'm going to say.

Be a **Stringbender**, stand up for your rights as a pavement management **RockSTAR** and say to the Naysayers, "I will NOT be getting my motor grader operator to survey my pavements, nor will I be using any old DOS based program as the pavement management software."

When you are segmenting your network, I'd rather you guys think like a contractor. Think about when you are hiring someone to come in and do a micro job, HA5, or hot in-place recycling. Don't break everything up into a third of a block because you are not going to treat it that way. I would much rather see when you go into a county, you do 2 miles because we know that the contractors do not like coming in and working in blocks of a tenth of a mile here and then going over there to do another tenth of a mile. Great job, Brian!

Brian Frix: I was going to point out one other thing, too. I didn't mean to pick just some FDR contractor to do the testing and the initial pre-design. You know, information you should be doing for all these counties and cities; you should be doing that for the heat scarification, for the microsurfacing, for anything you hire a contractor to do. I know, locally, for 1-2% of the construction costs, we are having a geotech come in and actually do the materials and field testing. I guarantee you will be glad you did. Just take my word for it. You will be glad that you did.

Blair Barnhardt: You may make that up on savings to your agency!

Brian Frix: Yes.

Blair Barnhardt: So glad you could be here, Brian.

See you over in Chapter 7, Part II, as we meet the folks from Boise, ID, during the actual day this book was conceived. Sure, I may have known for a decade that this book had to be written, but it was the crowd at IACERS in ID that helped get this thing started once and for all, and, to them, I am forever indebted.

# STRINGBENDERS UNITE!

*Author's note:* By definition, for the purposes of this book, I am using the term **Stringbender** as a name for all of those who choose to stand up to the Naysayers in the world of pavement management, in-place asphalt recycling and pavement preservation. *Jon Heese's added note:* **Stringbenders** are people who are not willing to put their head in the sand or simply follow the status quo. **Stringbenders** are the folks who are bold enough to stand and point out what is obvious to them: That the status quo is simply not sustainable. These guys realize that changes must be made. They prefer making the changes in an orderly fashion rather than have something imposed upon on them down the line. Everyone sees it coming; It's a mile away and coming like a slow moving train wreck.

Whether you have purchased the print or e-book version of this book, you will read or hear that I describe Chuck Berry as being the first, or one of the first guitar players, to actually record a bent string song. Thus he became a **"Stringbender,"** someone who refused to follow the norm, someone who changed rock and roll music, and every other genre recorded with guitars, from that day forth. As a musician, I recognize the innovation he made and the courage he needed to stand up and do something different. You see, if it weren't for the stringbenders back in the 50s, there may have never been Eddie Van Halen!

As a pavement manager and the author of this book, I am asking you to do the same. I WANT YOU TO BE A **STRINGBENDER**! I want all of the uninformed to become informed **Stringbenders**, and we **Stringbenders** don't have time to waste and we know what to do. We pretty much figure if two decades of successful implementation **The Three Legged Stool System of Pavement Management** is not enough to convince you to change, then you probably won't change until you run out of options. It's really that simple.

So, **Stringbenders** UNITE! Now is your time to stand up and join us to change the world together. And as a special token of our appreciation, we will have some cool swag, bumper stickers, t-shirts and other amazing things along with a very special short video message delivered directly to your inbox for all of those who will join us in signing our petition for better roads everywhere on this planet. So, come on over here and JOIN US at www.stringbenders.org. By the way, did I mention that we will change the world together and make it a better place for everybody with better roads?

Before we get started, and, to avoid any confusion, I do want to pay homage to Gene Parsons of the Byrds—musician, inventor, craftsman and creator of the StringBender device that allowed electric guitarists like myself to bend the open B string with a pull of the guitar strap for electric guitars. How about that for innovation! You can visit Gene over at http://stringbender.com/.

So let's get in the **Better Roads Bus** together and head on over to Boise, Idaho, to meet a bunch of **Stringbenders** that helped me to write this book! You can follow along here with the video playing as well by going to our YouTube Channel and looking up IACERS in Boise over here at www. youtube.com/ipmatv or just click here http://youtu.be/Cn4KNmCEFaU.

Here is a huge shoutout to Eric and all of the amazing **Stringbenders** I met while in Boise for the IACERS Conference! See you guys next year, and THANKS for helping me to write this book for all to share and enjoy!

I am going to let you guys read through the transcript from the live session here and see how this all played out. Since we are nearing the end of the book, and my editor is pushing me to get this thing done and up on Amazon so we can start helping folks out, I will take a little time to summarize this chapter before we leave on our journey.

But just know that this book is only the beginning of our relationship together! For all of those who have registered this book and signed up as a **Stringbender**, there will be plenty of great content heading to your inbox over the next year or so. This is just the beginning of our story together! I am also going to throw in a few BONUS chapters on the way out!

I see a lot of moonlit road signs in the better roads bus.

* HYPHEN CAUTION: If a link includes a hyphen as it goes to the next line of text, when you retype the link into your computer **do not include the hyphen**.

209

83,000 miles in one year = a thorough pavement management perspective

## Transcript Begins - IACERS Conference, 2013 - Boise

Blair: People ask, "Blair, how bad can this be?"

Well, I'm out here on the interstate that joins the west coast to the east coast, or east coast to the west coast, however you want to look at it, and, while we are worrying about building new highways and spending 57% of our GDP on 1.8% of our roadways in America (www.smartgrowthamerica.com) we are literally letting our interstates crumble in front of our very eyes.

People ask to me all the time, "How bad can this really be, Blair?"

Now, you may have heard the truck drivers talk about just how bad the situation is earlier in one of the other **IPMA** or **Driving America for Better Roads** www.drivingamericaforbetterroads.com episodes. This is not good for our country. We are trying to move goods across the country just-in-time so we can keep industry rolling and attract industry to our country. While other countries are building better infrastructure systems, we are letting ours fall to pieces.

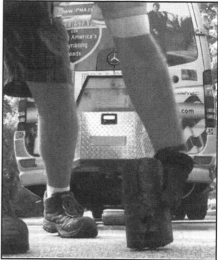

Feels like another 8" core coming on here

Yup, I was right – Why do we keep doing this over and over again?

Please stop the insanity – Stringbenders, unite!

We've got to do something about this, and the best way to go about it is to learn how to manage our pavements with eco-efficient, in-place asphalt recycling, pavement preservation and pavement management programs that do just that with **The Three Legged Stool System**.

How's everybody doing so far? We have come a long way, haven't we? Anyone ever take a flight from Phoenix to Flagstaff? When you get on that flight, they say if you are not on the right

* Hʏᴘʜᴇɴ Cᴀᴜᴛɪᴏɴ: If a link includes a hyphen as it goes to the next line of text, when you retype the link into your computer **do not include the  hyphen**.

211

plane, if you are not going to Flagstaff, now would be a good time to get off.  There are 8 seats on the plane, and it is 140°F inside the plane; it's a prop plane.

---

If you ever get a chance, listen to Ron White on the Blue Collar Comedy Network.  http://www.quotes.net/mquote/11187  Everything is true about that flight.  My buddy from Asphalt Institute, Wayne Jones, will tell you. I only tried the flight once. I refused to take it a second time!  (I can share that story over a bourbon.)

---

### Blue Collar Comedy Tour: The Movie [2003]

**f Like** 0

It had to happen: A national tour of redneck comedians culminating in this frequently funny concert film, shot in Phoenix. Ron White's scotch-and-tobacco-fueled, fatalistic world view gets things off to a good start. ("That last engine had just enou...more »

More Blue Collar Comedy Tour: The Movie quotes | Buy this movie now

- - - - - - - - - - - - - - - - - - - - - - - - - - - - - - - - - - - - - - - - -

**Ron White:**

So I flew in here to Phoenix from Flagstaff because my manager doesn't own a globe. He chartered one of those small private jets. I flew here on a plane this big, it was like a pack of gum with eight people in it.We were putzing along. We were going half the speed of *smell!* We got passed by a kite! There was a goose behind us and the pilot was yelling "Go around!" So about halfway through the trip, we start losing oil pressure in one of the engines, and the pilot says we have to turn around. It was a nine minute flight.Couldn't make it with that equipment. He came over the intercom and said "Hey, we're losing oil pressure in one of the engines," which I couldn't understand why he did, because he could have just turned around and said, "Hey, we're losing oil pressure." *"heard'ja"* Everyone else started freaking out, but I had been drinking since lunchtime, so I was like "Take it down! I don't care! Make sure y you hit something hard, 'cause I don't want to limp away from this!" The guy next to me is *losing his mind*. I guess he must have had something to "live for". He says, "Hey man, if one of the engines goes out, how far will the other one take us?" I look at him. "All the way to the scene of the crash! Which is pretty lucky, because that's where we're headed! I bet we beat the paramedics by a good half hour! We're haulin' ass!"

Blair: So, there's a lot of technical stuff we have to do here, and I'll tell you why in a second. Because, in this room, in the next hour, we are going to make history. How about that?

Now, if you guys are not brave and bold—you know what I'm going to say—I encourage you to get up and leave right now. There's going to be some sh*t up in this room in the next hour, okay? I swear. I'm not making this up.

So, now that I am old and I am forgetful, I actually put little pictures in here to remind me what I have to do next. Did you tell them we are going to give away a fellowship here? Okay, let's do this right now, because I will forget. I'll pass this book around. Now, I promise never to spam you. Don't take any notes, okay, because I'm going to send you a video recording of this seminar.

Because of the history-making change that we are doing, and the importance of all of this, and what is going to go on here in Boise, I tell you, I can't be more excited to be here today, right now. I've got a $2,000 scholarship to the **IPMA Academy** (www. ipmaacademy.com), and I'm going to give this away.

How many people have heard of **IPMA** or **IPMA Academy**?

That's perfect! Okay. It's the most comprehensive online training ever for pavement managers, okay? So, if you are interested in anything I say here, just know there are 70 hours of online training.

I spent my entire lifetime putting this together for you guys with the **International Pavement Management Association**.

Don't feel like you can't talk or raise your hand just because I've got the microphone, and, as we go through this, I'm going to tell you right now, I sat in this front chair earlier today.

What's your name? I sat right where Dan is two hours ago, and put the presentation together. I have no idea what direction these slides are going to take us. I don't know how long it will take. For the first 10 minutes you guys are going to help me make a legacy, okay, trust me. Watch what happens. I'm going to play this little video clip. It's my bio. There you go.

Video Bio: (Music interlude) I'm Blair Barnhardt, and I've got a vision. That vision is teaching normal citizens, just like you, how to get better roads for less money. Construction worker on the video: "You're watching **Driving America for Better Roads**."

* **Hyphen Caution**: If a link includes a hyphen as it goes to the next line of text, when you retype the link into your computer **do not include the hyphen**.

Each day I drive America, I watch your tax dollars being pilfered away doing conventional reconstruction techniques when we can be recycling in-place for less money and on a 65% smaller carbon footprint. In the last 3 months we drove over 25,000 miles in the Airstream teaching agency engineers and university students how to do more with less.

I promise not to rest until we have better roads, and I want to see one million people helping me with this effort. I've watched, first hand, for three decades, agencies save millions of dollars with less carbon footprint. I know we can make a change.

Will you help me? Let's stand together and change this country and change the world. We don't have to have crumbling roadways any longer. Put your name in that box and let's get started. (Music outro) (End).

Blair: Every day, 1,000 miles a day! How many of you people drive 1000 miles in one day? It's crazy, isn't it? Like, 15 hours. So much of the country I've seen in the dark. But, I'm not alone in this effort. People have told me, "Blair, the videos, man, you can't be reaching all the county engineers with videos."

I mean, how many of you guys are opening up the videos I am sending you at this time. Anyone? You know what engineers love? They love books! So, in a few minutes, we are going to make a little history. Let me get the actual program here because this will help me remember what I am here to talk about.

Are there any questions so far? Do you guys feel like you are in the wrong room and you want to leave now? Or do you know you are in the right room. (Laughter).

Engineer or musician all day, all night. Think about that, okay? There's no rest, ever. So, I'm here in this room today to create a little history. I've done this for 30 years. I think I'm probably one of the oldest people in the industry. In 1996 I got the call to go out and work on the full depth reclamation crew. Along the way, I've learned a few things. And, in a few short minutes, I'm going to share some of that stuff with you guys and hope you will join me in this movement.

214

I'm not here to talk about anything new. Everything we are going to talk about like everything Wayne went through, we've been doing this sh*t for 25 - 30 years. The Nevada DOT have saved over 600 million dollars alone (in the last 25 years doing this).

There are a lot of barriers out there, and, together, we are going to break down those barriers. We are going to take this session today to talk a little bit about how we are going to go about doing that, and you guys are going to be part of that.

I hope you will join me in this effort. So, a $2,000 scholarship. What I will do is, when we get the e-mails from you guys, we will send you a little BONUS offer. Bonus kitchen knives. We will give you 7 days to click on **IPMA Academy,** and join for $1,000. We do that everywhere we go so, don't let those guys at Northwest Pavement Association tell you that they got a deal and you didn't.

Tell them know you got the same deal. You have seven days to get in there and order this scholarship. (www.ipmaacademy.com) You can earn a plaque to hang on your wall, **Accredited Pavement Manager Certificate**, where you will be able to go to LinkedIn and search on **APM** and find all your peers and connect with them in a private forum.

We've had people from Cal-Tran, Canada, and local agencies go through the program. We've had 40, or so, people go through the program already (since we started a few short months ago). We've had one learner just finish the 21 week program in 5 weeks! He spent all his weekends going through the videos. It is all online training, and you can do MP3 downloads and take it to the gym with you as well.

So, you ask, "What is this all about, Blair?"

It is the integration of everything I've learned in 30 years, from people like Wayne and Eric and other really smart people like Shane up there from the Zipper folks. I know there are a lot of smart people in this room. In a second, we are going to do a little drill just to see how smart we are.

This is about taking all of the elements of cold in-place recycling, hot in-place recycling, full-depth reclamation, pavement preservation techniques and, you know what, having driven 83,000 miles in one year, I've learned a lot.

Everywhere, I teach. When I leave here, I'm going to Olympia, Washington (for the Washington Transportation Improvement Board (TIB)), to teach the Northwest Environmental Training Center (NWETC) in a 2-day class. Every time I teach these classes, I learn something new. I get more to share with you guys. I have this kind of continuing education brain that never shuts off.

So, how many people are allowed text on their phone? We always like to take a little survey. If you send a text message to this number, this is a easy way to get information and stay on the mailing list. You also can get updates on all the free PDH credit hours and stuff like that.

This stuff I'm going to show you is available by joining the association. The cost to join for an agency engineer is nothing. It's free. F-R-E-E, and, each month, we will send you a 1-hour PDH credit course: **The IPMA PDH Power Hour**. You will learn a bit about something. For example, with Wayne's permission, and you can tell me later, you don't have to answer now, but you may see

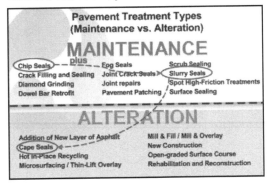

his presentation as a BONUS video. For example, the American Disabilities Act (ADA) is quite a topic right now.

I obtained permission from Federal Highways (FHWA) to do the 1-1/2 hour recording as an **IPMA Academy Bonus Video,** so, be sure to watch it if you are worried at all about ADA requirements. And you should be worried because it may double the cost of your rehabilitation projects: from microsurfacing and on up (where there is curb and gutter).

I know I talked to John about it earlier. Olympia, Washington, said for every 1 million dollar resurfacing project they were going to microsurface in 2014, the cost just doubled becauce of the ADA compliance requirements. John has a $50,000,000 backlog. Now, with the ADA compliance law, it just may have become a $100,000,000 backlog.

So, if you want to try it—and I didn't even know how to do this texting thing—text Tracy to get instructions. Now, the instructions are there. If you decide to do that later on, that's cool.

Cindy said we should try this little experiment. I've never done this before. I don't know how it is going to go. All my mentors say that city and county engineers and local agencies have no interest in music. I beg to differ because, guess what? Music should be a vital part of everybody's life, and this is going to be a metaphor.

This is going to be a little bit of a metaphor of what is going on here. ( Music guitar solo)

Chuck Berry, in 1952 or 1953, would listen to saxophone players. He asked, "Why do saxophone players get to bend notes with their saxophone? With the guitar we have to just keep playing the same notes, over and over." There's only notes A through C.

Chuck Berry must have sat in a hotel room one day, and went (Blair bends string on his guitar and makes it whine). What!! (guitar music). Then he started writing songs like *Johnny B Good,* right? Then, guess what happened? Had it not been for Chuck Berry and the legacy of bending the string for the very first time, the world's greatest guitar player, Eddie Van Halen—maybe you've heard of a little band called Van Halen—which Jean Simmons from KISS discovered at a party one night. He signed them to a contract immediately.

Eddie asked, "Why just bend strings with one hand?" (Blair does crazy leads).

So, as we go through the program over the next few minutes, this little legacy that we found out with Eddie and Chuck is going to apply to every single person in this room. How do you feel so far?

Audience: Good!

Blair: How many people think I'm crazy?

Audience: (Laughter).

Blair: Like, for 32 years she says. Every day. I'm amazed she is talking to me. The last thing I heard was, "Just text me."

Johnny Cash. What do you think his daughter had? What significance did his daughter have with Johnny Cash's career? Innovation at Sun Studios?

Audience: He put it in his strings!

Blair: Who said that? Huh? Damn! At 3:00 when we shut down this job . . . What's your name?

Audience: Eric.

Blair: What a blow! And you are an engineer, see! Yeah, at 3:00 we are going to do a live demonstration of acoustic guitar. What Johnny Cash did, can you sing a song, Eric? We'll do Folsom Prison Blues, half step down.

Eric: I prefer it in quarter.

Blair: (Laughter). Where was I going before all of this? I'll bring it all back in a second here. By the way, you guys, if you let me know, give us five minutes to three, because I want to play one more video. It will be the first time I ever played it in a crowd of this magnitude. Okay. So, I'm going to bring this all back.

You guys today are my **Stringbenders**! Here's what's going to happen with this little legacy right now. People are going to go back and see this video. They are going to go like 20 years from now. They are going to say, "That guy was off his freaking rocker, but that Eric, guy, was pretty smart. But, those guys in that room in Boise, Idaho, changed how we manage our pavements. That's

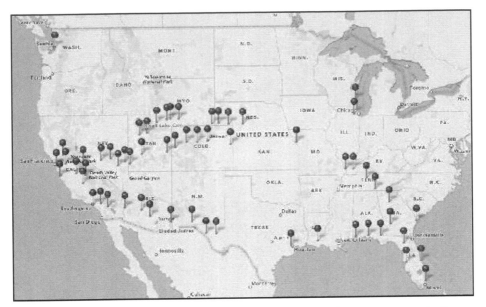

what they did. They changed how we managed our pavements."
They will say this Idaho Association or IACERS did it. We are going
to be the **Stringbenders** right now, in this room

I stopped using the iPhotos because the program crashes. I learned to load my photos right to the hard drive. The map above shows where I've taken pictures on my last 65,000 mile journey.

We taught along the way, and we've grown this circle of pavement managers. **Pavement Management Rock-STARS** are all over Canada, all over the USA, and all over the world. Hopefully we will get a lot of the **IPMA Academy** courses translated into foreign languages. Does anyone recognize that? You guys should know this because it was the guys in Vancouver last year (at NWPMA Conference) that told me to go see it. That's what Sam

Hill built in Washington State. That's the Stonehenge, a replica model of Stonehenge.

What's going on here? You've got a minute? Look at this. I get to meet so many cool people. Top left-hand corner, you might have heard a of thing called MicroPAVER. Sui, have you ever heard of that before? It is software for pavement management. That is Dr. Shahin, one of the inventors of MicroPAVER, and me with the US Army Corps.

You know we give away these **IPMA Academy Scholarships** along the way. There's Basem Muallem, District 8 Caltrans Director. Is Layla from LTAP in the room? There we go. This is Tina, from Colorado State University. Who's that Cindy? There's my good friend, Mary, over there. We will talk about her in a second.

So, what's my point with the plane wreck photo on the next page? This is real. This one I like. I was doing a pavement evaluation one day, and I had to pull over to the side of the road with this friend of mine—which is not easy because you need like 40 feet to get my vehicle pulled over—and I saw this sign about how you can learn to fly, nicely placed next to a plane crash.

If I ever learn to fly, I would want to learn from a pilot who knew how to avoid crashing. And I have learned a few things along the way, not because I'm smart, it is just because I'm old, experienced, and I know how to avoid pavement management crashes.

I got a chance very early in my own life to go out and do this thing called foamed asphalt or expanded asphalt (stabilization) up in Canada with the big pulverizers. I have continued to have this amazing journey of hot in-place, cold in-place, all the micro surfacing, pavement preservation techniques.

And each and every day, I'm still learning. So, I encourage you guys to share information so we can do better ourselves and work together to keep others from crashing.

Right now everyone in this room is probably doing pavement management, right? That's pretty darn good. Let's give yourselves a big round applause.

Audience: (Applause).

Blair: You guys, really. Many of the groups we talk to only 10%-12% of the agencies are doing pavement management. When I heard that figure the other day from this great bunch of speakers, Eric, when he said 66% of local agencies are doing pavement management, I knew this was the place, right here, to do what we are about to do.

Just so you know, I spent four days with my mentors in Santa Clara, California, last week. So, I'm wound up as tight as a . . . whatever you think right now, with all these ideas going through my head. I was given a mandate for 2014 to do things that were going to change this industry. When I got here, and saw who was in this room, as soon as I saw Cindy and Eric, I knew this is where we were going to do it.

That's why it took me until this morning to finish this. So, as we learn a little bit more about in-place recycling, pavement preservation and pavement management, as we get a little more confident, you might say, and we start to do a little crazy thing here and there, and then there's my neighbor, Tom, he said, "Hey if you can do it at this level, I'm going to try it there."

Then, I thought if Tom can do it there, I'm going to try it up here. All happens on Sunday afternoons. Yeah, there are a couple of beers involved (laughter). I won't lie to you.

Then my good friend Rocco pointed out, if Blair could do it there, I'm going to try up here. And what happens when you get this good pavement management, in-place recycling and pavement preservation, maybe after you've gone through **IPMA Academy,** you get the ability . . . (laughter) . . . to do things that you wouldn't maybe normally do. People have to have a lot of trust in you.

Do you call them "commissioners" here? Your commissioners, your city counselors, they are the people who take credit for everything that is a good idea—that you come up with—and give you blame for all the bad ideas.

You get this incredible responsibility, and you've got to take that with pride and with a lot of conscientiousness as well. Competent conscientiousness, so hopefully, after this session you will get the idea. Now let me just tell you, this is my brain and everything on that screen is in my brain 24 hours per day, 7 days a week because being an entrepreneur is hell. I would never, ever recommend it to anybody. You'd have to be crazy to do it, but I'm having a lot of fun doing it, too.

**The Barnhardt Pacific & Atlantic Divisions** perform about 6 pavement management jobs per year. I am not here to sell **The Barnhardt Group,** but if you want to get on next year's program let me know, otherwise there is no possible way we can get to you. We've been all over America doing that and The **IPMA Academy** (www.ipmaacademy.com) and the **International Pavement Management**

## Agency / Public Works Official Category:

F R E E. That's right folks. You heard it correct! All agency members and elected officials are free for life. What's the catch, Blair? Maybe you didn't hear us right ... we want you to be part of this amazing transformation while you learn how to do more with less and save your crumbling roads, once and for all. We don't care which part of the globe you're in, we all need to stretch our budgets further and get more done for less by implementing the Three Legged Stool Pavement Management System. You get the **same benefits** that we listed above, which gives you the ability to post all of your bid documents into a huge private forum of private sector pavement management experts. Each month we will provide free webinars and conference calls on all things pavement management, in place recycling, and pavement preservation. This is the biggest no-brainer in the history of time. We love to serve our circle of pavement managers. There are no strings attached. Okay, just one. You have to prove to us that you work for an agency, so when you register as an IPMA™ Agency Member using the button below, we're going to need you to provide us with a few details about your city, county, state, or country, or village. I mean, how else are we gonna get your name right on the certificate that Lea sends you next week? I could go on forever, but if you've watched *any* of our videos so far, you know this is the most exciting thing that's happened since the Wright brothers took flight in Kitty Hawk a few days ago.

Sign Up Now For FREE!

* HYPHEN CAUTION: If a link includes a hyphen as it goes to the next line of text, when you retype the link into your computer **do not include the hyphen**.

**Association** (**IPMA**) (www.ipma.co) which you guys are all able to join for free today and be up to date on all the great things.

---

The bottom photo on the previous page is really the impetus for where my career started in my own business. Literally overnight, I became the public works director for the largest privatized city in America, the City of Sandy Springs. I was called into a room. They said as of midnight on December 3rd, or whatever day it was, we are going to be incorporated. I said, "Yeah, that's great." The leader of CH2MHill, an engineering firm, who had the contract said, "Failure is not an option."

Great. So, you guys, how many of you feel that way every day?

Do you actually get people calling you and complaining from time to time? The same guys that complain about snow removal, complain about the roads, the gravel roads, the dirt roads and the pot holes? You sometimes feel like you are set up for failure? Who feels like they are set up for failure with the local agencies?

Be honest guys!! We'll turn the camera off for you guys to answer these questions, but, listen, if you thought you were screwed before with not enough money to go around, John, you're double screwed now with ADA legislation (clarification).

Audience Member: What is the ADA legislation?

Blair: Yes. Let's talk about that. And I'm not focusing on anybody with disabilities. Don't get me wrong, I focusing on the American Disabilities Act, Federal Highways, and the Department of Justice who just made clarifications about the law which forces you to spend more. I was recently on a 1-1/2 hour webinar about it, and here's what I found out.

The only thing you can do without spending more money (under maintenance in terms of the DOJ) is throw-and-go pothole repair with QPM, or UPM, or whatever the guys out there are doing with the cold mix.

You can do chip seals, you can do slurry, and you can do the High Density Mineral Bond like in Utah, St. George, with the Holbrook Guys (HA5). But, as soon as you go to micro, cape seal, or anything above that, you have to do every single ADA upgrade in your city of your county, every single thing.

226

If you have a 4 foot wide sidewalk (too narrow for passing places), it has to be 5 foot wide now to fit ADA compliance. If you don't have truncated domes (or bump pads), now you have to have truncated domes. It may double the cost of every single neighborhood paving job you do in 2014. So, now more than ever, you've got to take it upon yourself to do the pavement management and figure out now to maintain and preserve your roads.

Hire someone to do it for 2 cents per square yard and save $10 or $20/SY. It is almost like you cannot afford not to be involved all the way into pavement management. The thing about (the City of ) Sandy Springs where I worked, after doing that with 21 folks of my own, I didn't sleep. They did not have any tax base for the first year, but we promised (I didn't do this; they, the city officials did) the residents (ratepayers) that every pothole would be fixed within 24 hours of receiving the pothole location information. Plus we were to call and tell them we just fixed their pothole.

So, I've been through hell and back with the city, and I feel awful for you guys now, more than ever. John, we had this discussion inside. This is not going to go away like sign retroreflectivity. This is the Department of Justice putting their foot down and saying this is how it is going to be.

---

If you are members of **IPMA** or you get on the free membership there when I get a chance to produce that little 1½ hour webinar or video webinar, I will get that out to you guys.

---

So back in 1996, this was my life (see photo on the previous page). Here's 25 guys going out to pulverize. I knew it worked in 1996. Remember the numbers you were showing, Wayne? 30 % savings, 40% savings in a tenth of the amount out of time. I've been there for like 2 decades, and I try to tell every single person I know, and, it is not enough, so I need your help today, guys. We've got to get the message out.

There's an article that I wrote in 1999 **Asphalt Contractor**. I thought that surely by 2002 everyone will get it. Now, here we are and we are still only recycling 3% of our roads in-place. The Governor of Virginia in 1999 is saying this is amazing.

This is going to revolutionize how we do things in America. I'm thinking, dude, I knew that in 1999. What took you guys so long to figure it out?

Tell me the first thing you think of. What's your name, way up there? Stand up for a second, will you? Good looking kid, there all by yourself. What's your name?

Audience Member: Matt Mulder.

Blair: Matt! What do you think of when you see this picture?

228

Matt Mulder: It looks hot.

Blair: Kind of makes me depressed to think about it, right? Because, you know, like a third world country with a donkey trying to make hot mix asphalt. Thanks, Matt. Are you single?

Matt: I've got a girlfriend.

Blair: Oh, is she out here?

Matt: No.

Blair: Okay. I was going to say if anyone is single in the room, Matt there you go!

(Audience Laughter)

Blair: What are you guys thinking when you see this? Let's see. Are you okay back there? Are you changing your contact lenses. Oh, what are you thinking? What's your name?

Audience Member: Casey.

Blair: Casey! When you see that picture what do you think?

Casey: They are grinding asphalt.

Blair: They are milling it, right?

Casey: Yes.

Blair: You know what I think? I did the math on this job because at one point in my life I was an estimator, and that job wasted 6 million dollars!

I see this every single day of my life when I'm **Driving America for Better Roads** www.drivingamericaforbetterroads.com. On 23 miles of an interstate, they are milling up 4 inches of asphalt in the middle of a desert and putting it into a ditch, and pushing it over with a D6 dozer Casey. I did the math, 23 miles, four lanes, four inches thick. Asphalt is the number one recyclable resource in America. We only recycle 3% of our roads in place. It is a travesty.

We've got to change how we are doing this or we are going to be bankrupt. Every local agency is going to be bankrupt. There's no way around it. Dumping RAP (Recycled Asphalt Pavement) in the middle of a desert ditch and pushing it over with a dozer. It doesn't work for me. Casey, does it work for you?

Casey: Nope

Blair: I mean, really? Matt, what about you?

Matt: Doesn't work for me.

Blair: John?

John: Doesn't work for me!

---

Reminder that the video of this live recording is on our YouTube Channel at www.youtube.com/ipmatv or right here at http://youtu.be/Cn4KNmCEFaU

---

Blair: Cindy? Pat? This is crazy. So, everyone stand up.

Now I put these little notes on here to remind myself.

Meet the Stringbenders – IACERS Conference – Boise, ID - 2013

Sui this is a good time for you to take the camera and, first of all, let me just do one panoramic (with iPhone) okay. Steve Jobs, I mean think about it. We are still doing things and the same way we have been since 1956 with the paving (industry) and yet we all carry things like this (iPhones) in our pocket right.

Everybody keep standing, if . . . this will only take a second, and I'm not here to pick on anyone.

Don't get the wrong idea. It's not about picking on anyone. It is about helping to revolutionize what we do in America (and the world). This will give you a good chance to stretch out a bit and do a couple of windmills, but don't hit your neighbor beside you. Now watch how I multi task. So, video okay? Sui, you got this? Ready? Okay, keep standing, wait a second, let's record it. You see the little notes that I made for myself okay. So keep standing if you are doing pavement management already. What do we have in the room Sui? You think there's like 100 people here? Put up your hand if you're not here.

Audience: Laughter

Blair: Nice to see no one is checking their e-mail. By the way, you are welcome to record this yourself on voice memo or whatever. Keep standing if you are doing pavement management. So, everybody in the room is still standing, right?

Eric, that's freaking incredible. Okay, watch what happens now. Keep standing if you are doing pavement preservation somehow, way or the other and pavement management. Oh, my good Lord, so nobody is sitting down then. So, if you are still standing, nobody sat down yet right?

(Someone enters conference from doorway.)

Welcome, are you wondering what the hell is going on here? It's a cult!

Audience: Laughter

All right, keep standing if you are doing pavement management, pavement preservation and some sort of in-place asphalt recycling. (Many of the audience sit down at this point). Whoa, I was getting worried there for a second, and thought I was in the wrong group.

---

* **HYPHEN CAUTION:** If a link includes a hyphen as it goes to the next line of text, when you retype the link into your computer **do not include the hyphen.**

Okay, so we just dropped 70% of the people, right? Okay. So, let me do this. For those of you who are still standing, I want you all to give yourselves a big round of applause. You guys are awesome. Go ahead, no do it!

Audience: Applause.

Blair: This also gives me an idea of what it would be like to get a standing ovation, if I were so lucky. Now, let's sit down and carry on this madness. Wow! Whew! I hope this is my water and not someone's vodka. Okay. Thanks, Eric, for having me here.

Visit www.IPMA.co, it's free. If you go to the website you will see that Sui Tan of The Metropolitan Transportation Commission (MTC) was one of the very first to join as an agency member. By the way, Metropolitan Transportation Commission is an agency, and you should know this too, now, that I think about it because one of the speakers this morning touched on it.

If you are part of the Metropolitan Planning Organization, MPO, your funding is about to get drastically reduced if you don't have a pavement management system from 85% to 65%, or something like that, so please get involved in the **Association** (**IPMA**) and stay on top of whatever it is that is going on. We will try to keep you abreast of everything possible.

How many people, other than Shane, are industry people? Anyone? Okay, they have to pay $197 per month. It's not really that much is it? Wayne, what are you? You retired?

Wayne: Me?

Blair: Yeah, are you industry or academia?

Wayne: Currently looking for work!

Blair: Well, if we get a pavement management job out here, you can help me out.

Wayne: All good.

Blair: Okay. There's my great friend Mary (next page). When you see the video at the end of the seminar, right near the theme song, Mary's daughter-in-law is singing, Irene Boggs. I'm so blessed to have friends like this.

Right now, reach under your seat. There's 2 pages there, right? Get your pen out. If you are in a seat that doesn't have one, just reach beside you. Cindy put sheets at every second seat, so grab the ones next to you, if you need to. Thanks, Cindy, for handing those out. So, grab a pen, keep it face down, and don't look at the numbers. It's like the lottery, right?

Yeah, and, again, I've never even tried this before, so I don't know even what's going to happen. But, I'm going to give this book away to the person that gets the highest rate in this quiz, the best score. By the way what time is it? Okay, I think we are doing okay. I mean there's no agenda.

Audience: (Laughter).

Blair: I know engineers hate that. Really, no agenda here. Is anyone waiting for instruction now? What were we doing? So, you've got the sheets turned upside down? Who doesn't have a sheet? Do you remember that from last year? Okay. Everyone should have two sheets. Keep them face down. Take the first sheet. Let me just see that for a second (one of the sheets from audience member). So, take the first sheet. I'm going to get my iPhone timer.

Take the first sheet. You notice there are 50 numbers. We are watching you. We've got judges placed all over. Okay, fine. I'm going to give you 60 seconds to go 1 through 50. Don't do any smart stuff like just mark them all okay? Nobody do that. Be realistic okay. You are going to circle each number in order from 1-50 with your pencils starting now.

Go! You got 60 seconds to go 1 through 50. Mary is going to love you guys for this. She doesn't even know I'm doing this, but I will send her a copy of the video so she can see it. It seems to be going. That's a lot of time isn't it? Did it already go 60 seconds and I wasn't looking? Huh? That's a long 60 seconds. Maybe when you are doing it, it just doesn't seem really fast.

Audience: There's no number 10 on this sheet right?

Blair: There's a ten on there, I checked it last night. I was drinking when I put this together.

Audience: (Laughter).

Blair: You have 10 seconds. Now five seconds. When I say stop everyone put them down. This has got to be real. That's it.

Okay, stand up if you've got all 50 circled. Oh, my gosh, it's not supposed to be like this. Okay, so clearly you got the message. Nice. Okay. How many people got 40. Okay, good one. No one usually gets to 50. How many got 30. You can be honest with me 30. Okay good. Twenty or less? Okay those of you who got 10 or less you don't have to stand up.

Now, what I'm going to do is . . . if I can borrow someone's sheet . . . You did the first one already. Okay, this time I want you to do this a different way. I'll make it really easy.

---

Readers: Tear the next page out of your book, if you want to follow along, or e-mail me at blair@ipma.co and I will send you a PDF. For those of you who have already registered your book at www.thebookonbetterroads.com/register, Ben or I will make sure you get this page delivered directly to your inbox with the e-mail address that you provide our team. If you are listening in on the Audio CD Box Set, you can still register your book to get the free BONUS material such as this little quiz in PDF form.

---

I want you to fold your sheet in half then in half again. I have no idea what the purpose of doing this is. I knew it would waste some time (joking). No there really is a point here. Now you've got four quadrants right? You see that one? Now listen carefully so it will go quickly.

Look at your quadrants in order: one, two, three, four. Keep going clockwise. Note the patterns in the numbers. I'm going to give you 60 seconds again, don't start yet. Are you ready (looking at left side of room)? Are you ready (looking at the right side of the room)? Okay, go! Can you go 1, 2, 3, 4, clockwise and everything is in a quadrant.

One is in the first quadrant, two is in the second quadrant, three is in third quadrant, four is in the fourth quadrant, and so on. If you are doing this right, it should actually be a huge paradigm shift. We are only at 22 seconds and you probably are up to 30. How are you doing Casey?

Casey: Good.

Blair: Okay. Matt, you doing okay out there?

Matt: Getting along.

Blair: How would you (talking to Matt) like to drive the **Driving America for Better Roads Bus** up to Olympia? We are going to go to Helena (Montana) and then St. George, Utah, and Phoenix (Arizona) and then home to Atlanta (Georgia) for Thanksgiving. Ten seconds. Ten seconds everyone. Five seconds. And stop!

Okay. Now what do we have? Huh? So, put up your hand if you got 50. Everybody stand up who has 40 to 50. Who do you think got done the quickest? John? Here you go (Blair hands a copy of Mary's Book to John). Nice job everyone.

What did you learn from that? How many people got 30 to 20? Stand up. Stand up everyone 30 to 20. So, we had a significant change once you knew the path right? How many people under-stand the metaphor of where I am going with this? Okay, I should give you the book.

If you know the path, if you get clear direction in life where you are going, and you know where you're going to get that information, it becomes a very logical sequence, right? Even for people like me, who are, you know, not the brightest light bulb in the fridge. It is so easy once you know the path. I know Mary would have been really pleased to watch you guys do that. She's quite a motivational speaker.

So, I need your help to create this revolution. There are going to be 25 **Driving America Better Roads** episodes next year and I have been told by a really smart guy (Camper Bull http://www.camperonleadership.com/) that the only way for me to reach city

236

**The Stringbenders™ Test from IACERS Conference 2013 Boise, ID – Thank You to Mary Morrissey**
Feel Free to Tear This Page Out of Your Book to Do Your Own Quiz – Set Your Timer to 60 Seconds

38

37

18

17

34

25

21

6

30

49

46

5

14

1

22

9

50

41

10

45

13

2

26

29

42

33

4      16

23

11

31

32

12

3

44

47

24

15

8

7

39

48

20

19

35

36

28

27      43

40

www.ipma.co  blair@ipma.co  www.ipmaacademy.com  www.thebookonbetterroads.com  www.stringbenders.org
Excerpt From Chapter 7 Part II The Book on Better Roads© by Blair Barnhardt, APM Copyright 2014 All Rights Reserved

**\* Hyphen Caution:** If a link includes a hyphen as it goes to the next line of text, when you retype the link into your computer **do not include the  hyphen.**

**The Stringbenders™ Test from IACERS Conference 2013 Boise, ID – Thank You to Mary Morrissey**
Feel Free to Tear This Page Out of Your Book to Do Your Own Quiz – Set Your Timer to 60 Seconds

38

37

18

17
34

25
6

21

30

49
46
14

5

1

9
22
50

41
10

45

2

13
26
42

29

33

4
16
23
11
31

32

12
3
47

44

24
15

8
7
39

48

20
19

35

36
28

27
43

40

www.ipma.co  blair@ipma.co  www.ipmaacademy.com www.thebookonbetterroads.com www.stringbenders.org
Excerpt From Chapter 7 Part II The Book on Better Roads© by Blair Barnhardt, APM Copyright 2014 All Rights Reserved

and county engineers with **IPMA** and **IMPA Academy** is to write a 240 page book. We are going to go ahead and I am going to sequester myself in a room for 30 days and write this book, but guess what?

I have you guys to help me write it because you are going to give me the top 10 items that you want to know as pavement managers. I'm going to type them into my computer, and when you get the book delivered to your city, or your county, you are going to look at it and read about one day, a long time ago, in a room in Boise, Idaho, about a group of great people who gathered. It was like a cult. They came up with 10 things that made the framework of this book. Once they closed that door at 3:00, and played that Johnny Cash song with Eric, it was over.

So, I'll go and write the book, but wait, there's more. This book is going to be free to every city and county engineer in the world with $6.97 shipping and handling. Okay? Most authors are interested in getting rich. We are interested in saving America and saving the world's crumbling infrastructure.

There are no hidden catches. On top of that we will throw in the Popeils Pocket Fisherman (joking), and we will have a **Better Roads Radio** podcast so you will get a chance to hear people like

Eric and me, people like Wayne and me talking (about pavement management). We are going to have one hour episodes (www.betterroadsradio.com). We are going to produce about 50 episodes.

We are going to do an episode together with Sui (Tan) from MTC, and StreetSaver, I will get my buddy from Helena, Montana, Jason Sorenson, Montana DOT, whom I intend to do an episode or several with. Before you know it, we will have 50, one hour sessions. You can download them to your computer, or download them to your iPhone, and listen to them as you are driving over to the Couer D'Alene Resort Golf Course (http://www.cdaresort.com/).

Okay? On top of that the **Barnhardt Group** (http://thebarnhardtgroup.com/), like I said before, has 6 pavement management clients per year. We are a small boutique firm, so, once the book is written, and we start distributing it, and doing the lunch-and-learns and that stuff all over again.

Hey guys welcome back. (More folks come into the room.) Nice to have you here. You've missed a lot of sh*t.

Audience: (Laughter).

Blair: So, I have a $20 dollar bill. The person who gives us the best answer, by vote by sound of applause from the whole room, the person that gives us the best solution for the framework is going to win that $20 bill.

If I know a thing or two about computers, I should be able to go over this document. Oh, good, this is actually working. We still have some time left. Twenty minutes or so?

Number one, if you have a book in your hands called **The Book on Better Roads**, today, right now, Cindy, what would you want to know about how to implement your pavement management system based on the fact that 70% of you sat down when I mentioned doing recycling. That kind of tells me a thing or two. Help me get out of my brain as an engineer/musician and get into the brain of you local agency folks who are going to be getting the book for free.

Adam, what do you think these guys need to know about pavement management, in-place pavement recycling and pavement preservation? Just give us a nugget. A nugget. Somebody stand up.

Adam: Proper handling

Blair: Proper handling? Now we are talking about the whole **Three Legged Stool** thing, right? So, these are going to have to be the top 10 framework items.

Adam: Proper handling of emulsions.

Blair: You are talking about handling of your emulsions. How about foamed asphalt? Let's think about putting a system together.

I think somebody said you had to have really accurate survey data. Wasn't that something you asked, Layla? What about survey data, accurate survey data, when you are doing your road rating? Is that important? You can hold that (microphone). How to rate roads accurately. Okay, I'm putting your name status too.

Eric: Accurate road survey data.

Blair: Accurate road survey data. Sui, you are allowed to answer these too.

Sui: I'm in agreement with Eric on that. Quality data—that is very important otherwise you get garbage in and garbage out.

Blair: Shi**y data in and shi**y data out right? Should I put that in the book? (Laughter). Poor data in means poor data out.

## The Book on Better Roads
www.thebookonbetterroads.com

Top Ten Tips for implementing the **Three Legged Stool System of Pavement Management** to save local agencies from bankruptcy.

If you have already or are planning to implement a comprehensive pavement management system, what key elements and best practices would you like to share and/or learn about? Boise, ID, Nov. 13, 2013 LEGACY TOUR.

For details on the launch date of the book or if you wish to provide additional input please visit www.thebookonbetterroads.com.

### 1. Accurate Road Survey Data (Eric)

So, we've got a couple of minutes here to do a couple more. You can do two of them, Eric. We have a double chance of getting that $20 bill.

How are you doing, Casey?

Audience Member: Show me the money. (Blair is looking for the $20 bill, but can't remember where he put it)

Blair: I lose stuff inside a 23 foot RV. Think about that.

Okay, come on you guys, chip in here. What's your name. Come on, think of one right now. How many Erics are in this room? Okay, you guys are amazing. Just pass the mic around, okay, to whoever comes up with the best answer. I'm ready to type, Eric.

Pavement management, what do you want to know when you read this 240-page book? Bar charts, pie charts, am I saving money, what is a minimum sized job?

Eric: So, now that I know all these great recycling techniques, and how to do a good chip seal, and all of that, how do I know which one is going to be the most cost effective to apply?

Blair: I think what Eric is saying is show me a matrix of treatments I can use and where's my biggest bang for the buck? Okay?

Audience Member: Best application.

Blair: Oh, wait a second. I should look when I type. Okay, see I just want to keep this simple.

Audience Member: Best fix for the problem.

Blair: Best fix for the ... You know what I forgot to do? I forgot to turn on Screenflow. Let's see if I can do that now.

Audience Member: You also forgot to turn on spell check! (Laughter).

Blair: Go ahead just ridicule me! I knew this would happen. That was a combination of Eric and who was the fellow out there?

Audience Member: Jim.

Blair: Jim. Eric and Jim. I'm putting this like you will see this in the book. It will say Eric and Jim so if your name is spelled wrong, please let me know before it goes to print.

Okay, pass the mic down the row up there to the next person who puts their hand up. Okay, it took us a little while, but we've got the interaction going now.

Audience Member: How to educate the public.

Blair: Wow. What is your name?

Audience Member: Jay.

Blair: Jay. Well I tried for 30 years. It ain't working too well yet because when I asked you how many people have seen the videos no one stood up except for Shane. So, how to best educate not only politicians, but the general public. So, that would be a public awareness program. James?

Audience Member: Jay.

Blair: May I call you James? (Laughter)

Jay: No.

Blair: Now we are down to five, and we are 46 minutes into it.

I think we are going to conquer this. You don't want to sing, no? I'll call you up or come up here. Don't make me come up there. Okay, Wayne. (Blair runs up the steps.) Wait a second. Don't say anything. Wait. Wait until I start typing or I will forget.

Wayne: An old motto of UDOT (Utah DOT) was good roads cost less and if you take care of your good roads, it will be a cheaper treatment.

## *The Book on Better Roads*
### www.thebookonbetterroads.com

Top Ten Tips for implementing the **Three Legged Stool System of Pavement Management** to save local agencies from bankruptcy.

If you have already or are planning to implement a comprehensive pavement management system, what key elements and best practices would you like to share and/or learn about? Boise, ID, Nov. 13, 2013 LEGACY TOUR.

For details on the launch date of the book or if you wish to provide additional input please visit www.thebookonbetterroads.com.

1. **Accurate Road Survey Data (Eric)**

2. **Poor data in means poor data out (Sui)**

3. **Best fit for the problem (Eric and Jim)**

4. **How to best educate our public (Jay)**

5. **Good roads cost less, inexpensive treatments (congeal case studies) (Wayne)**

Cheaper treatments for pavement preservation will spread your dollars a lot further on keeping your roads good.

Blair: Okay, I'm going to resist the urge to use the word "cheaper." Can we use "economical" or "less expensive?"

Wayne: Inexpensive.

Blair: This is the framework for the chapters. This is ten chapters. Inexpensive treatments. The whole preservation thing.

Well, every one of the treatments in the tool box will save us money. I mean you showed it. We see it. Stuart is going to get us 262 million to spend. I told Stuart I said I want to help you spend it right. So, good roads cost less, and inexpensive treatments are the way to go. General awareness for the public, right? You want to get that out too? We need case studies, Wayne, would you say?

Wayne: There are plenty of case studies out there, plenty of data.

Blair: But they need to be in one book, right? I think that is the problem. There is too much information all out there. We will do around 10 case studies. Okay I'll do a two-day workshop, and people will say at the end of it, "Well, can you show us some proof, Blair?" Like the 30 case studies I just went over weren't enough?

I should have told Ken this morning when he talked about gravel roads, I came up with a little saying too, "flat roads fail first" because it always happens that way.

Okay, wow, so we are at six. Casey got anything to say up there? Rowdi, you are the kind of guy I want to go drinkin' with. Dude, let's get Rowdi. Let's get rowdy, baby!

Rowdi: Cost.

Blair: Okay, good, hold the microphone there would you mind? Because this is going to be pretty cool when it is in the book that your name is Rowdi. Is that your real name on your driver's license? Okay so costs and more costs. Proof in our industry, we talk about social proof so in addition to case studies, Wayne, let's drill down and go through the costs of every treatment.

So often we get in the room and people say, "Well, how much is the cold in-place recycling? How much is FDR?"

Matt, you've got something to say up there?

For about eight years we tracked the same price for full depth reclamation at $6.50 per square yard up until the time the asphalt prices went sky high (around 2008).

Is it almost time to quit, Cindy? I won't have to go to the gym tonight. Just let me finish Rowdi's before I say anything, okay? So, that was social proof and here we go, Rowdi. Okay, Matt I'm ready.

Matt: I think we need to talk about storm water. Water in the ditches, and keeping it away from the pavement. That affects the roads.

Blair: You know what Dr. John Emery taught me? The three most important things when you build a road are . . . ?

Audience: Drainage, drainage, and drainage.

Blair: Yeah. How do you write a book on better roads and not talk about drainage. I never would have thought about that. Two T's or one?

Matt: Two.

## The Book on Better Roads
www.thebookonbetterroads.com

Top Ten Tips for implementing the **Three Legged Stool System of Pavement Management** to save local agencies from bankruptcy.

If you have already or are planning to implement a comprehensive pavement management system, what key elements and best practices would you like to share and/or learn about? Boise, ID, Nov. 13, 2013 LEGACY TOUR.

For details on the launch date of the book or if you wish to provide additional input please visit www.thebookonbetterroads.com.

1. **Accurate Road Survey Data (Eric)**

2. **Poor data in means poor data out (Sui)**

3. **Best fit for the problem (Eric and Jim)**

4. **How to best educate our public (Jay)**

5. **Good roads cost less, inexpensive treatments (congeal case studies) (Wayne)**

6. **Cost, cost and more cost . . . SOCIAL PROOF (Rowdi) WINS 20 Bucks**

7. **Drainage, Drainage, Drainage (Matt)**

8. **Build the road from the bottom up, FOUNDATION (Dan)**

Blair: Because Mary's (Mary Morrissey's) son is M-a-t, so I ask. Okay, we've got three more to go. I'd like to wrap this up in the next three minutes.

Dan: A good foundation, meaning getting the base correct with the emulsions.

Blair: You can't build a road unless you work from bottom up.

Dan: I am an old concrete guy, you gotta have a good foundation.

Blair: What a great point. Foundation.

By the way is the book (Blair asked the attendees to put their names and e-mail address in a book he passed around) still going around with your e-mails? I forgot to ask you guys. If you want to win the $2000 (**IPMA Academy**) scholarship.

Cindy is going to draw a number randomly. It is going to be computer generated in the next couple of minutes here. We are going to give away a $2000 scholarship (http://www.ipmaacademy.com/).

Make sure your name and e-mail are in that book and we can read it. First name Rowdi. Rowdi@countyofwhatever?

Where's the mic? Matt get the hell down here! (laughter) What are you doing up there! Why am I running around? You're the mic runner for the last two (laughter). What the hell, I should know about delegation by now. Okay. What would happen if I were to have a heart attack and never got the book written?

Wayne: Time saving from traveling public during construction.

Blair: I'm from Georgia. You're going to have to talk a little slower man.

Wayne: Minimize public inconvenience with traffic.

Blair: Oh yeah, minimization because engineers like these kind of words that end with 'ion'. Minimization of public disruption. Minimize. Of public. We'll get the spelling right afterwards. And that was?

Wayne: Wayne.

Audience Member: That is a lot of work for a $20 bill (laughter)

Blair: One more and then we are going to vote for the 20 bucks.

Audience Member: Needs based, off knowledge.

Blair: You came in late didn't you. Huh? Should he be eligible if he came in late (asking audience)? I'm kidding. No, don't take me seriously okay? What's your name?

Audience Member: John.

Blair: Okay what was it?

John: Needs based, off knowledge.

Blair: Can you speak in the mic?

John: Needs based, off knowledge. What do we need to build, based on our knowledge.

Blair: Where you are going with this is everyone should go to **IPMA Academy** to get the knowledge. I like that one. Okay, needs based, off knowledge. That kind of has a ring to it. I should get that domain

## The Book on Better Roads
www.thebookonbetterroads.com

Top Ten Tips for implementing the **Three Legged Stool System of Pavement Management** to save local agencies from bankruptcy.

If you have already or are planning to implement a comprehensive pavement management system, what key elements and best practices would you like to share and/or learn about? Boise, ID, Nov. 13, 2013 LEGACY TOUR.

For details on the launch date of the book or if you wish to provide additional input please visit www.thebookonbetterroads.com.

1. **Accurate Road Survey Data (Eric)**

2. **Poor data in means poor data out (Sui)**

3. **Best fit for the problem (Eric and Jim)**

4. **How to best educate our public (Jay)**

5. **Good roads cost less, inexpensive treatments (congeal case studies) (Wayne)**

6. **Cost, cost and more cost . . . SOCIAL PROOF (Rowdi) WINS 20 Bucks**

7. **Drainage, Drainage, Drainage (Matt)**

8. **Build the road from the bottom up, FOUNDATION (Dan)**

9. **Minimization of public disruption (Wayne)**

10. **Needs based knowledge (John) i.e. IPMA Academy**

name. Needs based off the knowledge.com. Name again?

Audience Member: John.

Blair: Don't call me in late, John. Okay, everybody. One, two, three, four, five, six, seven, eight, nine, or ten. We are going to do a quick show of hands.

Number one? Just say, "Rah, yay, or ooo-yeah." No?

Number two? You have to vote for one of these. (Laughter)

Number three? (Applause).

How to best educate our public'– Jay? (Applause).

Good roads cost less, inexpensive treatments, congeal case
studies – Wayne, I better put your name down?
(Applause).

I just can't wait to hear what is going to happen next.

Cost, cost and more cost, social proof – Rowdi? (Applause).

Drainage, drainage, drainage – Matt? (Applause).

Build the road from the bottom up – Dan? (Applause)

Minimization of public disruption – Wayne? (Soft Applause
(Laughter).

Needs based knowledge' – John? (Applause).

Number four? (Applause)

Number six? (Applause)

One more time, number four, Dan? (Applause)

Number six, Rowdi? (Loudest applause)

Blair delivers $20 bill to Rowdi. Great, let me get my camera.

This photo will be in the
book. And then we are
going to wrap. There you
go. You go down here
and I'll stand up here.
(Laughter). There you
go. Okay. Look, I'll cover
your shipping and han-
dling okay. Is that good?
Okay. I'll sign that for
you later if you want.

Okay, Cindy so we've got five minutes left. We have time to
play the video. We are out of here okay? You ready? Here we go.

Thanks for coming up. It's amazing. I guess I have to press
play. And you guys are welcome to go get your cookies now, but
you don't want to miss this. You don't want to miss Eric and I singing and showing you the (Johnny Cash) trick. But, if you want to
go get your cookies and coffee, that's fine, too, we understand.
We'll be around here all day tomorrow if anyone has any questions.

Thanks for joining us today. I love you guys.

Video Playing: (Music – **Driving America for Better Roads** Theme Song with Irene Boggs and Blair Barnhardt) (End)

Blair: Thanks for coming out.

## Transcript Ends

---

Reminder that you can watch this video at the IPMA TV You-Tube Channel or you can simply click here at http://youtu.be/Cn4KNmCEFaU.

---

Thanks once again to everyone at the IACERS conference in Boise ID, November 13th, 2013, for creating a legacy with us. In the next chapter I will briefly cover these ten items from the marvelous folks in Boise.

I don't think I can do justice to our readers and the Boise Stringbenders by a couple of quick explanations with the few pages that we have left here in this book. So, I have decided that in addition to a short discussion here in the next chapter, I will take each topic back to **IPMA** Headquarters and get on the big-ass whiteboard to describe in detail along with some field video and perhaps some interviews.

---

All you have to do is—you guessed it—register your book with us to have these technical training videos specific to the Top Ten from BOISE, ID and our group of Stringbenders. www.thebookonbetter-roads.com/register.

---

Also just before I get out of here with this chapter, I will let you in on a little secret. You see, I was ever so slightly worried that the BOISE Stringbenders would come up a little short on their list, so I had a few items of my own up my sleeve in the same Word document that I was working on live with them.

Here is my list below that I was going to draw from if I had to in a pinch.

Think about all Top Ten Liabilities List (all things in ROW)

1. **Know your budget needs**

2. **Network level coring**

3. **Comprehensive detailed inventory for network (estimating)**

4. **Comprehensive decision tree**

5. **Proper treatment selection and planning (i.E. Co op bids)**

6. **Accurate distress survey data**

7. **Accountability watchdogs**

8. **World class certification program (i.e. APM Accredited Pavement Manager with IPMA Academy)**

9. **Contract incentives for pavement preservation and in place asphalt recycling**

10. **Qualifications based selection for consultants providing PMS**

11. **Workplace training Three Legged Stool (IPMA Tip of the Weeks, Driving, Podcast)**

Now in addition to all we have discussed in this chapter, we also polled our list of subscribers back at **IPMA** Headquarters to see what they might want to see as additional topics to be discussed in the follow up sequence to those that register their books. I am very happy to say that we have over 200 responses from that query as well. I guess what I am saying here is, we have plenty more material to cover in not only the follow up sequence for book registrants, but likely for two or three more books to be written over the next year or so.

# Chapter 9 – The Top Ten List From Boise, Idaho

Thanks to our **Stringbenders** in Boise, we have an excellent place to start digging in our heels and setting our practical pavement management plan into high gear. I will offer up a quick explanation for each topic, and follow up with a detailed explanation with field video and interview footage wherever possible for registrants of this book.

Here is the list again from the IACERS Conference in Boise, ID:

1. Accurate Road Survey Data (Eric)
2. Poor data in means poor data out (Sui)
3. Best fit for the problem (Eric and Jim)
4. How to best educate our public (Jay)
5. Good roads cost less, inexpensive treatments (combine case studies) (Wayne)
6. Cost, cost and more cost . . . SOCIAL PROOF (Rowdi) WINS 20 Bucks
7. Drainage, Drainage, Drainage (Matt)
8. Build the road from the bottom up, FOUNDATION (Dan)
9. Minimization of public disruption (Wayne)
10. Needs based knowledge (John) i.e. **IPMA Academy**

## 1. Accurate Road Survey Data (Eric)

During our pavement distress evaluations, we use DMIs (Distance Measuring Instruments) on all of our vehicles to get accurate linear measurements. The units we choose to use are the Jamar RAC units. If the road is a consistent width, we will generally take a width measurement with our Keson measuring wheels.

On occasion, we find a segment of roadway that is variable widths. When this situation arises, I will make a simple sketch in my field book and divide the length into 200 foot increments. At that point, our field crew will station the overall length of the road with white dots sprayed with our paint cans at the 200 foot increments.

You can use a simple dot in the center of the roadway; we usually put a dot and a number such as 2 and 2 dots for 200, a 4 and 2 dots for 400, and so on. At that point, we will drop back once our dots are in place, and the stationing is complete for that segment. This is a good time to have two folks doing the work, one measuring, and one writing the widths into the field notes. Ideally this would be done on a small notebook computer directly into an Excel, or Numbers spreadsheet if on a Mac.

The idea, here, is to think of your segment of variable width roadway broken into small strips 200 feet long and whatever feet wide. If there are islands in the center, you can simply measure up to the island curb, then jump the grass or pinestraw, pick up on the other side and enter that measurement as the total width. Be sure to make a note in our comments that you have jumped the islands, and it may be worth including the same islands in your sketches.

I will point out that we take the measurement in the center of the 200 foot strip. In other words, you are taking the average width of each 200 foot strip. Now along the walk up the road, or whatever transportation you choose to use, be sure to include all turn outs, decels, accels, etc.

Now is the time to make some standard operating procedures (SOPs) regarding your side streets and such. For example, when we do a road segment as the mainline, and it runs at a 90 degree angle to a homeowners association or subdivision, we have to make a decision in the SOP as to which segment will "own" the square yardage for the decel lane and accel lane. We typically will let the mainline square yardage end at the seam of asphalt where the turnouts start. You may want to employ this same technique.

What this means is that you would only reclaim, or preserve the mainline road during an upgrade. The pavement section that starts at the seam we discussed above would therefore be up-graded or preserved during the scope of work at the project level for the subdivision.

And finally, for all the radius filets at the intersections, we figure triangles of either 15 by 15, 20 by 20 or 25 by 25 feet. For example if we are on a 22 foot wide county road that joins up with another 22 foot county road, we will say that at either end of the segment there are two 20 by 20 squares, or 2 times 400 SF, for a total of 800 SF.

If we are in a subdivision with a 76 diameter cul-de-sac, we add 5,200 SF, and if we are encounter the occasional 96 diameter cul-de-sac, we add 8,000 SF. We have measured these to include the little filets that lead in and out of them, so you can use our same figures with confidence.

254

So, for an example, we drive the UTV (Utility Terrain Vehicles) into a segment in a subdivision. We measure as 21 feet wide from gutter to gutter. We add 5,200 SF in the 76 diameter cul-de-sac, and we add one 400 SF amount for the filets at the one stop sign where we start. The entire length up to the cul-de-sac start is 4,000 LF.

Therefore we get:

400. SF (filets)
84,000. SF (21 ft x 4,000 ft)
<u>5,200. SF</u> (cul-de-sac)
89,600. SF

This is the type of accuracy we look for when doing our boots on the ground pavement distress evaluation. Once the data is entered into your database, you may not have to repeat the measurements for the next project. We also teach these same principles as part of the **IPMA Academy Certification** during the online training.

Here is a photo of my calculator case with a page out of Dr. Shahin's book to remind me of how many units to inspect. Also, below are the actual Jamar RAC 100 Distance Measuring Units (DMI) units that we use on the job. Some use direct connections to the transmissions; some use OBD plugs and wires. The newer models are more expensive and can use GPS. (The survey

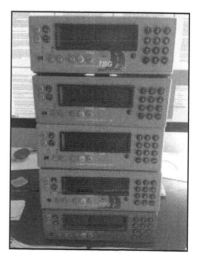

tape is so I can find it when the calculator falls down into the crevice beside my seat!)

Remember, at the end of your network level survey, the project managers who put the work out for bid are going to be relying on your square yardage takeoff measurements to go to bid with. If the pavement distress evaluation is done properly, there should be no need to reinvent the wheel, so to speak, when it comes to let the work to be performed. However, in some instances you will want to proof roll the roads at project level with a loaded dump truck, and, perhaps, do some more diamond coring at 500 or 1,000 foot intervals.

And though I haven't brought this up yet in the book, now is a good time to remind everyone that if you are out there doing anything in traffic, wear all of your Personal Protective Equipment (PPE), and have a second person with you, wherever possible, to act as a second set of eyes. I just read today about a construction worker that got killed on an Interstate project in Ohio. His family was awarded 19 million in settlement, and the construction firm that he was working for at the time were slammed with 20 million dollars in punitive damages for having the worker work in a very unsafe work zone. The driver that ran into the construction worker was not charged.

If I have learned one thing about safety in my three decades of construction experience, it is that no one just breaks a finger nail out here; they lose their limbs or life. So again, be on the lookout for any and all signs of vehicular mayhem.

Also, If you have ever thought about getting a carry permit for your weapon, now is also a good time to do that. It's a good idea to be prepared while you are working in strange surroundings in the middle of a county in anywhere America, or the world. If you ever run into Drew, ask him about the dog that came out and bit his leg while he was doing a pavement distress evaluation. Just when I thought I had seen it all . . . .

## 2. Poor Data In Means Poor Data Out (Sui)

Sui Tan is absolutely right. Funny story here, originally, when we got into the pavement management business, I was gun shy of all pavement management software that was cloud based. I went out of my way to ignore anything that resembled cloud, or virtual, in terms of pavement management software. Then, after a few "oh sh*t" moments, when things went awry on my computer based PMS (pavement management software), I called Sui up. We met, and the rest is like history. "If I had only known back then, what I know now," I say to myself. I met Sui almost a decade ago, and know now that, had I been more attentive, and less stuck on my idea of what the perfect set up for our business was, we may have had a lot fewer sleepless nights!

In any case, whatever PMS you choose to operate, one thing is for certain! If you collect your data as we have outlined in the book so far, and you are an accurate, methodical, double-checking, triple-checking, ethical, and conscientious person, then your final product that comes out of the PMS should be worthy of a round of applause by your ratepayers and politicians. If you take that one step further and dig into current regional unit pricing, and you load up your decision tree in the PMS with all of the available tools and their requisite unit pricing, and you carefully and methodically align all of those tools and unit prices with the correct functional class codes, pavement section types and surfaces, then you, my friend, are on your way to a standing ovation from your peers, and me.

If you continue to update your PMS annually, enter correct work history, and monitor the efficiency of all of those in your employ that take part in your pavement management, then you should get a raise.

If you do all of the above, and take part in an online pavement management certification program such as www.ipmaacademy.com, then you deserve a raise and a big promotion, right to the top, because you have now become a **Pavement Management RockSTAR.**

So, what I am basically saying here, is if you or your crew members do none of the above, you can expect your PMS to produce erroneous results that nobody will know what to work with because nothing will make sense.

On a similar note, anytime you set up any new data base in any industry, those who take a little extra time to follow standard operating procedures will always come out smelling like roses. Here is a simple tip to help you get started right out of the gate. And I owe this trick to Dr. Shahin and Scott McDonald for teaching me this the right way. We use this tip on every project we set up:

For road names, as you type them into the computer and set your data base up, always remember that in PAVER you have ten characters to work with as you set up your Section ID. So, we save the first six characters for the name, the next two for the prefix, like ST for Street, CT for court etc., and the final two for the orientation, such as SW, NE. Hence, Robertson Street Northwest would be ROBERTSTNW when we set it up, every time, no matter who on our team does it.

Another thing you will want to do is make some sort of video, or binder, with all of your SOPs in it. Then, as new hires come into the fold, you can get them up to speed quickly knowing that they are following the very SOPs that you have worked so hard to put into place.

Garbage In, Garbage Out. Simple, thanks Sui!

### 3. Best Fit for The Problem (Eric and Jim)

Great topic, Eric and Jim! Now don't shoot the messenger here, I get this all the time! People say, "Blair, just because it works in AK, doesn't mean it will work in FL." Good question. Even though I am aware that it works in CA and AZ and NV and UT, will it really work in GA and SC?

Everyone at every agency can rest assured that any of the treatments we talk about in the book, or in the follow up material for those that register their books, or in **IPMA Academy** or **IPMA** or **TBG** or **Driving America for Better Roads, Better Roads Radio**, basically anywhere you hear our voice, or our thoughts, know that we are never talking about anything new or unproven. All of these treatments work in every region, provided they are installed with quality contractors and equipment, and inspected and monitored as the materials go down.

---

They all have to be put on the right road at the right time with the right treatment with the right contractor for the right reason.

---

And, what Jim considers a high volume road, and what Eric considers a high volume road may differ. Let me give you an example of something to consider:

If you are a small township, and all you ever do is chip seal your roads, then an M&R (Major Rehabilitation) to you is a chip seal. To most others, a chip seal may be a preservation treatment. Some state DOTs apply chip seal to all of their state routes as the wearing surface on a hot mixed asphalt binder base. Others have concrete interstates and state routes.

In the case of the township above, that pavement manager may tweak his PAVER system, or whatever PMS he or she is using, to say that every time a new chip seal goes down, the PCI will be reset to 100. But, and this is a big "but" here, the reason for this SOP is the township superintendent knows this is the best it is ever going to get in his/her township.

The same chip seal going down for the neighboring county engineer may simply be a preservation treatment in conjunction with a crack sealing operation. So be very careful when you set up your system and decision tree as to what the best fit for the problem is. Recall that a sequentially overlaid HMA surface with multiple lifts can be a PCI 92 per my sketch several chapters before. It cannot just get a preservation treatment because the asphalt is already filling in the gutters in that example. Therefore, even when you set up your network level pavement management, careful consideration must be taken into account at the project level each and every time as to the best fit for the problem.

My best advice for those who are just setting up their system is, if you know someone who can help you set up the decision tree based on some fundamental knowledge of the implementation — a mentor or guru type, get that person to spend a few days with you. Get up to speed on all the treatments that are available in your pavement management tool box (or arsenal), and walk before you run.

For example, when our **IPMA** Advisory Board Member, Brian Frix, from Rockdale County, decided to begin his microsurfacing program, he was going to let about 300,000 square yards right out of the gate on his very first letting. I tugged on his arm a bit, and said,"Hey, Brian, let's consider doing 50,000 SY first, let the contractors know when they bid and perform the work that if it works out, and everyone is happy at the county, then we will rebid a larger sum of work."

Brian did this exact strategy with a great deal of success, and now has a very active and robust microsurfacing—and full blown preservation—program set up. He knows now which is the best fit for the problem at hand. I suggest you all do the same.

Here is another example:

Often when we implement a new PMS on the consulting side of our business (www.thebarnhardtgroup.com), we will make some key decisions such as: no longer will we just do hot mixed asphalt overlays on chip seal roads. We will simply chip them, or microsurface them, or maybe scrub seal them, or similar. We will take the hot mixed asphalt we would have put on the chip seal roads in the past, and use it in other parts of the county.

Now, this works most every time for most every county, but, sure as shootin,' there will be an anomaly along the way somewhere where this SOP that we have come up with doesn't work. But, for the most part, with simple decisions at the network level, implementation of your PMS can save you millions of dollars. Or another way of saying this is, you will end up getting more miles done with less money, or at least the same as you have been currently spending.

I will cover this topic in the **IPMA Studio** on the big whiteboard, and get you all a little video footage of some of the types of roads, and what treatments I would recommend, for those of you who register your book.

## 4. How to Best Educate our Public (Jay)

I have seen some really good publications in the past put out by local agencies, state DOTs and our US DOT, to name a few. However, while the publications are great at conveying the message about preservation, a few in-place pavement recycling techniques, etc., I have yet to see a comprehensive, easy-to-read publication about what we do and what we are trying to accomplish directed to the normal, everyday person.

My biggest fear is, even if this publication existed, the folks generating the educational material do not have access to large nationwide data bases. Even if they did, many don't quite understand the marketing and dissemination of said material on a broad scale.

But, the point Jay is making is taken to heart while I am writing this book. In fact, by this time next year, we will launch a book titled **Driving America for Better Roads** through Amazon.

---

We will distribute this book to a large list of everyday people in an effort to educate them on what it is that the **Stringbenders** are doing for our planet. So take a minute and register your book, and JOIN US over at www.stringbenders.org so that we can share your success stories in the next book, Driving America for Better Roads. Be sure to keep up with our movement at http://drivingamericafor-betterroads.com/.

---

### 5. Good roads cost less, inexpensive treatments (consolidate case studies) (Wayne)

Or: Good roads cost money. Bad roads cost more.

It is a well-documented fact that our US DOT (Federal Highways Administration) has proven that pavement preservation costs the end user less money in the long run. You can spend a day over here at http://www.fhwa.dot.gov/pavement/index.cfm seeing for yourself. I personally have been teaching this for two decades, and yet, it seems that some folks will never ever get it for some reason. But I have renewed faith in the masses. In fact, if you are reading this book, you likely have the desire to do what is best for your local agency or private sector firm.

I have already proven in previous chapters that pavement management costs pennies per square yard and offers you the opportunity to save millions. You have seen plenty of information in the first chapters about the benefits, cost savings and eco-efficiency of in place recycling of our pavement structures. You could therefore draw the conclusion that these inexpensive treatments cost less in the long run.

But like most folks out there, you may still need some convincing. For this reason I will continue to send out case studies in the form of Better Roads Radio podcasts, **IPMA Academy Training and Bonus Videos, IPMA Tip of the Weeks, Driving America for Better Roads** episodes, and, for those of you who register your book, I will send you a stream of case studies directly to your mail box.

---

* **HYPHEN CAUTION:** If a link includes a hyphen as it goes to the next line of text, when you retype the link into your computer **do not include the hyphen.**

You see, deep down inside, I am the same as you are. I will spend days on end on the internet trying to convince myself that what I am about to do or purchase is right. Then, I will ask a bunch of my colleagues and peers what they think. Heck, I may even call strangers to ask them what their experiences with the product or service is. I suspect you folks do the same.

But this pavement management stuff isn't rocket science folks! Let's face it, we are living in an age where we have put men on the moon, and we have self-driving cars. We are simply talking about putting a dollar per square yard treatment on the road to extend its life on down the proverbial curve so that we can prevent having to do a more invasive repair. In fact, some agencies are now specifying that preservation treatments be applied in as little as six weeks after the installation of new hot mixed asphalt pavement.

Funny, it seems that the private sector, the high end Home Owners Associations (HOAs), get this a lot faster than the local agencies.

---

Could it be that we have become so accustomed to wasting billions of dollars that we now accept this as the norm?

---

Again, if the nation was one big private sector firm, and the board of directors figured out that they could preserve their infrastructure with one dollar today instead of ten dollars a few years later, wouldn't they have done that decades ago? Of course, in this hypothetical scenario, if this private sector firm I speak of didn't preserve their infrastructure, they would have gone bankrupt years ago.

And, that is what is happening right now to our country, and possibly the world. Even though there is a solution, we are so disconnected from local agency, to state DOT to FHWA, with so much political rubbish in the way of real change for the better, we are sinking in our own puddle of mud (to put it mildly).

I have Google alerts set up on everything we talk about in this book, and, quite frankly, it is depressing for me to read the headlines of the stories I see each day on my computer screen. Yet, the majority of the stories are still based on the Google alert "repaving." It seems that when it comes to the politicians, and the normal everyday citizen, they just don't know that there are other options.

If I were to get on **20/20** or **MSNBC** or **60 Minutes,** I would be the first one to shout it out from the top of the rooftop, **STRINGBENDERS UNITE!** We don't have to have crumbling roads in this country any longer. There is a way—it is called **The Three Legged Stool!**

OK, OK, enough of that rant. Here are a few case stories to keep you going for now as we near the end of our book, again, many more to follow to registrants of their book as our journey together has only just begun:

---

On Mar 24, 2014, at 1:07 PM,
Shahriar Najafi <najafi@vt.edu> wrote:
Here is our experience for FDR/CIR Hybrid trial section on State Route 40 in Franklin County, Virginia:

---

— SR 40 is an east-west facility that runs through southern central Virginia approximately 35 miles south of Roanoke. This section has a combined annual average daily traffic (AADT) of approximately 4,400 (4% trucks).

— The FDR/CIR hybrid trial section was built on this route by the Virginia Department of Transportation (VDOT) during the 2008 construction season.

— Treatment consisted of pulverizing the existing bound flexible pavement layers along with a portion of the unbound layers (or all the unbound layers and a portion of the subgrade); adding a stabilizing agent; compacting the mixture; and surfacing with a new bound material layer(s) or surface treatment.

— Asphalt emulsion and foamed asphalt binder were used as the respective stabilizing agents on two sections within this project.

— The original pavement consisted of 5 to 6 in. of HMA and surface treatments over 6 to 10 in. of aggregate materials (consisting of crushed aggregate and uncrushed gravel).

— Prior to reclamation, the original pavement showed numerous structural distresses including longitudinal cracking and fatigue cracking within the wheel paths. Cores collected during the pre-reclamation site investigation showed multiple thin layers with some layers being completely debonded.

— The pavement was reclaimed to a depth of approximately 8 to 10 in., and a 1.5-in HMA overlay (following a leveling course) was placed as a wearing surface. Two treatments were applied at this site. The western half of the project (both lanes) was reclaimed using an asphalt emulsion, and the eastern half of the project (both lanes) was reclaimed using foamed asphalt as the stabilizing agent. The binder used during the foaming process was a performance grade (PG) 64-22 binder, and the binder used in the emulsion process was a PG 58-22. The reclaimer made two passes: the first pulverized the existing pavement, and the second added the stabilizing agent. Once the stabilizing agent was incorporated, the resulting material was shaped by a motor grader and compacted by pad foot, steel wheeled, and rubber tire rollers. The original pavement lanes were approximately 10 ft wide, and the reclamation process also allowed for an increase in width of 2 ft/lane. The stabilizing agent content was 2.7% and 2.28% for the foamed asphalt and asphalt emulsion, respectively. In addition, approximately 1.0% Portland cement was added within the foamed asphalt section. The reclamation process on the foamed asphalt portion occurred May 13 through 15, 2008, and on the asphalt emulsion portion from May 19 through 22, 2008. The HMA overlay was placed approximately 3 weeks later.

— The FDR assessment was conducted using a variety of methods that included gradation analysis; determination of resilient modulus, dynamic modulus, and indirect tensile strength; ground penetrating radar; falling-weight deflectometer testing; and LCCA (life cycle cost analysis). A hypothetical LCCA was also conducted to document the potential cost savings between a pavement rehabilitation schedule that included FDR with one that was based solely on traditionally used rehabilitation techniques.

— The study showed that pavements could be successfully reconstructed using FDR and that the structural capacity of FDR sections was dependent on both the stabilizing agent and time.

— The LCCA showed that if a pavement rehabilitation strategy that includes FDR is applied to a preliminary candidate list of projects on VDOT's primary and secondary networks, a 50 year life-cycle cost savings of approximately $10 million and $30.5 million, respectively, is possible when compared to a traditionally used pavement rehabilitation approach. A project-level investigation should be performed on any potential FDR site to verify that it is an appropriate candidate.

Source: http://www.virginiadot.org/vtrc/main/online_reports/pdf/11-r23.pdf\ Thanks, Shahriar

Here are some links for those on their Kindle book plus a case study:

A. From Steve Gorcester at Washington State Transportation Improvement Board talking about pavement management:

http://www.tib.wa.gov/media/newscontent/items/2014/TurningTheCurve.pdf

B. A case study from Don Clem, PE, from Portland Cement Association – Rocky Mountain Cement Council, discussing FDR in Utah.

### Concrete Pavement on an FDR Base – Built to LAST!

All across the Beehive State, thousands of miles of federal, state, county, and city roads are rapidly deteriorating and in need of immediate rehabilitation. The majority of these roadways were constructed utilizing flexible-granular base materials and were often under-designed for today's heavier traffic loads. The presence of ruts, potholes, and severe cracking are common problems that are usually maintained with additional asphalt patches and thin overlays. However, these problems often are not attributed to normal surface wear and may be the result of a failed or inadequate base course. When this situation occurs, it is important to fix these base problems in order to have long-lasting pavement rehabilitation.

Salvaging these existing failed flexible pavements is a good practice, both environmentally and economically, because they still contain good granular material that, when blended with Portland cement can be reused and recycled into a strong, durable new base. A process commonly referred to as full-depth reclamation (FDR) is a technique in which the old asphalt pavement and a portion of the underlying base, subbase, or subgrade materials are pulverized and blended together with Portland cement to create an enhanced roadway base material.

The steps for FDR consist of the pulverization of the existing materials, the incorporation of any additional materials, mixing, initial shaping of the new base mixture, compaction, final shaping,

* **HYPHEN CAUTION:** If a link includes a hyphen as it goes to the next line of text, when you retype the link into your computer **do not include the hyphen.**

curing, and the application of a new surface or wearing course. In Utah, FDR is performed on the roadway itself at depths typically ranging from 6 to 12 inches depending on the thickness and composition of the existing pavement structure.

In Salt Lake City, FDR has proven to be the engineering and economic choice for rebuilding both commercial and residential roadways. In 2006, an industrial section of 1820 South between 4100 West and 4130 West was reconstructed using FDR in a similar fashion to a residential section of 1300 West between 850 South and 700 South back in the summer of 2005. While projects like these in Salt Lake City typically use between 3.5 and 4 percent cement, the application of the cement is different.

For the larger industrial projects, contractors have applied the cement as a dry powder, while the smaller residential projects have been constructed by applying the cement in a slurry form. Both application methods are equally effective and illustrate the versatility of using cement as a construction material.

While normally thought of as a rehabilitation method for local and collector roads, FDR works just as well for arterials and freeways. In fact, in the summer of 2005, Granite Construction Company reconstructed a 10-mile section of Interstate Highway 84 near Huntsville to accommodate the nearly 15,000 vehicles that travel that section daily. The high traffic, coupled with the harsh weather environment in the section, had prompted Utah DOT engineers to seek a construction solution that would meet the demands of both strength and durability.

Research performed by Dr. Spencer Guthrie at Brigham Young University showed that by constructing a cement-stabilized base section using as little as 2 percent cement would provide adequate support for traffic as well as reduce any potential problems with moisture susceptibility. In fact, the strength supplied by the cement to the base layer through the FDR process allowed Utah DOT engineers to reduce the thickness of the more expensive asphalt surfacing layer.

John Coyle, Project Manager with Salt Lake City Corporation, understands perfectly well the sound engineering behind FDR with cement. Under Coyle's management, Randall Neal, Project Representative, recently designed and provided construction oversight

266

for four residential street projects in Salt Lake City: Forest View at 900 East; Judith Street and Hudson at 1100 East; Parkway Avenue at 1300 East; and 1900 East at 2100 South.

Each of these projects included about 12-16 inches of pulveri-zation of the existing asphalt and base course, followed by removal of some unsuitable materials. Then, approximately 6- inches of the reclaimed materials was treated using 4% Portland cement by dry weight. The wearing surface for each project was a 6 inch non-reinforced jointed concrete pavement. This FDR section saved the taxpayers about 30% when compared to the conventional removal and replacement of the aggregate base course.

Not only is there a cost savings up front, the residents along these improved roadways will enjoy decades of superb perfor-mance, with minimal maintenance disruptions. Coyle maintains that "when properly constructed, the City will get a much higher return on their dollar, while ending up with a roadway section that will surpass the older flexible pavements in terms of longevity."

Whether Interstate, industrial, or residential, Portland cement is the key to reconstructing flexible pavements that have failed. The incorporation of the cement with the old base course mate

John Coyle, Salt Lake City Project Manager, reviews work completed along Forest Street.

rial, often including the old asphalt surface, provides a versatile, practical, and cost-effective means of strength-ening worn-out pavements. The cement binds the granular particles together to form a paving material capable of withstanding moisture infil-tration and degradation. It increases the strength of the base without the need for removing the old material and hauling in large quantities of expensive new base materials.

The reclamation of failed flexible pavements using Portland cement has many advantages: the conservation of non-renewable resources through the reuse of existing materials, the elimina-tion for the need of new granular base

267

materials, a reduction in both hauling and energy costs, and the elimination of bumps, dips, ruts, potholes, cracks, and preliminary patches. In addition, the new stabilized base course can be shaped to restore the desired surface crown and cross-slopes, preserve drainage flow at curb and gutter sections, and retain adequate clearance at overhead structures.

C. A link out to a story on hot in place recycling from my friend Andy Pujats over at iBuildroads, www.ibuildroads.com:

http://www.ibuildroads.com/hir-solves-cost-challenge-to-runway-reconstruction/?utm_content=buffer765de&utm_source=buffer&utm_medium=linkedin&utm_campaign=Buffer#%21

D. A link from the Salmon Arm Observer talking about hot in place recycling in Canada:

http://www.saobserver.net/news/231000441.html

E. Take a look at this graphic that pretty much sums up the state of our infrastructure here in America:

http://www.bestmswprograms.com/infrastructure/

I will put a few more case studies in the BONUS Chapters .

## 6. Cost, Cost and More Cost...Social Proof Winner (Rowdi)

Rowdi hit the nail on the head, and won the coveted prize for coming up with the best topic to be covered here in the book.

---

Here is the link from the craziness in Boise, ID, at the IACERS Conference: http://youtu.be/Cn4KNmCEFaU.

---

The short answer is you can have your entire network of roadways evaluated and managed for about $.02/SY, and save $10/SY down the road by selecting the right treatment on the right road at the right time with the right contractor for the right reason.

Further, you can spend a dollar per square yard today on a preservation treatment or two that will ultimately save you ten dollars per square yard down the road.

Moreover, when you have to do a major rehabilitation project, you can select the in-place pavement recycling usually for 30% less money than conventional rehabilitation techniques.

Now, let's discuss specifics:

I will list as many tools in the toolbox that I can think of along with their associated unit prices. Now, wait a second here, don't start getting uptight with me and shouting out that you get things done for less, or, it cost you twice as much. As an estimator who used to bid 50 million dollars of this type of work each year, I know first hand that it "depends" on a lot of factors. So, this list is not meant to be all-inclusive, all encompassing, or in any way, shape, or form an indicator of what you should be paying. I am just trying to answer the call from Rowdi. After all, he did win for best answer!

Furthermore, this list is based on contractors or service providers coming in and doing a decent size job for your local agency. And, here is a little secret that I will share with you all, for those pavement managers who give their contractors a lot of grief for no apparent reason, us estimators have been known to add a certain percentage to their bids to offset the additional cost of aggravation that we intend to encounter on your job site if we are lucky (or unlucky) enough to get the work awarded to our firm. (LOL.)

Again, I want to emphasize, if I didn't put a particular treatment on the list, or, if the unit price is too low or high based on current day market conditions, don't sweat it. I did my best to cover what is current. I am the same person that used to get the nasty comments on the NHI evaluations because the case studies and unit prices were two decades old, even though that curriculum wasn't in my control at the time of delivery.

If I use certain name brands, remember I am not here to promote or endorse ANYONE or ANYTHING, just that, some of these are sole source, or single supplier. The treatments below do not include their requisite wearing courses where required. I also based these unit prices on the current asphalt cement prices and fuel costs at the time of writing. Also, with many of the techniques listed below, milling would be required to eliminate surplus material, so you would have to add the two unit prices together to estimate your cost of reconstruction. (Be sure to read the disclaimers and legalese)

| Treatment Type | Unit Price Range per SY (Unless noted otherwise) |
|---|---|
| Crack Sealing (per LF*) | $0.50 - $1.50 |
| Fog Sealing | $0.60 - $0.90 |
| Rejuvenating Agents | $0.80 - $1.20 |
| Rejuvenating Fog Seal | $1.20 - $1.50 |
| Cold Milling (Edge Mill) | $1.75 - $2.25 |
| Single Chip Seal | $1.40 - $1.80 |
| High Density Mineral Bond | $1.90 - $2.45 |
| Slurry Surfacing | $1.10 - $1.90 |
| Single Micro Surfacing | $2.25 - $2.90 |
| Double Micro Surfacing | $2.45 - $3.30 |
| Scrub Seal | $2.20 - $2.70 |
| VDM (Variable Depth Milling) | $2.75 - $3.75 |
| Cape Seal | $3.30 - $4.00 |
| Hot in Place Surface Recycling | $3.75 - $4.50 |
| Thin Overlay | $4.50 - $5.80 |
| Cold in Place Recycling | $6.00 - $8.00 |
| Full Depth Reclamation Chemical | $6.50 - $9.00 |
| Full Depth Reclamation Bituminous | $6.50 - $9.00 |
| Ultra Thin Bonded Wearing Course | $6.50 - $8.00 |
| 2" HMA Overlay | $7.50 - $9.00 |
| HIR Re-HEAT (no wearing course req'd) | $9.00 - $12.00 |
| Deep Patching (mill and fill 4") | $22.00 - $25.00 |
| Remove & Replace Sidewalk (per SF) | $8.00 - $10.00 |
| Remove & Replace Curb & Gutter (LF) | $23.00 - $28.00 |

In future editions of the book, we will add and alter the list of products and unit prices as the market dictates.

*NOTE: Here is a tip for you to consider when estimating how many feet of crack sealing or crack filling you need to do, thanks to my GA Tech Intern Scott Horvath (we spent a day measuring this stuff). You can use the multiplier chart o the next page to estimate linear feet of cracks to seal or fill:

## Block Cracking Liner Feet Multiplier Chart —

LF of the block cracked area is determined by multiplying the SY of the distressed area by the following multipliers:

| | |
|---|---|
| Low Severity* Multiplier | 0.30 – 0.50 |
| Medium Severity Multiplier | 0.60 – 0.80 |
| High Severity Multiplier | 0.90 – 1.20 |

*Block cracking severity is based on PAVER guide.

We will take a hypothetical example of a roadway with medium severity block cracking that is 22 ft wide and 4,000 ft long, with one pair of filets 20 x 20 SF, and one CDS of 76 LF DIA. (Refer to page 251 for cul-de-sac SF.)

$$4,000 \text{ ft} \times 22 \text{ ft} = 88,000 \text{ SF}$$
$$CDS = 5,200 \text{ SF}$$
$$Filets = 400 \text{ SF}$$
$$Total = 93,600 \text{ SF} = 10,400 \text{ SY (divide SF by 9)}$$

Now all you have to do is take 10,400 SY and multiply it by the multiplier that Scott and I devised:
$$10,400 \times 0.60 = 6,240 \text{ LF}$$

In this example we chose the lower end of the multiplier. We will assume we are paying the contractor $0.50 per LF to crack seal:
$$6,240 \text{ LF} \times \$0.50 = \$3,120.00$$

You now have a close estimate as to the cost of preparing the road, and crack sealing it. Remember to leave a few months in between crack sealing/filling operations and your intended preservation treatment. Also, wherever possible, crack filling and sealing is best done in the spring and fall when the cracks are not at their narrowest or widest.

OK, Rowdi, there you go!

Let's go down and talk about drainage for Matt.

## 7. Drainage, Drainage, Drainage (Matt)

I can't think of a more important thing, maybe next to construction safety than drainage. Remember the phrase I coined, "Flat roads fail first!"

Nine times out of 10 when I go out to look at a failed road, it is usually a casualty of a drainage problem of some sort. Could be a failed culvert, a spring underneath the road, a plugged inlet, a reverse crown from a sunken sub base and on and on.

The trick going forward as we rehabilitate our roads is to look for potential drainage problems before any and all other things. Note that I didn't say preservation candidates. You see, we shouldn't be trying to fix drainage problems with preservation techniques, short of maybe a little rut filling with the microsurfacing rut box technique. But you all already know that after getting this far in the book!

271

I like to see asphalt roads at a minimum of 2 percent cross slope and concrete pavements can be a little less, but always more than 1 percent. Also, wherever we see high levels of pavement distress on roads with an inverted crown, we are always best to recommend changing to center crown where possible during the rehabilitation stages.

Think about it, the inverted crown pits our two worst enemies together, a cold seam in the asphalt pavement, and debris clogged inlets (pine straw, grass clippings, etc.). The pavement section is set up to fail from day one. Then, worst case scenario, someone starts putting a bunch of poor patches in the center of the inverted crown. Next thing you know you have bird baths (standing water) and an overgrown mosquito breeding ground.

One of my colleagues from a county in Wyoming used to grade all his dirt roads to a 6 percent cross slope. He said there was never any trouble with them in the summer as far as wash-boarding and such, but he did point out to me that he brought them back to 3 percent for the winter time, otherwise he may have cars sliding into the ditches in icy conditions.

So, as you are out there doing your pavement distress evaluation, whether in house with your own crews, or with your favorite consultant, make a drainage survey part of what you do at the time. After all, there is no sense in preserving and recycling our roadways if we are simply going to return them to a poor grade once they are done.

It doesn't matter if it was a design flaw, or whether the road simply sunk in the middle, do not replace poorly drained roads with poorly drained new roads. Get yourself a digital, 4 foot level from Lowes or Home Depot, and be on the lookout—always. Be sure to keep the level behind your seat at all times, and calibrate it regularly as recommended by the instructions that come with it at time of purchase.

You cannot get water to run up hill! Many have tried. Even in new construction, some areas on the blueprints are designed for minimal fall, don't make the mistake of building it that way just because it was designed that way.

One time, as VP of a paving and reclamation firm, I was asked to price the overlay for a gated community of high end town homes in the Metro-Atlanta area. The binder asphalt had been done several years before, and for whatever reason, that company was no longer around to perform the final wearing course.

So, I measured the job and submitted the price for acceptance. Our folks went down and performed the work, and two weeks later I got the call to visit the site and see the "defective" pavement that wasn't draining.

The bad news is, I should have caught this on my first visit, before any of the work was done. The good news is, I had my 4 ft digital level in my truck. I measured the areas that weren't draining properly. By the way, did I mention that this was an inverted crown design?

At the point of fall away from the garage door jambs out to the inlets, the digital level showed a mere 0.50 percent cross slope at best. Dismal. There was no way to get the water out to the inlets where it was supposed to go. Then I started asking questions to the home builder and his project manager. I found out after several minutes of questioning why the design was so flat. He told me the original drawings from the engineer called for twice as many inlets.

Really?

"Yes, that is right, Blair. We find that with all those drains in our town home developments, the road goes up and down a lot and it looks bad."

So, I say, well, sorry about that, we will get the guys to heat up the final wearing course with a propane torch and try to put a little swale in there, but that is about all we can do when you only put in half of the amount of inlets that are required to get 2 percent cross slope.

And the moral of this story is, never let someone else's problems become your problem!

As one of my mentors, Dr. John Emery, always drilled into my little brain: drainage, drainage, drainage. Those are the three most important things to consider when building a road. Enough said!

## 8. Build the Road from the Bottom Up, Foundation (Dan)

While this motto applies to most of our roads that fall under the critical PCI range of 55 or less, it is good for all of us to burn this into the back of our brain for each road we look at in the course of the day.

For the sake of brevity, I will focus on the opportunity that presents itself when we specify FDR (full depth reclamation) for our standard "go to" complete restoration. As a reminder, I did ask everyone reading this book to stand up, put their right hand up and swear, "I promise, never, never, never to dig up and haul off to a landfill site a roadway section that I have already bought and paid for. I promise to only use FDR as the rehabilitation method for my worst roads."

Now, aside from the fact that FDR is more economical, faster and more eco-efficient, I want to point out that it can double or triple the layer coefficient of the in situ pavement section. But wait, there's more. And no, it is not the kitchen knives. The great thing you will find about having a 800 HP pulverizer (often called reclaimers) on your job site is, after the road is pre-pulverized in advance of the stabilization operation, you will be able to deal with soft subbase problems immediately and effectively.

The analogy I use here is like a good painter coming into your house and spackling the rough spots and divots in your wall prior to putting on the coats of paint. More often than not, the soft sub base and trash pits that we all know exist under the paved surfaces in our cities and counties, go undetected over the years because the in situ asphalt surfaces (and sometimes concrete) mask, or bridge over, the troubled areas. This was clearly the case on the Natchez Trace Parkway project I described in a previous chapter.

So, after the pavement structure is pre-pulverized, get out there with your 30 ton rubber tire roller or a loaded dump truck and proof roll the heck out of it. Be on the lookout for deflection of the sub base. Isolate the areas, mark them up with paint or stakes offset at the side of the road, etc. Then drop the pulverizer back and put seven pounds of Type III Portland Cement (Type I if you can't get III) per square yard per inch of depth in advance of any stabilization that you are proposing in the contract.

So, if the soft spot is down 18 inches, you will put 18 x 7 = 126 lbs/sy into that area of soft sub base. Now you may experiment a bit with this formula and drop back to 100 lbs/sy in this case. But if you absolutely want to take care of this problem once and for all, go big or go home.

The next day all of the soft sub base problems will have conveniently disappeared, and you can move onto the balance of the contract doing the bituminous or chemical stabilization that you originally were contracted to perform.

A good rule of thumb for those pavement managers setting up these jobs at the project level would be to allow for 5% of your overall square yardage on any one job to be candidates for deep base stabilization. When I used to bid this type of work, I would simply add a by-the-ton price for each ton of cement that we would use for this purpose. That price-per-ton included all of the incidental costs of compaction: mixing, grading, cement, water etc.

Now, if you are thinking for a second that this is an expensive repair, think again. Consider the other option: digging to an indefinite depth filled with tree roots and stumps, for an indefinite amount of time, in uncertain weather conditions, incurring potentially expensive dump fees, then replacing it with new select fill, granular base rock, and new pavement . . . need I say more?

Dan, you are absolutely correct that a solid foundation is essential to having a long lasting road. It's much like building a structure such as a skyscraper or tower, spending a little extra time with the equipment that we already have on site is not just an option; it is an essential ingredient in a successful long term project.

I will also point out at this time that I used Portland cement in this example, but we have also had great success with lime, lime kiln dust (LKD), calcium chloride, magnesium chloride, fly ash and various other combinations of stabilization agents. Even if you only decide to add RAP, broken concrete, or aggregate to the mix, the fact that you are performing FDR with the mechanical technique in this case, it is far better than building a road over a suspect sub grade.

Again, I will point out that whenever you are doing this type of invasive work, especially in an urban environment, always "call before you dig" to get locates. Better yet, call in a GPR (ground penetrating radar) crew to determine locations and depths of utilities.

---

Also, if you would like to learn more about any of the techniques we have discussed so far in the book, there are 70 hours of online training that we developed just for you over at www.ipmaacademy.com.

---

## 9. Minimization of Public Disruption (Wayne)

I think back to times when we sat down in the estimating war rooms, putting our bids, and options together, and discussed staging of traffic in Metro Atlanta or some other large metropolitan cities.

It is always an uncomfortably amazing picture to imagine that if you were to block a section of collector road that adjoins a major interstate, you could actually have cars lined up on the shoulder of the interstate for several miles during your construction project.

Even with proper staging and dozens of variable message boards placed in advance, off and during the project, when you start clogging up roads with 30,000 cars a day, you can create havoc beyond your wildest imagination.

For this reason alone, even if FDR was the same amount of money per square yard as conventional rehabilitation, because it gets done in a tenth of the amount of time, it still comes out a significant winner. But wait, you may be saying to yourself, "What if we actually preserved these roads so that they never deteriorated?"

Well, in that case, you are absolutely correct.

Wayne spoke up in Boise and said, "How do we minimize the public disruption?"

You know we are living in a day and age of just-in-time delivery. Everything that we touch in WalMart or Target is arriving at the exact time we need it, not a day later or earlier. So, it is imperative that we keep, not only our normal citizens moving with the least amount of disruption, we also have to keep our commerce rolling with minimal construction delays. So, going forward, let's all agree we should at least get our pavement networks evaluated, and come up with a game plan we can follow verbatim. This way we know, with scientific evidence, we are putting the right treatment on the right road at the right time with the right contractor for the right reason.

And here's a good word of caution from Jon Hesse: "Watch for pitfalls here folks. Don't forget the part about going out and looking at your roads before making any final decisions. At the end of the day your focus should be on managing pavements, rather than on Pavement Management, if that makes any sense. The PMS should work for you and not the other way around."

---

Then, let's agree to get in, get out and stay out!!

---

I mean, let the decision tree prevail at the network level, but, if you know that you are about to build out a 600 lot subdivision at the end of the road, or a new quarry is coming into town next year, then build and rehabilitate accordingly. Yes, the algorithms in the PMS are there to aid us in our decision making, but our common sense and engineering judgment has to take precedence at the end of the day.

---

Now that we have all agreed on those two points, let's once and for all make the pact that we will preserve the good roads to make them last longer, and we will recycle in place the asphalt roads (rubblize the PCC roads) and follow **The Three Legged Stool System of Pavement Management** to make our world a better place.

---

Another excellent perspective from Jon: "In today's environment, with so many competing priorities and pressures, what if Pavement Managers were always thinking, 'This is important work that is ultra visible to the public. Let's see how good we can get at this.'"

Finally, think about this, what motorist would be upset with you as a pavement manager if you were spending their money in the wisest manner possible, keeping construction delays down to a minimum by using expedited methods that were less money, less carbon foot print and less time? Next!

## 10. Needs Based Knowledge... i.e. IPMA Academy (John)

There are many training opportunities out there for everyone in every conceivable niche you may be interested in. You can go to seminars. You can attend webinars online for an hour at a time. You can visit job sites like when we have the **IPMA Lunch and Learns**. You can do web based mini courses and certificate programs. Yes, you can literally spend the rest of your life and tens of thousands of dollars learning from a bunch of different sources who claim to be unbiased. Some good, some bad, some indifferent. OR...

---

You can enroll in www.ipmaacademy.com and receive the most comprehensive online training ever produced. If you have enjoyed any of the wisdom and knowledge that I have shared in this book, and if you wish to learn more outside of the free BONUS material we will be sending to your inbox upon registration of your book, then you will likely want to learn more about the **Accredited Pavement Manager (APM) Certification Program at The International Pavement Management Association's IPMA Academy**. Go ahead and put your first name and e-mail address in the box over at www.ipmaacademy.com and we will send you some free pavement management training videos.

---

Thanks for reading (or listening), for those who wish to continue on I have included a couple of BONUS CHAPTERS for your perusal. Any questions, blair@ipma.co. See you soon!

**\* HYPHEN CAUTION:** If a link includes a hyphen as it goes to the next line of text, when you retype the link into your computer **do not include the hyphen.**

# Bonus Chapters —

# Bonus Chapter #1

## Dr. Michael Heitzman, NCAT – "Rehabilitation Type Selection"

This presentation is a transcript of an **IPMA Academy LIVE** training event. You can order the HD DVD Box Set at http://ipma.co/marketplace/ if you would like to see all of the amazing training that took place in Georgia and California. Thank you to Mike, NCAT and Auburn University for allowing us to share this presentation in our book with you.

# Transcript Begins

[Theme music]

You wanna be a pavement management rock star,

and you say you wanna go real far?

Well, you gotta learn your skills right now,

we're about to show you just exactly how

at **IPMA Academy**. Yeah, **IPMA Academy LIVE!**

[Theme music]

Mike: Well, good morning, everyone, I think we'll have some others coming out, but I'll just do some quick introductions before I get into the slides. Are you able to see all right? All right.

---

* **HYPHEN CAUTION:** If a link includes a hyphen as it goes to the next line of text, when you retype the link into your computer **do not include the hyphen**.

281

My name's Mike Heitzman. I've got quite a colorful background; in fact, as much as Blair's getting things thrown at him for going out and saying we need all this money, my original career was with the Federal Highway Administration. How many were here back in the early 1990s, during the scrap tire mandate?

Oh, not too many people remember that. All right. Well, one time, a certain Congressman needed to have a solution to his problem in his state and decided to put the entire nation on a scrap tire mandate to where crumb rubber had to be used in every ton of asphalt that was produced. I went into Washington, D.C., at that time, and my original--my only task for my four years there—was to explain that to all the state agencies, and then duck, because they'd start throwing things at me.

After my 18 years with the Federal Highway Administration, I went out to Iowa DOT, spent nine years there, as their Bituminous Materials Engineer. That was one of the first times Blair and I were together. He was doing the NHI course on pavement rehabilitation, and then I took that series around the state to all the local agencies. For the last six years, since my children all got out of school, Dr. Randy West, who's the director at NCAT (National Center for Asphalt Technology), called me up and made me an offer I couldn't refuse. So, as my children left the house, I became an empty nester. I just decided to move the nest as well, so we're down in Auburn at NCAT.

## Overview

- Background
- Pavement Management System (PMS)
- Pavement Condition
- Pavement Performance (what is performance?)
- Rehab Types (tools in the tool box)
- Rehab Type Selection
- NCAT Lee Road 159

National Center for Asphalt Technology
NCAT
at AUBURN UNIVERSITY

2

This particular presentation is not just mine; it has a number of authors. Dr. Ray Brown, who is the past director at NCAT, and Dr. Mary Robbins are also a part of what's going to be shown here this morning. My intent here is to give you a quick kind of perspective on a very broad basis of why this is needed. A lot of the same things that Blair was talking about, but maybe a little bit more on the technical side. We're going to talk about the background.

Some interesting numbers here that we had to put together for a low-volume roads report. We'll talk a little bit about pavement management and pavement condition. Hopefully these are not new terms to you. What I want to try to do is put them all together and indicate to you that you've got to look at all these different things.

**Pavement performance.** If every one of us had a piece of paper and had to write down a definition of pavement performance, I can guarantee at least ten different definitions. As it should be. Performance in a large, parking lot full of heavy equipment is a lot different than a road in a National Park. So, pavement performance is really relative to the conditions you have to work with.

There are a lot of different rehabilitation types, and it is important that, in fact, we understand all those tools and try to use those tools when they're most important. It is not uncommon to see tools being misused, and that's essentially a waste of money for all of us. Eventually, we do have to build a proper pavement.

Lastly, what I will do is share a case study—what we call "Lee Road (Lee County) 159." NCAT now has an actual pavement preservation test study going on there. It started in 2012.

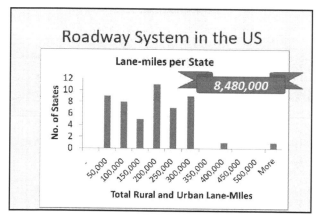

All right, so a little background. We have about 8.5 million lane miles in this country. Depending on the state, you can see a lot of them are somewhere between 50,000 lane miles and, say, 300,000 lane miles. We do have a couple of clicks way out there on the upper end; you can kind of guess which states those might be. California and Texas come to mind. So, there's a lot of lane miles out there. There are also, within those lane miles, a lot of different types of roadways

The type selection is probably the most difficult thing, particularly for a public agency. You have to convince both politicians and

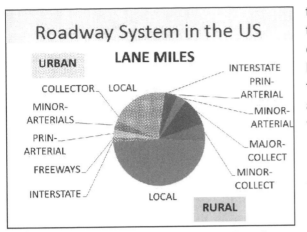

the public that you need to put some money on fairly decent roads because if you're going to do pavement management correctly, you want to keep that good road in good shape rather than spending all your money on the worst roads. If you follow "worst first," you are guaranteed to doom because there's no way to keep up with the money that's needed.

Particular emphasis here is, if you look at the rural local and the urban local roads, that's better than 75% of the system, in the way of lane miles. What about vehicle miles? Well, vehicle miles are spread a lot differently. The local urban certainly has quite a bit of vehicle miles to them, but you look at the locals for the rurals, which is right down here in that lower right-hand corner, not a lot of vehicle miles representing that 50% of our system. If I combine those two, now things get really serious. In fact, this

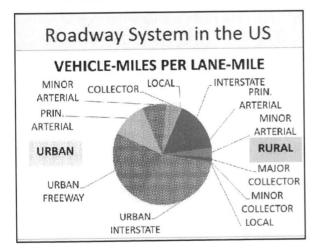

is why it's extremely important for those that have such a large part of the system but such small money to work with, that in fact, you use that money wisely, because this is the rural local work network, and you can see on a vehicle miles-per-lane mile, that it's almost non-existent.

And, quite frankly, it probably pretty well represents that pie is how the money is distributed for roadway efforts. So, the individuals with the highest percentage of the miles also have probably the lowest number of dollars to work with. So, it's even more important that we're well educated, knowledgeable and make some very good decisions about how we're going to spend those few dollars.

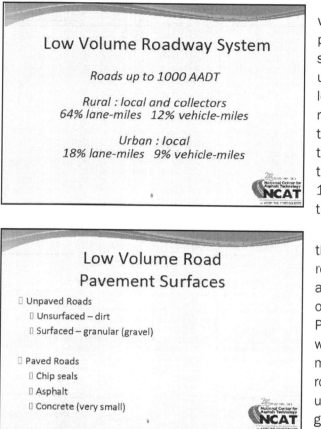

So, what is a low-volume road in this particular study? We said anything that's under 1,000 ADT is low-volume: that represents 64% of the total lane miles on the rural system, and that represents only 18% of the miles in the urban system.

So, what about these low-volume roads? A lot of them are unpaved; the other part is paved. Paved roads start with chip seals and move up; unpaved roads could either be unsurfaced altogether or could have just a granular-type surface on them. Of the unpaved roads, most of those are going to be rural. I think we could all expect that.

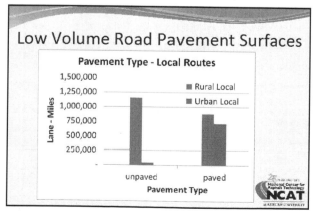

But when we look at the low-volume roads that are paved, about half are urban and the other half are rural. If I start breaking that down, some of those are collectors, but actually those are local roads themselves. So, the

285

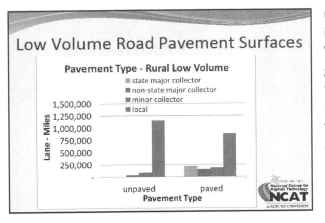

unpaved roads are going to be local roads. We're not probably going to do too much with those, as far as upgrading them, if, in fact, we've got a large system that's already paved and we're trying to maintain it. Are the politicians and the public going to agree with that? Probably not. If one neighbor got his roads paved, why can't we pave the next road? There's some real reasons for not doing that if the budgets can't handle it.

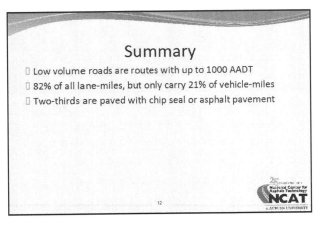

So, in summary: for the low-volume roads, giving it a set amount, at least that's what we did at NCAT, and that amount was a thousand ADT, that determined what was "low-volume."

There are probably some states in the northeast that would say, 2,500 ADT is low-volume. Again, that's a lot of perspective depending on what part of the country. The summary, or the bulk of that, though, is any 2% of our lane miles only carry 21% of the vehicle miles. And consequently, that gets reflected in the amount of funding that generally gets to us in order to work with these lower-volume roads.

All right, let's move on.

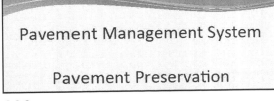

In pavement management we have to learn how keep the good roads good, and then deal with the poor roads as we can — a very

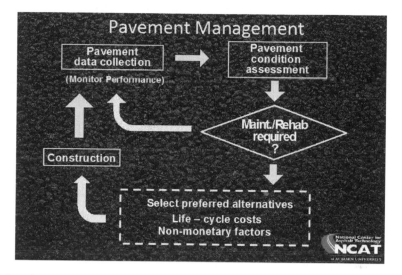

simple concept of how pavement management works. Up in the upper left-hand corner, we have to understand the condition of our roadway. We have to collect that data. It could be very simple; it could be literally driving it and taking notes; it could be much more sophisticated if the system is larger. We then take that information and just define what is the condition of the pavement. And if I'm doing huge parking lots, what I consider to be a part of that condition is different than doing a National Park Service road, or even a city road. So I just have to define what are those criteria that I want to have in my pavement condition assessment.

From that, then, I look at the entire network, and I say, for each section, does this require rehabilitation or maintenance? If the answer's no, I can move it back into collecting more data. But, if I do have to do some maintenance or rehabilitation, then I go into the toolbox. When I go into that toolbox, then I can look at which one of those particular tools, which one of those maintenance strategies, preservation strategies, rehabilitation strategies, which one best fits for the condition of each of those sections. Are we going to be able to do them all at one time? No. But I can, at least from that, make some decisions about what ones I will select.

When I was with the Kansas Division of the Federal Highway Administration (FHWA), Kansas DOT did a pretty good thing. Their central office would do the pavement management portion of this and would select a group of pavements in each one of these categories. They would give that out to the district and say, "Look, here's the list, here's your ten in the maintenance category, and you have this amount of funds to work with. You choose which ones you want to do within that category, but you have to do the maintenance on those." There would be a category for the minor rehabilitation, and a category for major rehabilitation. So the districts had some responsibilities, some ownership about the selection, but they did have to follow this concept of a pavement management strategy.

Of course, once I get that strategy done, then I go back to making some decisions. Oh, there are some non-monetary factors that might go into those decisions; one of those might be politics. Funny how that tends to work. So, eventually we get to construction. Then we take that cycle and we keep going, year after year after year, to keep track of whether I'm making any headway in my system.

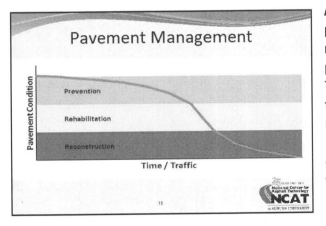

**All right. Classic pavement management, pavement performance curve.** This is a very simplistic view, but basically, in theory, when my pavement is originally constructed, I have very good performance. My pavement conditions factor is going to be different depending upon our interests, right? Eventually, it's going to perform, and it'll start to taper off. We're still into the area where I consider prevention. Just like changing the oil in your car, we want to keep that engine working as fine as we can. We have got to spend money on prevention. Even though the pavement may look very good, we've got to spend that money in prevention just to keep it maintained and stretch it out as long as we can. Eventually, we get into rehabilitation; we've got minor rehabilitation and major rehabilitation. I can't let something go longer and still expect to use a small, minor rehabilitation strategy. I'll talk a little bit more about that.

Eventually we get to the point that we now have a pavement that's not going to perform as needed, and we're going to have to do some kind of reconstruction.

Probably on the very end of what we consider all these rehabilitation strategies, I consider full-depth reclamation, straddling the fence between rehabilitation and actually reconstruction. Because I am literally building a new pavement when I do full-depth reclamation (FDR).

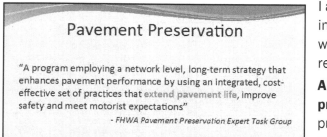

Pavement Preservation

"A program employing a network level, long-term strategy that enhances pavement performance by using an integrated, cost-effective set of practices that extend pavement life, improve safety and meet motorist expectations"
- FHWA Pavement Preservation Expert Task Group

**All right. Pavement preservation**. A program employed at network-level, long-term strategy that enhances the pavement performance by using an integrated cost-effective set of practices that will extend the pavement's life. And the key here is we have got to extend the pavement's life with each of these strategies that we select.

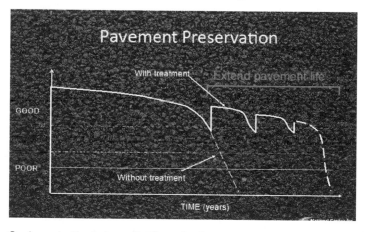

So how is that done? There's that pavement where I first built it, and it's in really good shape, but I can see that it's starting to go downhill. I'm starting to get some levels of distress that are important to me. Taking a rehabilitation or maintenance step at this point is a lot cheaper and a lot more cost-effective than it is waiting until I get down here to where I now have to do reconstruction. If I can, in fact, manage my system well, and do these smaller maintenance and minor rehabilitation steps early on at a lower cost, I can

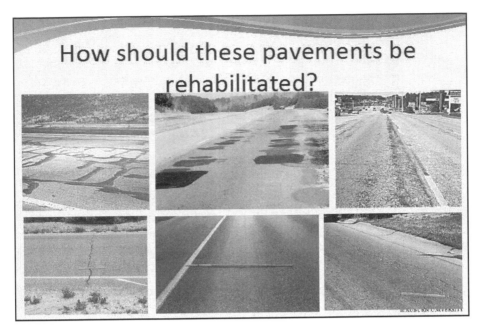

How should these pavements be rehabilitated?

extend that pavement life out much better than if I simply wait until it falls apart, then try to go back in and do something.

**So what is pavement condition?** That slide didn't turn out too bad in the lighting we have here. I'm sure each of you could, in fact, say, "I've seen one of these before." The point of the slide is there's no one particular rehabilitation strategy that's going to take care of all of these. You really do have to understand what's behind each one of these distresses before I can actually make a selection. If I just have an old-aged pavement, I've got block-cracking. I'm going to treat that differently than if I'm down here in the lower right-hand corner where I have fatigue cracking in the wheel paths. If I've got a rutting issue, I darn near need to know why it's rutting before I select what I'm going to do.

And I have a great story from Iowa; they had an interstate pavement for ten years and suddenly it had a rut like this. The maintenance people said, "Oh, we're just going to mill the high spots off to make it smooth again." I said, "Before you do that, let's cut a trench to see what's there." So, we cut a trench. This pavement was about a five-inch overlay on top of a continuously reinforced concrete pavement. The rutting was coming from the 3 inch intermediate lift below the surface lift. It was stripping out. So, maintenance was basically going to take the band-aid off of the wound. Had they gone ahead and just done the milling, we'd have just lost the entire pavement. So, you do have to understand what's going on.

In the South, we don't see too much of this, at least not major issues, but low-temperature thermo-cracking is an issue as you go farther north. You don't treat that the same as you do fatigue cracking; they're not the same things. Certainly, raveling near the longitudinal joints on asphalt pavements is probably the biggest thing we're now having to deal with. We've got a lot of other things somewhat solved. The point of the matter is, we have to understand what our condition is before we can take that next step.

There's another one: I've got asphalt literally crawling out of the

lane and coming up onto the curb section. I need to know why that asphalt's moving out there before I can simply go in and do some type of rehabilitation.

Good example: ended up with longitudinal cracks in the wheel path, something you normally don't see by themselves, and these were fairly early on. A little bit of investigation always helps. We found a lot of stripping in that intermediate area right below that surface layer. I have to go in and take care of the

problem with my rehabilitation. I can't simply overlay it; that's not going to help at all. I can't do a minor rehab or a thin lift over that to help it. I have to know where the problem is and try to address that particular problem.

## Pavement Distress

◻ HMA Distress
  ◻ Rutting, Friction, Fatigue, Thermal Cracking, Aging
◻ PCC Distress
  ◻ Faulting, Cracking, Fatigue
◻ Premature vs Normal Distress

Match Distress with Maintenance/Rehab Techniques

**So what is pavement distress?** We each have our own ideas on what are major distresses and minor distresses for what we have. Certainly, rutting is the one that was early on the really big factor with hot-mix asphalt. Friction can be a problem; that's one of my particular areas. I'm doing a lot of work right now as far as research goes. Fatigue is where we eventually want to get with our pavements. if we make it, design it properly, we can make sure that it's going to go through the entire fatigue life: thermal cracking, aging. Aging is something that's going to happen. Whatever we can do to improve that surface or maintain that surface is going to be important to reduce that aging effect.

Concrete pavements, faulting, cracking, even fatigue in concrete pavements is an issue. One of the other things we have to understand, though, is the difference between premature distress and normal distress. When you're building your pavement management system, if you've got some sections that have failed prematurely, for whatever reason—poor design, poor construction, poor materials, I caution you against putting those into the pavement management system and determining the normal curve for a pavement. It's going to skew the numbers low compared to what you really ought to be expecting out of your pavements.

The bottom line: you've got to match the distress with the maintenance rehabilitation technique. If you don't do that and you simply go out and do the same thing year after year, you're not going to be getting the most cost-effective use of the funds.

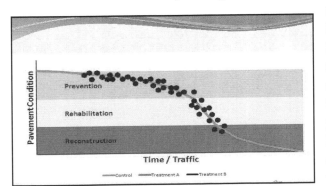

**So, what is pavement performance?** For each of us, that's a little different. That performance curve, that pavement condition index, whatever you're going to use on this wide part of the scale, that is your criteria

.In Iowa, you know, when I was there, I fought very hard—didn't get very far—but I fought very hard against their pavement management pavement condition index. The true predominant factors they had in there was ride and age. Well, ride is important to the public, but age tells me nothing about the pavement. But the statisticians said, "That's the one that correlates the best with all my pavements." But it doesn't tell me, as an engineer, very much.

That pavement condition index (PCI), whatever you use, has to reflect the critical parameters that you have for your pavement.

Now, if you're in the park service, ride is certainly going to be important. All right? Structure may not be as important, because there are not a lot of loads. If I'm working on a large parking lot with very heavy equipment, the ability of that parking lot to hold the load may be a lot more important than whether it's rough on the surface. So, there are different factors depending on what conditions you have to work with.

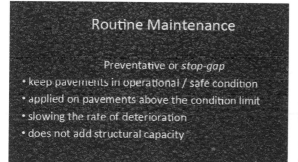

Routine Maintenance

Preventative or *stop-gap*
• keep pavements in operational / safe condition
• applied on pavements above the condition limit
• slowing the rate of deterioration
• does not add structural capacity

**Rehabilitation tools.** We'll get into it; I'm just going to group these into categories, and the rest of the day is going to take these into more details. There are things that are considered routine maintenance. By definition, these are going to simply maintain the pavement, as it is, keep it in the safe condition, and keep it operational. There's a limit as to when I can and can't make these effective. They will slow the rate of deterioration.

As I tell the graduate students in the pavement construction class, what's the first three things they need to know about the pavement design? **Drainage, drainage, and drainage**, right?

So, whatever I can do to get the water out and to keep the water out is very important. Because once I allow the water into the pavement, I am going to lose some of my performance one way or the other.

**Routine maintenance, though, will not improve or change the structural capacity—the ability of that structure to hold the loads or handle the loads.**

### Minor Rehabilitation

- Generally applied to the entire pavement section with the primary goal of slowing the rate of deterioration
- Applied on pavements above a condition limit
- Include the following types of treatment:
  - Fog seal
  - Rejuvenators
  - Slurry seal
  - Surface treatment

National Center for Asphalt Technology
**NCAT**
at AUBURN UNIVERSITY

**Minor rehabilitation.** I've gone a little bit further now. Typically, minor rehabilitation is going to be something that's full-lane width. It's not going to be spot-type techniques. It's going to be full-lane width applied to a longer section. Fog seals, rejuvenators, slurry seals, surface treatments tend to be lumped into that particular category.

### Major Rehabilitation

- Applied to improve structural and / or functional requirements.
- Applied to deteriorated pavements, pavements deteriorating at a rapid rate, and pavements subjected to a change in traffic.
- Includes: Overlays, Pre-Overlay Repair, Reflective Cracking, In-place Recycling

National Center for Asphalt Technology
**NCAT**
at AUBURN UNIVERSITY

**Major rehabilitation.** Now we're getting into things that are going to do more than simply maintain the existing structure. We will improve the structure; we will improve the function one-way or the other. At this point, I do have some deterioration; the amount of deterioration is such that the routine maintenance is no longer going to be of any value to me.

I need to spend just a little bit more money in order to make it function properly. Now we start to talk about things like overlays; we talk about overlay repairs; doing major repairs; we talk about reflective cracking issues; we talk about in-place recycling techniques—there's a whole bunch of different tools here which have to match what is the distress. It has to match the problem I'm trying to solve. And if I simply bury my problem, I have simply tossed the coins into the water, and have really lost the value from those funds that I have.

**Major Rehabilitation**

- Applied to improve structural and / or functional requirements.
- Applied to deteriorated pavements, pavements deteriorating at a rapid rate, and pavements subjected to a change in traffic.
- Includes: Overlays, Pre-Overlay Repair, Reflective Cracking, In-place Recycling

NCAT

**Rehabilitation Methods**

- Crack sealing
- Chip seal / Slurry seal
- Cape seal / Scrub seal
- Hot In-place Recycling (HIR)
- Cold Recycling (In-place or Plant)
- Full Depth Reclamation (FDR)
- Thin Lift Asphalt Concrete

**So, what are rehabilitation methods?** We've got everything from crack sealing, chip sealing, cape seals, slurry seals, scrub seals. . . . The list goes on. Hot-in-place recycling, cold recycling—that's kind of the new term. Cold recycling, because you can either do that at the plant or you can do it in-place. You have full-depth reclamation, which from my perspective kind of gets us into that next realm of potential reconstruction. And, of course, you have thin-lift asphalt concrete overlays.

**So, how do we select the correct "type"?** Go back to pavement management. I have a pavement condition (PCI) rating; I know what this particular section is like; I can look at prediction models for that particular section based on each of these rehabilitation strategies. If I've got a pavement that's fatigue cracked, and all I'm going to do is crack sealing, I have not improved the ability of that pavement to handle the load. In some parts of the country, like Arizona, that may actually be fine, because it's so dry. They've got enough structure underneath that pavement so it will literally

## Project/Treatment Selection Strategies (NCHRP Synthesis 222)

☐ Current condition rating
☐ Prediction models ("What if" scenario)
☐ Network Optimization models
☐ Find treatment that addresses deficiencies (may be affected by local policies/mandates)

just sit there. In other parts of the country, up in the mid-west where you've got a lot of wet, freeze/thaw cycles, that pavement is not going to last once it gets to that fatigue state.

Eventually, I have to do what's called **network optimization**. This gets into the part of pavement preservation which is a little bit beyond what we can talk about. You've got to keep the engine oil replaced, and deal with changing your tires. If I delay the engine oil change because a year from now I know I will change the tires, I have really detracted from the ability to maintain my car.

The same thing with pavements. We've got to be able to do optimization: that's where the best dollars are spent. And the best dollar spent includes a certain amount of pavement preservation, pavement maintenance. These are things that the public says, "Why are you putting that money over there when I've got all these potholes over here?" Well, we have to be able to balance our money and efforts if we're actually going to get the overall condition improved.

I'm going to go through a number of tables of cost factors. And I'm doing a number of different tables for the sole purpose of saying, there is no one table that's right. Depending upon where you are in the country, and depending upon what technologies are readily available to you. The costs you're going to see are going to change.

## Cost Considerations

| | |
|---|---|
| ☐ Fog seal | $0.15 / yd² |
| ☐ Sand seal | $0.35 / yd² |
| ☐ Crack Sealant | $0.60 / yd² |
| ☐ Slurry seal | $0.85 / yd² |
| ☐ Chip seal | $0.90 / yd² |
| ☐ Db. chip seal | $1.15 / yd² |
| ☐ Micro-surfacing | $1.30 / yd² |
| ☐ Cape seal | $1.70 / yd² |
| ☐ Mill and Inlay | $5.80 / yd² |

Here's one table. In this particular table, the mill and inlay is $5.80/SY.

Here's another table (see next page) In this particular case, the overlay now is only $1.75/SY. We're starting to see some expected lives of the treatments.

We just completed the NCHRP synthesis for low-volume roads.

| Treatment | Costs $/sq.yd. | Expected Life of Treatment, yrs | | |
|---|---|---|---|---|
| | | Minimum | Average | Maximum |
| Crack Treatment | $0.50 | 2 | 3 | 5 |
| Fog Seals | $0.45 | 2 | 3 | 4 |
| Slurry Seals | $0.90 | 3 | 5 | 7 |
| Microsurfacing | $1.25 | 3 | 7 | 9 |
| Chip Seals | $0.85 | 3 | 5 | 7 |
| Thin HMA Overlay | $1.75 | 2 | 7 | 12 |

2000 Study

Actually, it would be more correct to say we just looked at thin-lift asphalt applications. The expected life of each one of these different treatments varies dramatically across the country.

In this particular case the average life of this crack treatment is 3 years. Average life of the overlay was seven years, but seven years would range from 2 to 12 for the overlays, for example.

And part of this gets back to my earlier comment about being very careful about looking at sections that prematurely fail. Microsurfacing's a good example of that. When we were doing micro-surfacing in Iowa, sometimes you just got a bad microsurfacing application, and it would fail very rapidly. I didn't put that into my pavement management strategy as a typical type of performance. I have to discount that for what it was.

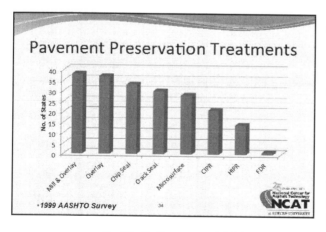

Pavement Preservation Treatments

•1999 AASHTO Survey

Here's another study. What was actually being done by the states in 1999? Mills and overlays, overlays, and chip seals certainly were very predominant, and then as you got into the cold-in-place, hot-in-place and full-depth reclamation, they were very small. Well, that was 1999. I am certain that these particular charts, or these particular levels of effort have probably changed by now. Everyone needs to be able to put all these different preservation treatments into their toolbox and use them appropriately.

## Preservation Treatment Life

| Treatment | Expected Life | Range |
|---|---|---|
| Thin Overlay | 10.7 | 7-14 |
| Chip Seal | 4.1 | 2.5-5 |
| Slurry Seal | 3.2 | 2-4 |
| Microsurface | 4.7 | 4-6 |

**Pavement preservation treatment life.** Thin overlays. Now we've got 10.7 years on this particular study, ranging from 7 to 14. A lot different. Microsurfacing, almost 5 years. Ranging from 4 to 6. Again, depending upon where you're at, your climate conditions, the pavements that you typically work with, these rehabilitation strategies will change. The caution here is if you read a report that's talking about this particular pavement strategy, and the report says it doubled the life of the pavement, well, make sure you understand a little bit about the conditions that report was written around.

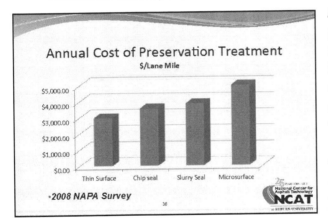

Annual Cost of Preservation Treatment
$/Lane Mile

•2008 NAPA Survey

**Annual cost of the preservation treatment.** Well, this is a NAPA survey, okay? So, you would expect the thin lifts for asphalt to look pretty good. Be sure to look at the source of the report to see if there's any particular biases with what they're doing and how they're collecting their data.

## 2009 FHWA Survey

| Treatment | Initial Cost ($/SY) | Expected Life (yrs) | Annualized Cost ($/SY) |
|---|---|---|---|
| Crack Seal | 0.32 | 2 | 0.16 |
| Fog Seal | 0.99 | 4 | 0.25 |
| Chip Seal | 1.85 | 6 | 0.31 |
| Microsurface | 3.79 | 6 | 0.63 |
| Slurry Seal | 4.11 | 5 | 0.82 |
| Thin Overlay | 5.37 | 13 | 0.41 |

FHWA survey, again, this gets back to the one I had earlier. You got a fairly high cost per square yard for thin overlays. Crack seals were pretty low, and you had expected life

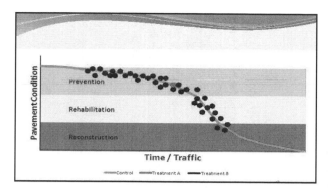

and annualized cost which depends upon the performance area where this data came from.

One of the things we did was we divided the data into the various climate zones. We were amazed at how much difference there was between pavement performance results in those different climate zones.

All right, so as you're making your pavement-type selection. So, of all my sections that I have in my pavement management system, they all tend to go somewhere on that curve. If I were to select this particular selection, or that particular section, and determine what are going to be the best strategies for that section, I might choose one pavement preservation technique and, through my performance history, I can say, "Yeah, I'm going to be able to stretch that out pretty good."

But I might look at another alternative as well, and even though it's not going to perform quite as well, maybe it doesn't cost as much. So, now I've got to start balancing out my cost and the expected life when I make those decisions. **But the trick is to do most of your work up at the top of the curve, and not down at the bottom.**

---

If we constantly do "worst first," we're never going to get ahead. The math shows that. There's no way to go backwards and try to get things from worst first. We just don't have the funds.

---

A little bit of summary. I want to go to NCAT Lee, Lee Road 159 The NCAT Test Track was built in the year 2000; actually, about 1999. The first sets of test sections were placed and started trucking in the year 2000. This is a 1.7-mile, full-scale two-lane facility. 1.7 miles long. The loop, and every 500 feet, is a different section. And, within those test sections, we have the ability to look at various types of treatments.

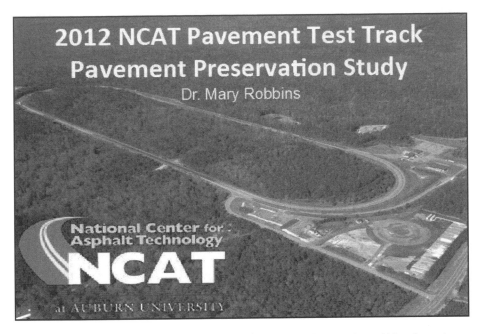

Originally, this first set of studies was for rutting. What's going to be the best mixes to handle rutting? Some of these pavements are very thick, so, we are only looking at the ability of the asphalt mixture. The test track runs on a 3-year cycle. It runs from six months of construction, 2 years of loading, and six months of forensic studies.

During the 2 years of loading, from 5am to 11pm, five days a week, Tuesday through Saturday, we have five triple trailers. Each axle loaded up to 22,000 pounds. Those five trucks with triple trailers go around from 5am to 11pm. There are two sets of professional drivers. They take their breaks. They do everything they would as a professional driver. A triple trailer, fully loaded, is not a fun thing to drive, okay? But, their job for two years, is to load the track. And we have all of the instrumentation in the track.

Every Monday, that is the day to go out and look at all those sections, to look at the stress levels and see what kind of things have occurred. The buildings are over here on the right side, and here is a great big pad that was originally designed to be the location for a hot-mix plant. We've been using one of the local plants for the most part, as opposed to having something staged on-site.

Every three years, we've gone through a cycle. We're now completed 80% of the trucking on the 2012 track sections. And very

**2012 Preservation Group (PG) Study**

☐ Quantify life extending benefit of study treatments
  ☐ Time/traffic to return to pretreatment condition(s)
  ☐ Test sections on the Track and Lee Road 159

☐ Sampling/testing for construction quality

soon we'll be looking at putting in new sections for 2015. With the 2012 track, we started converting to some pavement preservation techniques. Some are on the track, but there's also a preservation group study that was started up. That particular study is looking at, seeing how, the different treatments actually extend the life. We're monitoring them on a weekly basis, just like the test track.

We also look at the time and traffic. We know what the precondition issues were on this section; we've got them well mapped out. There are sections on both the track and on Lee County 159. And Lee County 159 is where I want to emphasize a little later.

We do sampling and testing during construction; we do more sampling and testing during construction on 250 feet than you generally would do on multiple miles. In fact, it generally takes us about three times the amount of quantity before the actual section goes in, because with 250 feet, it's got to be right. So there's a quantity that goes out just to see if the mix is close, adjust the mix, put some more mix out, maybe even pave it up on the lot. See, if we're going to get density, and then once we're all comfortable with the criteria, then we finally go in and pave our section on the test track.

This is an aerial view of Lee Road 159. This is another major county route here. This little stub that goes back to a Martin Marietta quarry is about half a mile long from this intersection back to about here, which is the gate in to the quarry. That is the section we are using for our study of pavement preservation treatments. There are only about three

**PG Sections on Lee Road 159**

Martin Marietta Quarry

Asphalt Plant

Lee Road 159

• Low ADT roadway
• Very high % trucks
• Load data provided by quarry and asphalt plant
• No traffic control needed for data collection

homes on the entire route, so where's all the traffic coming from? It's coming from the quarry, and it's coming from the hot-mix plant. So, we've arranged with those two companies to get all the information as to how many trucks are going in and going out of those facilities.

Okay, so while this road has low ADT number. If you drove by it, you'd never see a car, right? It does, however, have very high truck traffic. As such, then, we get to see how the load is impacting each of these rehabilitation strategies. We get the data provided by the quarry and the asphalt plant. Mary and I have had a number of conversations— she's very detail-oriented—and occasionally the paper information coming from the quarry doesn't agree with the visual surveys we've gathered as trucks have been going by. Apparently what we saw was not the same truck they thought it was. Well, you have to deal with the realities in the real world and try to collect this data as best you can in order to come up with the overall loadings.

The nice thing for us, from NCAT's perspective, something you would all appreciate, we don't have to deal too much with traffic control. So, if we were to do this on another route that had a higher ADT, we'd be constantly having to do traffic control. We would not only put our own staff at risk with traffic going by, but we'd put the traveling public at risk as well.

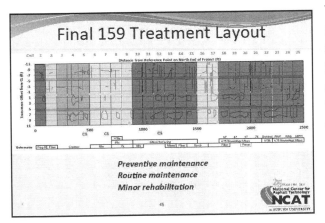

These are the half-mile research track sections. We have broken them up into one-hundred-foot increments, and each one of those 25 increments, then, has a different combination with pavement preservation techniques. Everything from fog seals to ultra-thin bonded overlays to thin overlays, microsurfacing, fog seals, scrub seals— 25 different combinations across there. We have very good ideas of what distresses are already there. The ones that look like boxes and areas, that's fatigue cracking.

So rather than showing every crack, they usually show that in an area. The incoming lane, surprisingly, doesn't have a level of fatigue cracking. Why would that be? There's no load, right? The trucks are coming in empty; they're coming out heavy. So you can see this progression of fatigue, and you can have essentially across those two same types of pavements, you've got the unloaded or the light-loaded condition as well as the heavy-loaded condition.

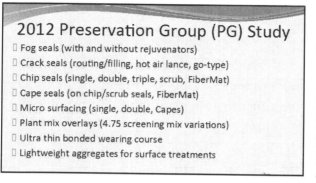

### 2012 Preservation Group (PG) Study

- Fog seals (with and without rejuvenators)
- Crack seals (routing/filling, hot air lance, go-type)
- Chip seals (single, double, triple, scrub, FiberMat)
- Cape seals (on chip/scrub seals, FiberMat)
- Micro surfacing (single, double, Capes)
- Plant mix overlays (4.75 screening mix variations)
- Ultra thin bonded wearing course
- Lightweight aggregates for surface treatments

**Preventative maintenance?** Yes, there's some sections set up with preventative maintenance. Some have routine; some have minor rehabilitation; each of these are techniques to try to see how they're going to perform side-by-side on these particular sections.

So, this is what we have in this 2012 preservation group. There are fog seals, crack seals, chip seals, cape seals, micro-surfacing, plant mix overlays, ultra-thin bonded wearing course, and lightweight aggregates for surface treatments as well. Those techniques are all being used in different applications in different combinations.

### Rates Checked Prior to Placement

We do look at the rates that are being applied, such that we know exactly what went down in one of those sections, and yes, they are only 100 feet long, so we had to make sure everything was right before they actually came into that particular section. I'm sure a lot of you have seen, you know, checking chip spreaders, for example, to make sure that they are applying the right amount of chip. Because this is an NCAT research study with a number of sponsors, there's a lot of data that's collected during construction.

Actual Rates Verified During Placement

If you do get down to Auburn, give us a call. I'm sure one of us— and particularly Dr. Robbins, if she were available—would be able to take you over to the site. It's actually not too far from our offices. There are a number of different sponsors for this preservation study: Alabama, Mississippi, Missouri . . . . You see a number of different states there.

Lee Road 159

Pavement Preservation Experiment

to Reduce the Cost to Maintain Your Roads

Funding Provided by:

Alabama, Mississippi, Missouri, North Carolina, Oklahoma, South Carolina, Tennessee, and FP2 via Auburn University and the Lee County Commission

The Lee County Commission is certainly involved. They provided us that site from within their structure. Each one of the sections has its own sign posted next to it so you can really get a sense, as you go down the road, what research is being done on each of the sections.

L1 – Rejuvenating Fog Seal

Chip seal. Untreated control. I actually think there's three control sections along those 25 different sections, so we can look at what would have happened to this roadway had we not done anything at all. So, we can make those comparisons, then, with the different treatments.

L2 – FiberMat Chip Seal

Crack seal. Chip sealing. Chip seal with crack sealing. A triple-layer chip seal. Double-layer chip seal. Cape seal, which is a microsurfacing on top of a chip seal. Just straight microsurfacing. Another microsurfacing, only

it was crack sealed ahead of time. Double layer of microsurfacing. Microsurfacing on top of a Fibermat. Microsurfacing on top of a scrub seal.

Lots of different combinations. Some of you may have applied some of these before; others, these may be somewhat new to you. Just a straight scrub seal. Here we're looking at a control section; you've got the distressed data demonstration. We can show how the distressed data is different in one location versus another.

We get into thin hot-mix overlays over Fibermat. Straight thin hot-mix overlay. And here we put in essentially what amounts to a cold in-place underneath the asphalt thin-lift overlay. That, we did have to go back in and treat the existing pavement.

We do have a polymer modified thin overlay. If, in fact, I can make the band-aid stronger, if I want to use duct tape instead of masking tape, do I get better performance? Is it worth the additional cost of using that higher-priced material?

We have a bonded, thin asphalt overlay. We've been in some thin overlays with a fairly high percentage of RAP (Recycled Asphalt Pavement) in the mix. They can be done. You don't do it with normal operations; you've got to think about that in order to do it right, but it can be done.

We have a section with RAS. Is anyone familiar with the term RAS—Recycled Asphalt Shingles? We're now replacing a portion of our asphalt binder with waste shingles, not only from the manufacturer waste, but also using the post-consumer tear-off shingles as well.

Another thin asphalt overlay.

## 159 Testing Overview

☐ Weekly
 ☐ ARAN Van (rutting, roughness, texture)
 ☐ Video for crack mapping
 ☐ Visual inspections with notes/pictures
☐ Monthly
 ☐ Wet ribbed surface friction
 ☐ Subgrade moisture readings
 ☐ Falling weight deflectometer (FWD)
☐ Other
 ☐ Ground penetration radar (GPR)

So, what are we doing out there? We are testing on a weekly basis. We have an ARAN van that goes out and records the rutting, roughness and texture, and gets results for us quickly.

The ARANs, Automatic Road ANalyzer vans, take a video of the cracking that's occurring. The drivers do a visual inspection as well. Quite frankly, we're still to the point that you can do all the really high-tech video that you want, but our eyes do a heck of a lot better job of finding cracks, in some cases, than a high tech video.

On a monthly basis, we friction-test. They check the subgrade moisture and determine that cyclical cycle—that change in moisture through the course of the seasons. And we do have our FWD (falling weight deflectom-

ARAN Van for Roughness/Texture

eter testing) that goes out and does our structure. And structure's important. I'm from Missouri so I can talk about Missouri, but they've had a plan for a long time—you just continually put down single-lift overlays on their system. They know they're only going to last about 4 or 5 years. and then they'll put on another one. So for them, ride is very important, but they're losing their structure as they do that.

We also used some **ground-penetrating radar** (GPR). I'll show you that device in a minute. If you haven't seen an ARAN van in the past, there's our ARAN van. There's instrumentation in the front panel, and on the back. These are two lane lines lasers that measure rutting. So, we get a continuous rutting measurement across each one of the wheel paths.

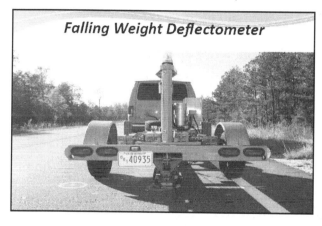

*Falling Weight Deflectometer*

If you're not familiar with the **FWD** (falling weight deflectometer), this is kind of a tough picture to see it, but basically, we have a plate sitting down on the pavement; we lift up a set of loads; we drop them down to the plate; and we have instrumentation going ahead at that for about six feet. And that instrumentation is measuring how much that pavement deflects when I drop that load on there. It gives me a good idea of what the structure is like and whether it's improving or not.

Lee 159 Testing

Ground Penetrating Radar
By 3d-Radar
Dec. 3, 2012

**Ground-penetrating radar.** We just finished a SHARP-II study. This was one of the devices we used. This was a ground-penetrating radar array. There's about twenty different radar antennas within that trailer. We can get a continuous six-foot wide, actually, they can do a full lane width, that provides about a half a lane width image. We did the entire section to see what the condition was underground.

Here's what it looks like on the surface after a rain. Everything always shows up right after a rain. The tracks show up; you can tell which is the outbound lane and which was the inbound lane. Again, you can see where, as I put a treatment on, I've got a crack here, and I can start to monitor how that crack is going to grow into that rehab section.

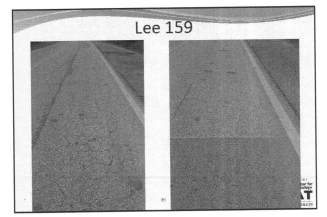

Within each of our 100 foot sections—Mary actually has this broken up into ten-foot increments, and she is actually identifying distress within, basically, a five-foot by ten-foot area. So, every one of those 100 foot sections has 40 different distress areas that we're working with. She can keep monitoring

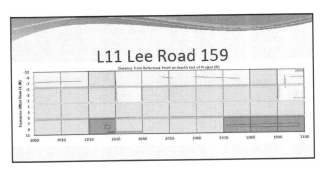

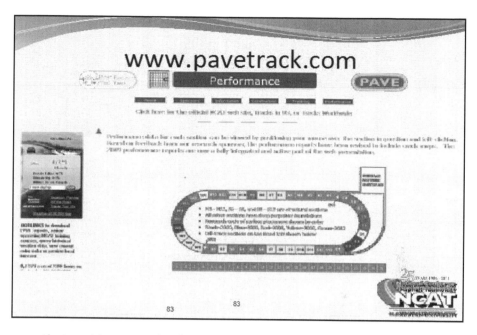

that and keep track of whether or not the condition is good, bad, or indifferent.

That slide didn't turn out all that well. But if you want to get in and check out either the test track, or the Lee Road 159 sections, go to www.pavetrack.com that is our website for the test track, and you can go in there and look at what the construction conditions were. You can look at some of the distress as well, to see how that's put together.

And I think with that, I'll thank you for your time, and I'll address any questions you might have.

[Theme music]

## Transcript ends

## Bonus Chapter #2

## What the Folks in Arizona Want to Know

### The Better Roads Radio Podcast: www.betterroadsradio.com

★★★★★

"The ONLY podcast on the planet dedicated to saving our crumbling roads."

Get it FREE on iTunes

Following is the actual Word document that I typed up while doing a lunch-and-learn for the folks in Arizona. During this lively session, and prior to the official launch date of the Better Roads Radio Podcast, I asked the 50 or 60 folks in attendance what would they like to hear about on the only podcast on this planet dedicated to saving our crumbling roads.

What follows is their feedback, which I immediately typed into this document. We also recorded the event on video, and it is sitting on a LaCie hard drive somewhere in my office. When we get that video produced, we will be sure to share it with you all! Thanks to the folks in Peoria, AZ, for helping us get the **Better Roads Radio Podcast** out of our brains and onto your airwaves! We will be constantly referring back to this to make podcast episodes for you all, hence the inclusion as a *Bonus Chapter* in our book.

### Transcription begins

The only source you need for real unbiased advice from pavement management experts across the world to help you save your local agency from bankruptcy. Available on iTunes in 2014 (actually available right NOW), and downloadable from www.betterroadsradio.com. This program was developed in conjunction with input from the amazing APWA AZ folks during the November 25th 2013 LEGACY TOUR with Blair.

* **HYPHEN CAUTION:** If a link includes a hyphen as it goes to the next line of text, when you retype the link into your computer **do not include the hyphen**.

313

If you have already or are planning to implement a comprehensive pavement management system what key elements and best practices would you like to share with others and/or learn more about? i.e. ADA Legislature?

Maher - ADA Legislature and how it will impact local agency budgets.

Tom – "Worst first" is not always best case with examples.

John A – What would be a good sequence of events to circumvent the ADA (several episodes)?

Joe S – Politics versus the actual needs of the pavement inventory demands.

Ed – Understand life cycle management (PCI and RSL) and how we buy back pavement degradation.

Leon – Strategies of utilization of the various tools in the toolbox and how they are leveraged with price per sy per year (Roger Cox).

Matt – Social Proof City of Mesa bond election; Mayor is trusting the leadership (do episode).

Matt – You get what you inspect, not what you specify.

Craig – How do you get innovative products specified in the public works system? – Maher change state law.

Eric – PWKS Directors are scared to death to try different technologies – i.e. HIR, CIR, FDR i.e. Mayor of Greenville. Politicians want to hear from other politicians.

Mark – Distinguish between turning a road black versus actually extending the RSL – i.e. Hockey Pucks.

Steve – Why is there so much emphasis with funding on new roads? See The Hamilton Project (get them involved). – What is the REASON? Why are we not spending more on preserving what we have, i.e. MAP 21?

Mat – Jason double chip seals, why are the Feds now issuing grant money for this all of a sudden?

Bob – User costs – show me the real unit costs for the treatments, as well as the longevity of the treatments – get in, get out, stay out . . . Show me how to spend wisely with least amount of user delay.

David C – How to educate the public as to why you are doing the methods you are that calendar year on roads that appear to be fine.
Lou – What do you do when you run out of roads that don't have sidewalks or curbs, i.e. County level, do you add new? Or ignore if there is no demand? One part of the road may be ok for ADA, while the other side may be in need. Do I try to pull off stopgap measures and hope for the best? Reminder about the penalty.

Robert (BCEA) – Portland, topography, affluent neighborhood, alternative standard was implemented, published report, in Portland News, late 90s. Extensive input from the residents who don't think that DOJ would allow this today. (This would be a good one for Diane to do.)

Craig – Will the ADA Clarifications have an impact on St. Ives or private gated communities?

Tom – In a perfect PM world, we would focus more on the term service delivery. – We should be wrapping our efforts around service delivery goal. – What are the elected officials saying out there? – Are you going to have the Cadillac or the Chevy? – Base it on the pavement condition. – i.e. don't spend too much time focusing on the RSL, focus on the three outputs.

Elvira – I know what I have to do to fix it, but why did it get like that in the first place? Educate the public: this is why your HOA went bad – i.e. irrigation of the green space island

Steve – Breakdown on the techniques. – Blair, walk me through the toolbox, and what the decision making process is for selection.

Lou – How do you implement the tools for small cities, cooperative bidding? (Steve Gorcester)

Robert – Contractors doing extra work for Cities and Counties if the agencies are part of the state sharing program.

Charlene – Maybe we need to change and prioritize what and how we do. . . . . Some planning ahead at the beginning of the year.

Jack – Material sources – educating the public on getting material sources – i.e. mines and hot mix plants.

John G – Funding sources, co-op bids, state DOT, FHWA?  Green grants?  MTC – i.e. Napa Sonoma, 2 million dollar grant, how'd they get that one?  Sui Tan talk about grant funding.

Robert – That's not the way my grand ditty did it, Blair.

Craig – Better understanding of asphalt rubber, testing, Rubber Assoc. session – i.e. I -40.

## Transcription ends

## Bonus Chapter #3

## The Request for Case Studies Message From IPMA HQ

Following is a transcript of the e-mail request that went out to our entire database of subscribers. Thank you to everyone who participated and offered feedback. If your case study did not show up in the book, it will likely show up in the near future in some type of curriculum that we offer.

## Transcription begins

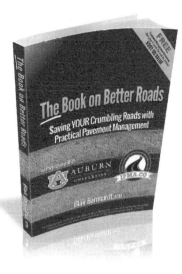

Hey, folks, you are going to receive a few extra e-mails from us over the next few weeks because there are a lot of cool things going on over here at the **IPMA HQ!!!**

As I sit down to write **The Book on Better Roads** (http://ipma.co/betterroadsradio/the-book/) for worldwide distribution on Amazon, I have a special request for you all and hope you can help me out. One thing I have learned from the feedback so far is that folks want to hear about current, real-life case studies, overall treatment costs, unit prices, eco-efficiency, and speed of construction with all things pavement management, in-place recycling and pavement preservation.

So I humbly ask for your feedback. Could you take 10 minutes and send me your favorite case study details, in a simple bullet form e-mail or paragraph so I can include it into the next printed edition or the online version of The Book (http://ipma.co/betterroadsradio/the-book/)? Just hit reply on this or send your case study to blair@ipma.co.

Readers will want to know how you saved time and money using your pavement management program, in-place recycling and/or preservation efforts. And for those of you **APM Alumni** from **IPMAAcademy** who are already following **The Three Legged Stool System of Pavement Management**, please send me your incredible success stories for inclusion in YOUR BOOK (http://ipma.co/betterroadsradio/the-book/.)

While you are driving to work this week, go ahead and listen to our latest guests talk about all things pavement management here on the only podcast on this planet dedicated to saving our crumbling roads www.betterroadsradio.com

(Episodes 1-6 at the time of this writing).

Later this week (it is live now), Ben will post episode 6 which was recorded live from Purdue Road School as I explain the Three Legged Stool Vision in 50 minutes. Rocco will also be making a video of this for the Purdue ePubs learning platform.

Stay tuned for some very exciting news about our new partners at **IPMA** and a very special shout out to our newest Partners and Charter Members, Gallagher Asphalt, Hot In-Place Recycling, Prevent Potholes, Utah Asphalt Pavement Association and Western Emulsions.

**Thanks for all your help everyone!!**

Blair

---

If you want to get **APM Certified** and enroll in **IPMA Academy** while you are at it, or learn more, you can click right here IPMA ACADEMY 70 PDH Hours (https://ipmareferral.myquickcheckout.com/). If you have been waiting for the link to register TODAY, here it is IPMAAcademy Registration. (https://ipmaacademyreg.myquickcheckout.com/) Also, we have some amazing news coming shortly about your next APM Certificate!)

---

We love to serve our circle of **Pavement Management RockSTARS,** thanks for all you do with so little!! If you are in trouble right now with your hundreds of millions of dollars worth of infrastructure and need to talk, call me at 404-323-5974, or blair@ipma.co. I will be flying and driving all over America this year and would love to stop in and see you if we can help in any way!

# Transcription ends

* HYPHEN CAUTION: If a link includes a hyphen as it goes to the next line of text, when you retype the link into your computer **do not include the  hyphen**.

# Bonus Chapter #4
# Award Winning Cold-in-Place Project in Canada

For those of you who don't know me, I spent the better part of my career in Canada growing the pavement management, in-place pavement recycling and preservation business across the country. I also spent several years on the board of directors with www.arra.org as the CORE Chairman, the committee on recycling education. I am putting this Bonus Chapter in for several reasons, some of which I will keep to myself, some I would like to share with you.

One, anyone in this day and age can set up a Google Alert on pretty much any topic they so desire. I choose to set up a handful on all things that we talk about in the book. So, today, as I write the final chapters, I am sharing information with you from the internet that is current as of today's date. You can see this just like me right here at http://www.bayshorebroadcasting.ca/news_item. php?NewsID=65323. Thanks for sharing this story with our audience, Bay Shore Broadcasting in Canada!

Two, for decades I have asked local agencies to embrace pavement management, in-place recycling and pavement preservation. **It works!** There are counties and cities across the world doing it! **It is not new!** Let me repeat, it works, there are folks just like you doing it, and it works!

Three, this is a great example of a success story. Reputable contractors are teaming up to share their knowledge with the world via the internet. This same type of internet sharing of knowledge that will eventually show enough **Stringbender** success stories to crumble down the walls that the Naysayers have put up. Trust me on that one!

Four, we need more stories of success just like this one to CRUSH THE NAYSAYERS!

Five, when I listen to the MP3 here http://www.bayshorebroadcasting. ca/downloads/audio/mike_alcock_award.mp3, it reminds of when I used to live in Canada, LOL!

Six, I immediately recognize all of the names in the story, having spent many long days working for these same folks at some point. Many who used to be local agency folks are now working on the private sector side of the fence! Hope you all are doing all right up there, folks!

Seven, I wanted to remind the readers and listeners that in addition to **IPMA,** where local agencies join for free at http://ipma.co/, there are many other great trade associations out there. I have tried to stay on the high road throughout the book, and want to end on that positive note by asking you to consider taking part in other trade associations such as http://www.arra.org/ and http://slurry.org/, so you get a chance to hear things from a different perspective and formulate your own unique blend of wisdom back there at your office!

Eight, this is a great example of industry partnering for a common goal. We need to all work together if we are to resurrect our economy. As the author of this book, I want to remind the readers that we are willing to partner with any reputable association, firm, or person that will further our movement – blair@ipma.co.

Nine, the consulting side of the business at http://thebarnhardtgroup. com/ works anywhere in USA and Canada to serve our local agencies in any way we can with their pavement management. I didn't want you folks up there to feel left out in the book. Our RV can travel wherever we need to be to save our crumbling roads.

Cold in-place train in action - Canada

My Crew - Region of Sudbury, Canada - mid 90s – FDR w/Foamed Asphalt

# Driving America
# For Better Roads
## SAVING AMERICA'S CRUMBLING ROADS

Also, we did a really cool session on CIR for the Driving America for Better Roads (and Canada) series from Niagara Falls (Canadian Side) a while back. You can watch it right here http://drivingamericaforbetterroads.com/home/driving-america-for-better-roads-episode-7/. please share and enjoy!

So as you listen to the transcription of the award winning CIR job description, please think about the reasons above why I chose this article.

**Stringbenders UNITE! We can defeat the Naysayers!**

\* HYPHEN CAUTION: If a link includes a hyphen as it goes to the next line of text, when you retype the link into your computer **do not include the hyphen**.

321

# Transcript begins

### Huron Wins Asphalt Award

Thursday, April 10, 2014, by Rick Stow

Dave Laurie and Mike Alcock receive award for asphalt recycling

http://www.bayshorebroadcasting.ca/downloads/audio/mike_alcock_award.mp3

Huron County's Public Works Department has copped an industry award for its asphalt recycling program.

At Huron's Committee of the Whole Day One session Wednesday (April 9th), Bentley Ehgoetz of Lavis Contracting and Trevor Moore of the Miller Group made the presentation to the County's Dave Laurie and Mike Alcock.

Alcock explains that the County's Cold In-Place Asphalt Recycling Program, in operation since 1998, has won the 2014 Charles Valentine Award for Excellence.

The annual accolade is a presentation of the Asphalt Recycling and Reclaiming Association (ARRA), and submissions are made from all over North America.

The County's Civil Engineering Technologist tells Bayshore Broadcasting News that fully half of Huron's 730 kilometre road network is topped with the recycled asphalt mix.

Alcock says the process saves money by re-using the asphalt with new emulsion.

He says the blend is less prone to cracking.

Trevor Moore, the Corporate Director of Technical Services with the Miller Group, notes that Huron County was a pioneer in the use of milling machines to achieve a wider road swath during the paving process.

# Transcript ends

* HYPHEN CAUTION: If a link includes a hyphen as it goes to the next line of text, when you retype the link into your computer **do not include the hyphen**.

# Bonus Chapter #5

# Roads & Bridges Magazine article on HIR Re-HEAT

**Greenville Goes Green.** Mississippi town shows how new asphalt recycling process saves time, money.

APRIL, 2011. BY BLAIR BARNHARDT, APM

Over forty years ago, a small businessperson in America ran out of hot mixed asphalt on a paving project he had to finish before winter. With no hot mixed asphalt available to his forces, and a pending driving blizzard, this young man rallied his troops to bear torches, hand rakes and used motor oil to heat up the old asphalt in-place and rejuvenate it on site. That following spring, there was no discernible difference in appearance with the new asphalt and the recycled asphalt on the project. This small businessperson went on to build his first hot in-place asphalt recycling train. More-over, this same person was one of the three founding fathers of our Asphalt Recycling and Reclaiming Association (ARRA), the voice of our recycling industry in North America, and the world. ARRA and Federal Highways Administration (FHWA) wrote the **Basic Asphalt Recycling Manual (BARM)**, the textbook that we use in our National Highway Institute Training Workshops.

Two score of years has passed, and this person's son has built the premiere set of machines to perform what he has coined, Re-HEAT. It's a 100% hot in-place asphalt recycling process. Unlike its predecessors in the industry, this equipment does not employ the three well-known ARRA sub disciplines that we teach in classroom (scarify, remix or repave) rather we refer to this as a newly formed hybrid process. The Re-HEAT equipment train heats the in situ asphalt roadway up to 600°F, picks up the hot asphalt from the road base, rejuvenates it in an on-board mixing drum, and redistributes it at consistent 300°F via a conventional paving screed. Once conventional compaction equipment compacts the 2 to 3 inch thick layer of fresh recycled Re-HEAT asphalt, the traffic can begin to use it immediately.

By definition, the Re-HEAT process is an on-site, in place, pavement rehabilitation method that consists of heating the existing pavement with a thermal transfer of up to 600°F, removing the aged and distressed surface course asphalt, adding a polymer modified asphalt-rejuvenating emulsion, mixing the material uniformly in an on-board mixing drum, re-laying the recycled material, followed by conventional compaction equipment.

Unlike some of the other in-place recycling trains that are well suited to long stretches of county and state roads, the Re-HEAT units occupy a mere 200 linear feet and can articulate, when required, to get in and around city cul-de-sacs and traffic circles. Moreover, the Re-HEAT train is capable of literally peeling off an asphalt overlay from an underlying concrete pavement, tack the concrete, and reapply the rejuvenated hot mixed asphalt to the agency's street.

In the case of Greenville, MS, their city engineer headed up a pavement evaluation study and selected the most appropriate streets for the Re-HEAT process. Mr. Anderson states, "While the work is ongoing at the time of this article, and weather has caused some delays, some of the streets that have been rehabilitated to date are Robertshaw from Hwy 1 to Colorado, Trailwood from Reed Road to Anne Stokes St. Also, a typical cross section of the road is 24' wide, 3" of asphalt and 8" of crushed stone."

Unlike other methods of in-place recycling, such as heater scarified hot in-place, cold in-place recycling and full depth reclamation, the Re-HEAT method does not require a final wearing course, such as microsurfacing or hot mixed asphalt paving. While all of the recycling techniques just mentioned will always save 30% to 40% in comparison to conventional rehabilitation techniques, the Re-HEAT may offer the greatest savings of all to the agency provided the in situ road section is an appropriate match for the process. (The author would like to stress the importance of a comprehensive pavement distress evaluation married to the most appropriate recycling and pavement preservation strategy at the correct time to achieve the maximum savings and service life.)

While I get frustrated, at times, having spent the latter 15 years teaching asphalt recycling and pavement preservation across the country and seeing only a low to moderate interest for processes that could potentially save agencies 30-50% of their annual budget for roads, I am inspired by the latest developments in this equipment and how one agency had taken full advantage.

**Rebuilding and Saving.** Much like the story of the young businessperson above who persevered to build his small business innovations into eco-efficient asphalt recycling machines for the world to embrace, the City of Greenville has grown into a prosperous place perched on the highest part of the mighty Mississippi River between Vicksburg and Memphis. Located in the heart of the Mississippi Delta, Greenville is a town of spirit that has survived flood, fever and fire. In many ways the city has not changed. It is the same city led by the spirit of men who built it, those weary men who, returning from the Civil War, found their homes in ashes and rebuilt it.

The city of 130 years is now face-to-face with another rebuilding of sorts, not unlike that of its ancestors. As the largest port on the Mississippi River, Greenville has a plethora of aging infrastructure and 150 miles of roads that require rehabilitation. I sat down recently and had a candid conversation with Mayor Heather McTeer Hudson and her City Engineer, Mr. Lorenzo Anderson, PE. The Mayor and her staff make an exemplary case study of how any city or county in America can save millions by implementing a solid pavement management, recycling and preservation program. Our United States Department of Transportation (FHWA) has long since proven that this type of "three-legged stool" approach can save agencies millions by using green recycling techniques coupled with life extending pavement preservation techniques.

**A Green Challenge.** Several years back, Mayor Hudson challenged her department heads to come up with methods of rehabilitation for their infrastructure that would not only save money but also be more energy efficient and sustainable. "Going green and the economy are synonymous. Lorenzo brought great ideas to the table including job creation, costs savings and benefits for the community", says Hudson. The Mayor also gave the city engineer the go ahead to purchase MicroPAVER pavement management software during this period, and her staff went out, gathered pavement distress survey data, and began to load it into the computer software. Their average network level pavement condition index (PCI, with 0 being impassable and 100 being new or having major rehabilitation) was in the high 50s.

325

"Once we settled on the Re-HEAT method as the most suitable means of in-place rehabilitation for our streets, we started the bid process. As we were the first agency in Mississippi to implement this hybrid type of hot in-place recycling work, we called agencies such as the Florida Department of Transportation (DOT) and Ohio DOT to obtain historical information on their experiences with this process and guidance. Since we do have a local paving contractor in the City, we also allowed for the option of a two inch mill and inlay bid in lieu of the Re-HEAT process at the time of the letting," states City Engineer Lorenzo Anderson.

---

"Based on the competitive bids that we received, we were pleasantly surprised to see that with the Re-HEAT process we could plan to do 43 city streets instead of the original 20 that we had budgeted with the conventional mill and inlay process used in previous years. With the 50% savings we are getting, we can do over twice as many roads," proclaims Mayor Hudson. "This is great for our people, our businesses and growth in our city! Now I can say that green is the new green."

---

"When the equipment arrived on the first section of work, and we all went out there to see it, touch it, and watch it in action, we couldn't believe how fast and efficient Re-HEAT turned it (the old road) over into a new street without the long line of trucks and noisy, dusty milling equipment," emphasizes Mayor Hudson.

"In fact the local state-wide paving company CEO visited the job site and got a vision of how everything was going to go and got a good idea that recycling is the way to go," says the Mayor. "During a trip to France last year, I saw firsthand how advanced some European agencies are when it comes to asphalt recycling and sustainability. We have a great opportunity with our city to get everyone on board and be at the forefront of it, not necessarily putting someone out of a job. With Re-HEAT it is good for the community, environment and the future by using our resources most wisely," reiterates the Mayor.

**7-point solution.** Recently appointed to chair the Environmental Protection Agency's (EPA) Local Government Advisory Committee (LGAC), Mayor Hudson comments, "Since the Re-HEAT train emits 65% less emissions than a stand-alone asphalt plant, and has 80% less of a carbon footprint because of its eco-efficient design, that means a lot to me and the colleagues that are part of my committee. This in-place process eliminated the trucking of over thirty thousand tons of millings and asphalt on one job alone. That equates to over 2,000 truckloads of resources that will not be driving over our other streets and damaging them to get to and from the project. Our committee has discussed emissions problems in North Carolina and west coast states, but we feel that if there are problems with pollution in some parts of the country, eventually it will become a problem nationwide."

---

Lorenzo Anderson adds, "Our network PCI ratings are increasing about 7 points a year since we implemented the MicroPAVER pavement evaluation and management system and combined it with asphalt recycling."

---

"While we do some of our worst streets with a reclaimer (full depth reclamation is another discipline with ARRA), our biggest cost savings comes with the Re-HEAT train. Once the road is hot in-place recycled, we reset the PCI in our software to 100, and fully expect to see a 12-15 year life cycle similar to that of a mill and inlay at half the cost."

It is worth noting that streets typically fall about three PCI points per year when left unattended, so the fact that Greenville streets are going up 7 points a year on average is a huge testament to their overall approach. Mr. Anderson plans to implement other pavement preservation techniques such as microsurfacing and thin overlays in the future once their backlog of poor condition roads are rehabilitated with the Re-HEAT process.

For the past few years, Lorenzo Anderson has been using asphalt millings to make his gravel roads last longer, and used full depth reclamation for his roads with PCIs fewer than 50. He also plans to use the Re-HEAT process once the initial contract is finished. "I especially like the idea that the Re-HEAT layer offers twice the crack mitigation against the underlying cracks versus a conventional mill and inlay," states Mr. Anderson.

**A good neighbor.** Combining a solid pavement management program such as MicroPAVER, asphalt recycling and pavement preservation have certainly helped Mayor Hudson save millions of dollars for her citizens in Greenville.

---

Mayor Hudson touts, "Green is the new green!"

---

When I asked the Mayor, a member of the Alumnae Association of Atlanta's Spelman College, what advice she would give our Atlanta City Mayor Kasim Reed, she said emphatically, "Get recycling asphalt!"

"This is an easy way to make a big difference with our environment; we were the first city in Mississippi to use the Re-HEAT process to recycle our roads in-place without a wearing course. I will tell anyone who will listen—the LGAC members, county commissioners, city politicians—this is a no brainer for us! This process takes so much less time and it is in and out of neighborhoods quickly. The time savings is not something that everyone talks about, but community members are well aware of the long delays, limited access to driveways, messy tack coat, dust, lines down and noise from conventional mill and inlay projects. They appreciate what we have done, so far, with one-day traffic control in neighborhoods. Once they pass their house, they are finished. The residents leave on an old road in the morning and return to a new road that afternoon."

---

Mayor Hudson and City Engineer Anderson would welcome any questions that the reader may have regarding this article. For further information, please contact the author of this article blair@thebarnhardtgroup.com. Mr. Barnhardt is a National Highways Institute (NHI) Certified Instructor for Federal Highways Administration (FHWA), Local Technical Assistance Program (LTAP) National Instructor and a course designer and instructor (pavement preservation, recycling and management) for a prominent USA University. His consulting firm also specializes in MicroPAVER and StreetSaver pavement evaluation services.

---

**Re-HEAT HIR train in action**

Here is the link to the digital version at **Roads and Bridges** http://www. roadsbridges.com/sites/default/files/60_PE%20Market_0411RB.pdf

## Bonus Chapter #6
## IPMA Tip of the Week Sample Episode

Hey, everyone, if you are still hanging in here after 300 plus pages, and tons of links to extra curricular activity, I commend you! YOU are one of one percent of the pavement managers in the world who have the desire to take your game to the next level. Following is a transcript of one of my favorite episodes that we did for the **IPMA Tip of the Week Video Series**.

I am sure there will be some doozies going forward with new episodes, and we will be sure to share those with all the members of **IPMA**, www.ipma.co, but this one will always remind me of the power of the internet!

You see, shortly after we released this one to the general public on our YouTube Channel, **IPMATV**, it got placed on the World Highways Website! Before you know it, the guests in this video were getting calls from all over the world. So, as you listen in, or watch, or read this one, remember, we are not alone here. This is not a vacuum we are living in. People are watching, reading and listening to us **Stringbenders**.

The topic in this **Tip of the Week** is HIR with the surface recycling technique. Listen or watch right here if you are connected: http://youtu.be/I5Nw_oF2T_Y. Here is the link to the World Highways posting as well: http://www.worldhighways.com/sections/general/news/ipma-provides-video-on-in-place-recycling-of-road-surfaces-video/.

Please share and enjoy all!

* **HYPHEN CAUTION:** If a link includes a hyphen as it goes to the next line of text, when you retype the link into your computer **do not include the hyphen.**

# Transcript Begins

Blair: Hey, this is Blair Barnhardt, Founder and Executive Director of the **International Pavement Management Association** with your Tip of the Week, and I've got Brian Frix from Rockdale County to talk to you about . . . .

---

(Music and intro roll) It's time for your **IPMA Tip of the Week**, where we teach pavement managers just like you to do more with less. Here's your host, Blair Barnhardt.

---

Brian Frix:  Heater scarification, did I guess it, did I guess it?

Blair Barnhardt: Yes, that's right, Brian has been a big advocate of the **Three Legged Stool (System of Pavement Management)**. He's done plenty of bids for microsurfacing and some of the other surface treatments and a lot of the other in-place asphalt recycling.

In Georgia, especially, we've seen the full depth reclamation (FDR) take off for several years now.  Brian, I'd say that's a main stay in the industry now, but what we're seeing is a sudden surge for counties just like Brian's to do the surface recycling (HIR). That's one of the three sub-disciplines. We've got the surface recycling, remixing, the repaving operations, and part of that group of hot in-place sub-disciplines is the Re-HEAT process.  But, today, Brian is going to talk to you specifically about his experience with surface recycling, hot in-place recycling, here in Rockdale County.

Brian Frix:  Well, first of all, if you compare, you know, do a cost analysis on the heat scarification versus milling and inlay or mill and overlay, you're going to find that the heat scarification (method) is much more cost-effective, number one.  Number two, it is eco-friendly. Obviously that's a big deal, you know, for the green folks out there.

Blair Barnhardt:  We're saving trees, and we're saving our carbon footprint because we're not hauling.

Brian Frix:  Absolutely.

Blair Barnhardt:  Well, first of all, we're not making a whole new bunch of asphalt.

Brian Frix: Absolutely.

Blair Barnhardt: I guess that's a big part of it, and we are not burning a bunch of diesel fuel to get a whole bunch of new material to the job site.

Brian Frix: That's correct, and, you know the other thing is, it's a really fast operation. It's a single pass operation that heats the road back up, melts the asphalt, and adds some asphalt rejuvenating agent to it. It provides a year to three years crack mitigation, depending on your online structure

Blair Barnhardt: (speaking from a different job site) In advance of the surface recycling operation, I just wanted to point out a couple of best practices in terms of this particular project. This is a 4-lane, undivided collector; I guess you would say probably 30,000 to 40,000 cars a day out there. The manhole frames and grates have remained exactly in place, so, once the hot-in-place surface recycling has been done, and when the one and a quarter inch hot-mixed asphalt inlay has been placed, riser rings or adjustments will be made to the manholes.

But, what I want to point out here is that along the gutter line, both edges of these drive lines have been taper milled. We've gone from an inch and a half on the gutter pan here, out to zero, just as we get close to the first twelve foot division here.

The two centre lanes show environmentally distressed block cracking and a lot of weathering and the likes of that (are visible). The existing (HMA) mix is pretty much on the fine side, as with all these southeastern mixes, it seems as opposed to maybe some of the coarser mixes I see in the northeastern region.

In any case, as you'll notice when we do the surface recycling down here, we'll have the travel lanes on both sides of the gutter back down to the original grade to allow for the inch and a quarter inlay. Notice I said "inlay" so, when we talk about milling these edges down, and putting a mix into the milled area or the void space, we call that a mill and "inlay" as opposed to a mill and "overlay" (when in a curb and gutter or some type of gutter bound pavement section i.e. granite header curb).

Breakaway Footage with Blair: In this scene, Blair is referring to the deep patching that went on ahead of the hot in-place surface recycling work. This hot in-place surface recycling, in this case the contractor is Gallagher Asphalt Corporation (http://www.gallagh-erasphalt.com/ and www.hotinplacerecycling.com), and C.W. Matthews (http://www.cwmatthews.com/) for the inlay, but, the point is that, because we're using three or four inches of 19 mm binder, we will have a really good structure underneath for the surface recycling. However, if this was going to be an HA5 (High Density Mineral Bond) or a microsurfacing on top as opposed to an inch and a half overlay or an inch and a half inlay, you'd probably be best to go with the 12.5 mm or even a 9.5 mm patch in that area there that's been milled and deep patched. (Back to Interviews with Brian Frix.)

---

Brian Frix: You know you have to patch all your structural deficiencies on the roadway, which we did with a local contractor, and then the out of town contractor, Gallagher Asphalt, came in. There are others out there I'm not advocating them, but there are others out there depending on where you are in the United States. They came into town, heat-scarified this road right here, and then we had our local contractor come back with hot-mix.

Now HMA is not the only surface treatment you can put back on this. We've got microsurfacing as an option, as well another treatment that we have been recently looking into, HA5, which is a High-Density Mineral Bond. We are considering that as well. But, you know, we are letting another contract here in the next few months where we are going to heater-scarify (HIR) some roads. We will be microsurfacing those roads or providing a hot mix over the top, so there are options out there, depending on your budget. I'm sure that's a big issue for everyone out there. You know how to save money.

Blair Barnhardt: Well, I think a lot of times people really just keep doing the same thing over and over. Nothing against them. The county engineers out there, Brian, they just maybe don't know of anything different. I mean, look at us, we're out there on the front edge with **IPMA,** and trying to learn all these new techniques how we keep up?

* **HYPHEN CAUTION**: If a link includes a hyphen as it goes to the next line of text, when you retype the link into your computer **do not include the hyphen**.

Brian Frix: That's correct!

Blair Barnhardt: You know, I've got a feel for these people who don't know all the different options. I'm so glad you're here today to discuss one of those options, and, again, this is only one tool in the toolbox.

Brian Frix: That's correct!

Blair Barnhardt: If you look at the **IPMA Academy,** we talk about this stuff for seventy or eighty hours online, but for this five minute session for this **IPMA Tip of the Week**, one thing, surface recycling (HIR) could save you upwards of a million dollars this year!

Brian Frix: Absolutely, I mean we're looking at a thirty percent savings, but you know thirty percent of a million dollars is quite a bit of money.

Blair Barnhardt: Absolutely, so, just recapping here in Georgia. In Georgia alone, I know this is going on in all the States all across America, but specifically in Georgia over the last three or four years I think we've got upwards of 75 miles (center-lane miles) of roadway at the county and the city level down in the surface recycling hot in-place recycling.

Breakaway Footage with Blair: What we have here is the surface recycling hot in-place operation. In this particular example we've got the two units we're got one preheater and a heater unit with the integral screen; the paving screen attached to it so the first unit is going to heat that asphalt up to about 270 degrees Fahrenheit and the second heater is going to heat the asphalt up again sequentially to about 330 to 340 degrees Fahrenheit at which time the tines can get in there, the spring loaded tines, the rejuvenating agent can be added with this rotary spinner cups and at that point the material is lubricated with the rejuvenating agent and softened with the sequential heating.

Now, remember, we don't want to heat things up too quickly, like, we don't want to roast a marshmallow over an open fire on a campsite too fast because it'll burn. But if we gradually heat it, then, we soften up that asphalt, and introduce the rejuvenating agent into the final sequence of heaters.

Now, when we're doing extra depth, or in colder climates, or in wet conditions, the contractors may elect to bring in a third, or maybe even a fourth pre-heater unit and spread that train out. For this particular example, a single pre-heater followed by another heater unit which is all within, I'm going to say 100 to 110 feet of area that they are taking up,

---

Back to interviews with Mike Lehner, Cobb County, GA

---

Blair Barnhardt:  And, in terms of traffic, I think it's worth noting here that if you have 30 or 40,000 cars a day, you don't seem to have any upper limit to the roads. In other words there's no cut off point here in Cobb (County, GA).

Mike Lehner:  No not at all, it's working out really well; we're pleased with it. The pilot project was in 2007.

Blair Barnhardt:  That's a long time ago!

Mike Lehner:  It was like we did a pilot project over 50,000 SY and over laid it (with HMA). To this day, there's no problems, whatsoever!

Blair Barnhardt:  Well, my math first thing in the morning, and all about . . . 6 years?

Mike Lehner:  6 years this summer; it will be 6 years!

Blair Barnhardt:  So, this summer, it will be 6 years, the same type, it wasn't milled was it?

Mike Lehner:  It wasn't milled. It was a curbed subdivision, and we, actually, just went the surface course and took all that out with HIR instead of patching.  So, we saved all those patching dollars. It was a subdivision that was alligatored, it was stressed, but we didn't have any deflection or any base failures, so it was an ideal candidate for that.

Blair Barnhardt:  So, no reflective cracking in the subdivision.  Do we still have the busy trash compactor trucks, or Home Depot trucks and the likes of that going through these subdivisions here? Usually, so you know, if you're not from the southeast they only have one type of egress, or one means of cars coming in and out of the subdivision.

Mike Lehner: Sure, that is true!

Blair Barnhardt: That's a pretty good testament if you've got very little, if any, crack mitigation—cracks coming up after 6 years so . . . .

Mike Lehner: That is true, and you don't have all the trucks and the milling crew coming out through our neighborhoods.

Blair Barnhardt: That's being said, I don't think we're here to bash the hot-mixed asphalt industry. In fact, I think we're actually going to say here again if we adopt the **Three-Legged Stool (of Pavement Management**), we are actually going to get more hot-mix asphalt for the contractor to put down because you can stretch your budget further.

Mike Lehner: Right, well, not every road is a candidate for this process, and so you have got to know which is good and which is not, and we do rely on our contractors to assist. We've got two of the largest paving contractors in the southeast that are headquartered right here in Cobb County.

And, this is going through those paving contracts so those contractors are the prime. You can use this (hot in-place surface recycling). We've got a spec written, and added a line item in a bid. We leave it to the contractors to select who they want, so long as they are approved and . . .

Blair Barnhardt: Right!

Mike Lehner: . . . in the industry.

Blair Barnhardt: Awesome! So, wrapping up, I'd like to thank you so much for joining us, Mike, and you'll probably get e-mails from people from all over the world . . . .

Mike Lehner: That's fine.

Blair Barnhardt: With the **IPMA Academy** learners and all that, I encourage you guys to get on the e-mail. Mike will give you his e-mail address in a second. Just get on there and contact him, and ask him any questions. He has already been through this for the last five or six years, so, if you're just jumping into any the recycling techniques, Mike is a great candidate for a question-and-answer period.

I'm sure he's learned a few things, and I think we're all learning in this business, Mike, on a regular basis. What advice, or what words of wisdom, might you have for a county in a similar situation?

There's one I know, I think he only has one paving contractor locally. They want to keep them involved in the loop, but they also want to branch out and do things that are more cost-effective and eco-efficient. What words advice would you have for a agency like that?

Mike Lehner:  Well, as always, it depends on the streets you are looking to do.  This is a great process, and most of our roads are great candidates that would support this process.  There are areas that if you have base failures, or other problems, you don't need a surface treatment. You just need to mill it, and replace it.  There are areas you may not need anything but an edge mill, if it's curbed, so there are a lot of different scenarios. But it is definitely something Cobb County has adopted to do.

We're going to keep HIR surface-recycling in the program. Cobb County has got a very aggressive, multi-year paving program on our SPLOST (special local option sales tax – see transcript of article that Blair wrote on this subject in another chapter in the book), and a large percentage of our SPLOST, upwards of a hundred million dollars, is dedicated to resurfacing, and in rehabbing our streets.

Blair Barnhardt:  Ok would you mind giving our learners your e-mail address?

Mike Lehner:  All right, my e-mail is mike.lehner@cobbcounty.org.  You can call me in my office 770-528-3681.

---

Breakaway Footage with Blair:  (Speaking from the Cobb County job site) And traffic control is running quite fine, again sequentially heating that asphalt, gradually getting it introduced to the screed, and the spring-load at tines—where it can be scarified with the spring-loaded tines—and then compacted as conventional asphalt would be compacted.

---

Blair: Now, we're in the outside lanes that have already been milled by the contractor, which in this case was C.W. Matthews, and, as a result, those outside lanes are going to turn out to be ever-so-slightly coarser because of the underlying 19 mm stone (in the 19 mm SP HMA patching). In this case, once Gallagher Asphalt completes the (HIR) surface-recycling, a finer mat will result in the center two lanes. It will be similar to that of a brand new asphalt, but their work is all going to be the leveling course. You heard Mike, Cobb County, and Brian, Rockdale County, talk about this.

This is going to provide an excellent crack mitigation layer to the underlying cracks, increase the life and basically ensure this asphalt overlay, this asphalt 12.5 mm overlay, which, incidentally, the contractors have been using a shuttle buggy to put down, so it's going to be an incredible ride out here with a very durable asphalt for long service life.

Let's go take a closer look here . . .

---

Back to Interviews with Brian Frix.

---

**Brian Frix:** Well, that goes to show you know HIR is making its way in the southeast more and more. Individuals, municipalities and agencies are finding the value in this, and, you know, I think it's coming. You know it's going to make its way. More and more people are going to start investing in this. More of the locals are going to have to figure out how to bring this equipment into their operations.

**Blair Barnhardt:** We just don't have enough money to go round anymore at the county level, do you?

**Brian Frix:** That's right, exactly!

**Blair Barnhardt:** Not saying you ever had enough to begin with, but one thing for certain, Brian has done great justice to his county by doing the pavement management, the pavement evaluation, pavement preservation and in-place recycling!

Kudos to you, and for those of you who don't know this, Brian also sits on the **IPMA Advisory Board,** so for all of you **(IPMA) Academy Learners** listening in, Brian will be one of the people reviewing your **IPMA Academy Certification** (www.ipmaacademy. com) for **APM (Accredited Pavement Manager).**

So, in any case, just wrapping up, Brian, if anyone's sitting there back at home watching this **(IPMA) Tip of the Week,** if they have any questions and they are sitting on the fence, what advice would you have for them?

Brian Frix: Well, you know, you can feel free to shoot me an e-mail. If you have any questions that you know Blair hasn't covered, or you'd just like a little more information on the heater-scarification process, my email is brian.frix@rockdalecounty.org, and, of course, Blair is obviously an excellent resource.

Blair Barnhardt: blair@ipma.co

Brian Frix: There you go . . .

Blair Barnhardt: I don't think they want to hear from me anymore!

Brian Frix: They don't?

Blair Barnhardt: They want to hear it from the "real people."

Brian Frix: Well, hey, I'd be glad to provide any help I can, I've certainly had help along the way!

Blair Barnhardt: Great, so anybody who needs help or questions about putting their bid document together, Brian's been a great resource to all the people here in the southeast. Thanks for that, Brian!

Brian Frix: No problem.

Blair Barnhardt: Thanks for joining us today on the **IPMA Tip of the Week**. We'll see you guys next time on this is Blair and . . .

Brian Frix: . . . Brian Frix.Blair Barnhardt: Signing out!

* HYPHEN CAUTION: If a link includes a hyphen as it goes to the next line of text, when you retype the link into your computer **do not include the hyphen**.

Hot In-Place Surface Recycling in action

Brian Frix, APM, IPMA Advisory Board Member with Blair

# Bonus Chapter #7

## For the Contractors: Profit is NOT a Dirty Word

So far, the entire book has really focused on saving money for local agencies, and that is really where the biggest bang is going to happen for the planet. However, contractors struggling to make a living can also take full advantage of the **Three Legged Stool System** that I have developed. Let me give you an example below:

### Case Study:  Atlanta Technical College, GA

During the letting of this project, the owner was not able to accept alternate methods of rehabilitation due to time constraints on the bid and scheduling of the work. At that time, prices for liquid asphalt cement had sky rocketed, and conventional rehabilitation was very expensive. We went ahead and bid this project as a conventional undercut along with some thin overlays for the parking lots. Our final prices was about $900 K, or so, with half of the price for the contract being for the dig out of the main bus route.

I knew time was of the essence because the off-season for the college semester was a short one. You could say I rolled the dice a bit, but we bid the job straight up as it was let with the intent of proposing a change order to do FDR (full depth reclamation) in lieu of the conventional undercut.  Experience had shown us we could do this work for substantially less money in a tenth of the time normally allotted. We also knew that the owner would likely be enticed by the fact we could complete the project ahead of schedule.

So, in a time when our competition was literally beating themselves up with little or no profit margin, we secured the work. We also successfully switched the project to the scope we knew would make us the most amount of profit, while providing the most value for the customer.

Bottom line here is, as a contractor, it is okay to make profit, which is not a dirty word by the way— provided you can give value to your customer. In this particular example, we also gave the Atlanta Technical College President a check back for $25,000.00. She, in turn, requested we do an additional parking lot resurfacing project and used that credit up. She said to me during the punch list of the project, "Blair, I have been doing this job for 25 years, and you are the first contractor who has ever given me money back!"

To this day, this is one of my favorite case studies as it exemplifies how business is supposed to work. As a business owner, you provide solutions for your customer, they get value at a reasonable price, and you make a reasonable amount of profit in return for providing that service.

So, if you are sitting on the fence deciding whether or not this pavement management, in-place recycling, or pavement preservation thing is for you, think about this little story and how it could affect your bottom line back at your office. We did this work in harsh economic times, but made more profit in one month than most small business firms made in an entire year in that season.

Below are some of the photos and facts from the project. If you are a consultant, contractor or service provider and wish to discuss how to grow your business with anything that was covered in this book, please e-mail me at blair@thebarnhardtgroup.com to discuss in detail.

Atlanta Technical College-Marta bus route-before FDR

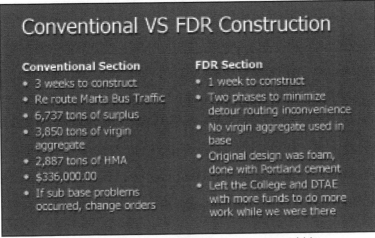

# Conventional VS FDR Construction

**Conventional Section**
- 3 weeks to construct
- Re route Marta Bus Traffic
- 6,737 tons of surplus
- 3,850 tons of virgin aggregate
- 2,887 tons of HMA
- $336,000.00
- If sub base problems occurred, change orders

**FDR Section**
- 1 week to construct
- Two phases to minimize detour routing inconvenience
- No virgin aggregate used in base
- Original design was foam, done with Portland cement
- Left the College and DTAE with more funds to do more work while we were there

Comparison of conventional vs. FDR method $$$

Before FDR and HMA inlay

19 mm binder going down on FDR w/cement

Final wearing course, speed table, striping complete

If you are in the contracting business and haven't been involved with an in-place recycling project in some way, you may want to consider doing so in the near future. There are plenty of ways to provide value to your customers while making a very good profit margin, with little risk of failure or warranty work.

# Bonus Chapter #8
# Case Study – High Density Mineral Bond (HA5)

While traveling in the **Better Roads Bus** out West, I came across a breakthrough in pavement preservation especially targeted for residential roadways. This same product, however, can be used as a wearing surface for hot in-place recycling and cold in-place recycling. I let the owners of the Holbrook Asphalt firm know this may be an area they may want to invest in by doing some additional R&D.

Just goes to show you once again, perception. . . . Had I not driven 83,000 miles across this great country, I may have never discovered some of these products and services. Again, this is something new to me, but these folks in Utah, Arizona and Nevada have been using High Density Mineral Bond for over a decade.

If you haven't heard of this product yet, I am almost certain you will as demand for this type of preservation treatment is growing nationwide. Again, classified officially as a High Density Mineral Bond with a specification produced by the American Public Works Association, it's more commonly known as HA5 as that is the name of the only product at this time currently meeting the High Density Mineral Bond specification.

People ask me all the time, "Blair, why is this HA5 such a game changer in the world of pavement preservation?" Well, I may very well be one of the biggest skeptics out there, and, after seeing what I saw, and talking to the folks who have been using this treatment in the states that we visited, I can tell you why!

In fact, I can let you watch the same thing I saw while teaching at the Utah Road School and going out on the field trip with all the folks there. (Who doesn't love a good field trip!?)

Check out the YouTube video right here http://youtu.be/RJOrVVZ4Dcs and/or the photo on the next page.

After 30 years in construction, it takes a lot to get me excited about a highway seal coat, but you sure can see in the photo. It is easy to identify the difference in longevity and performance of the two treatments. And, by the way, this type of proof of performance is what I subscribe to most. That is, in the field, real world performance evaluation, rather than laboratory test results.

Premium Seal Coat left / HA5 right – Both in service 4 years

One of my main mentors, Dr. John Emery, used to always say to me, "There are three ways to do a job, Blair: you have got the classroom and you know the books; then you have the laboratory results of how things should go; and, then, **most importantly**, you have to know what actually goes on out there in the field!"

This is an untouched picture of a high-end subdivision road with HA5 compared to a premium asphalt emulsion sealer. Both treatments were installed within one week of each other in 2010. Initially, the differences were minimally discernible. However, after four short years, the HA5 is still effectively preserving the pavement and will for many years to come while the non-HA5 treated section is exposed to the environment and is experiencing oxidative damage once again.

The main benefit of the preservation treatment is the HA5's ability to reduce the aging characteristics of the asphalt pavement. In fact, recently, an independent engineering firm, reported 9 times less cracking in the HA5 treated section compared to the section receiving what has been considered premium asphalt seal coat.

The bottom line here is that the residents of this, and every other subdivision in America and the world, embrace the deep black color as their desire aesthetics above all desires with their roadways. Public agencies benefit from lowering their cost of pavement ownership by preserving the good roads and keeping them out of the critical zone of no return.

Effectively extending the life of our asphalt roadways and reducing the need for major rehabilitation or reconstruction, we impose fewer costs on taxpayers. To view additional videos of the entire tool box of treatments such as this High Density Mineral Bond treatment, be sure to register your book at www.thebookonbetterroads.com/register.

# Bonus Chapter #9

## Our Set Up – Easy Equipment Implementation

Over the years a lot of folks have asked Jason and me about our set up in the field for the RV, the Rhino, the core drills we use, the measuring wheels, the distance measuring instruments, etc.

As you may have already figured out by now, I am basically an open book in this respect—pardon the pun here. What I mean is my underlying goal in life is to get this country out of economic disparity by creating better roads for less money, and, any one task that moves us closer to that goal, whether it is shortening your pavement management learning curve, hanging out with you in your city or county to help you put the pieces together, or to hand over the keys to the equipment that we use on a daily basis, my only goal is to provide you with the tools to get you to pavement management **RockSTARDOM!**

So, I just took a few minutes in the yard the other day, gathering up all of our tools, so Jason and I could start a new project in Colorado this week. So, below is a bunch of photos of our set up for boots-on-the-ground expert pavement distress evaluation. You can replicate this set up for under $20,000 and be performing your own work in two weeks. I went ahead and put a photo in of what some of our **IPMA Academy** are doing for their set up as well just for comparison's sake.

Keson Model R318 N – Remember to Order Metric Model Outside of USA

I think you know this already, but if you should have any questions at all along the way, shoot me an e-mail 24/7 at blair@ipma.co and I will get you the answer you need to set up your own equipment. I have provided our most up to date equipment photos, along with some upcoming equipment that we plan to acquire. If you are a consultant, or agency person, I hope this bonus chapter helps you with your decision making process. There is no sense recreating the wheel here, and with 4 million miles of roads in USA, I think there is plenty of pavements to be managed by all!

Yamaha Rhino 660 – 2000 watt generator

Rear of Rhino – Hilti DD 130

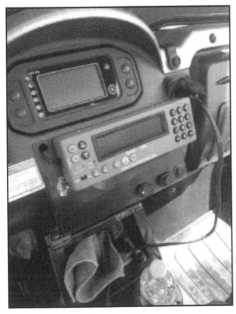

Jamar RAC – 100 DMI –
velcro mount to dash

Signal lights installed on Rhino
front & back

Props for crack measurement

Hilti DD 130 Setup – probing rods –
straight edges – levels

14 ft. Interstate Pro-Series
enclosed trailer

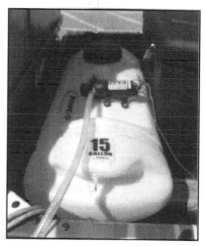

15 gallon water tank for core drilling

Pavement coring trailer, Piqua, Ohio

PIQUA PHOTOGRAPHS COURTESY OF DOUG HARTER, PIQUA STREET DEPARTMENT

353

Driving America for Better Roads – The Fleet

Dyanamax Dynaquest from Camping World

So, if you have any additional questions about any of the equipment that we use, from the software we use to make our videos, the microphones we use to record our podcasts, or the tires that we mount on our RVs, blair@ipma.co. We will try to answer everyone who e-mails us! After all, we have spent thousands of dollars getting geared up, seeing what works and what doesn't, so you don't have to figure out what is right for you. Simply replicate our list of what to get, and get-r done!

# Bonus Chapter #10
## Stringbenders vs. The Naysayers — Reprisal

So, you have three types of pavement folks out there: the **Stringbenders**, the Uninformed, and the Naysayers. Having driven 2,480 miles over the last three days, I got to thinking: How will you know who is who when you are sitting in a board room somewhere? Then it occurred to me, I simply need to give you an idea of the types of things you may hear coming out of a **Stringbender** versus what you may hear coming out of a Naysayer.

So, in the left hand corner, weighing in at 177 pounds, we have Brian Diefenderfer, **World's Greatest Stringbender** of all time, all the way from Virginia DOT, please give him a warm welcome!

Here are some of the highlights from a brief video interview I had with Brian shortly after he won the **Roads and Bridges** Award for In-Place Recycling from ARRA. You can watch the entire video here at our YouTube Channel http://youtu.be/Ee4LAD3ykV4. Brian is, to this date, one of my favorite **Stringbenders** ever! FYI: Several weeks prior to the work being let and performed, the contractor who performed the award winning project flew in to watch Brian and me do an NHI Recycling Workshop in Baton Rouge, LA.

Kudos to the VDOT folks for combining cold central plant recycling, cold in-place recycling and soil stabilization in a single project. It saved millions on their I-81 Interstate Project! And special kudos to Richard and all of the folks at Lanford Brothers (http://www.lanfordbrothers.com/), the contractor who took the plunge to invest in the equipment and bend strings with the state officials! When will everybody get this?

## Transcription begins

Blair: Hey, this is Blair and we've caught up here with Brian Diefenderfer at the ARRA (Asphalt Recycling & Reclaiming) convention where he just accepted the annual award with **Roads and Bridges** giving him a great trophy for his efforts here in Virginia DOT. Brian, you did a great service for the industry by putting three different process together. Give us a brief synopsis, please, and then we'll get into the case study.

Brian: We had a project on VDOT's Interstate 81 where we were looking at rehabilitating the pavement, especially the right lane, down to a deep depth, down to the unbound materials. Traffic on this section of I-81 is about 23,000 vehicles a day, about 28% trucks, and that's a directional traffic count for the south bound direction. That's where the project took place.

Projected reconstruction time was in the neighborhood of a four month process. The right lane consisted of deep-milling 12 inches of full depth reclamation using Calciment stabilizing agent. The milled material was processed in a mobile plant off the edge of the project, brought back and repaved to a 6 inch depth. That cold central plant material was stabilized with foamed asphalt and Portland cement. That was covered with a 4 inch layer of hot-mixed asphalt.

The process shifted over to the left lane where a 2 inch milled process happened first. Then a cold in-place recycling process at a 5 inch depth using foamed asphalt and Portland cement stabilizing agent, again. That was capped with 2 inch, hot-mixed asphalt layer.

Traffic ran on that section for about 3 months then was capped again with another 2 inches of asphalt. So, the total pavement structure in the right lane would be 6 inches of asphalt over 6 inches of cold central plant (mix) over top of 12 inches of FDR.

In the left lane is 4 inches of hot mixed asphalt on top of 5 inches of cold in-place recycled mix over the top of the existing pavement structure.

It was a very interesting project for us to work on. There was a lot of lab testing, with core sampling after the project was completed as well as sampling ahead of the project. So, we've learned quite a bit. Our goal is to develop specifications and guidelines for our district folks to use. We are trying to do an even better job of pavement recycling around Virginia.

Blair: Well, and one thing I give you credit for too, Brian, you had many agency people walking up and down the job. Students (http:// www.ipmaacademy.com/) are going to see pictures of all the white hard hats. Did you find that there was a lot of positive feedback with people coming from local agencies and other state agencies? Were they getting on board with the processes?

Brian: I think so. I think there's always a hesitation to look at a new process when you've only seen it or heard about it. When I say see it, maybe you've seen a presentation or read about it some place in the paper, but, when you actually get out and look at the process with your own eyes, taste the dust, get your hands dirty, I think it takes that experience before you really get on board. You can actually see what things are possible, and what really worked for us.

When we went to the ARRA (http://www.arra.org/) workshop up in Harrisburg, Pennsylvania, the other year—several of us went— I think we got really motivated to work on this process a little harder. It came out of this and also some other demonstration projects that we had. We also had a great group of contracting folks on the project. They provided a lot of assistance as well.

Blair: Well, that certainly tells a story as far as outreach efforts go. I'm always saying, especially to Mr. LaHood (former United States Secretary of Transportation) and the likes of that, there's not enough money to go around for training. The very fact that you sat in a one day seminar in an ARRA workshop and, this is living proof, you've taken it to the limit.

I think you've done more in this combination efforts than anybody I've ever seen. Based on Sohila's (Bemanian) experience in Nevada, I think you've brought the level up to the very top. Looking forward to what you do with the ongoing rut testing and FWD (falling weight deflectometer) testing, perhaps, if you work out some layer coefficients of the cold in-place mat, based on what I've heard so far, it sounds as if the cold in-place mat gave us some pretty positive results, as far as a the rutting, or I guess, anti-rutting characteristics?

Brian: Well, our main concern was rutting or destabilization, or however you want to look at it, in the early life of the project. Again, these materials cure over time. They stiffen with time, and we had a concern to start with, and so, I mentioned that during the construction. There was a 2 inch overlay that was finally placed. We had about a 3 month time window between when the recycling was finished and initial overlay was placed. Then, before that final overlay was placed, we went out and did manual rut measurements. In the right lane we did manage to do rut measurements again, manually, in the right wheel path. I saw, on average, prob-

357

ably about 15 hundredths of an inch, two-tenths of an inch, in that range, and I calculated in those over 10 to 12 weeks that about 400 to 450,000 trucks had passed over (the CIR mat).

Blair: Gosh.

Brian: So, for a lot of projects that may be a three-year life, we saw that it in several weeks.

Blair: That's amazing.

Brian: So, we thought that if we don't have any issues at that point, we've got good confidence that we're going to have a long lasting project.

Blair: Well, kudos again to you, Brian. Thanks for taking the time to talk to us today, and you are number one in my books!

Brian: Thank you.

Blair: Thank you so much, enjoy your afternoon!

## Transcript ends

Now, in the right corner, dressed in black trunks, and wearing a constant frown on his face, and exuding negativity all around him wherever he walks, all the way from Some-state-dot-office on this planet, Ned the Naysayer!

Please note that the above is a fictitious person from a fictitious location. However, below is an edited post from a reply to an online newspaper article somewhere in USA. Following, therefore, is a perfect example of what type of venom you may hear someone spew in an online blog post, or the next time a group of **Stringbenders** gets together at a local conference or Commission meeting.

## Transcript begins

DECEMBER 11, 2013, AT 9:31 AM

*Asphalt Daddy*: The reason there were no bids for resurfacing \*\*\*\*\* Rd. is because of the heater scarification surface recycling that Sammy Stringbender and Sally Stringbender are specifying, in spite of competent professional advice against it.

Heater scarification surface recycling involves heating the top

1″ of the existing pavement structure to approximately 300°F by subjecting the surface to temperatures approaching 1000°F. Then the top 1/2″ – 1″ is disturbed with spring-loaded, steel tines. A "so-called" rejuvenator is added, and the pavement is re-screed to a semi-smooth, temporary, wearing course. Since heater scarification surface recycling destroys the elastic properties of the asphalt cement, which is not mitigated by the rejuvenator, the resulting pavement is brittle and prone to cracking and rutting immediately after paving.

Additionally, there are no quality control measures in place to check for density, smoothness or mix consistency. There is no tack coat applied between the layers. As such, the recycled pavement is porous, has no structural value. It can't resist rutting, cracking or slippage, and must be resurfaced almost immediately or risk losing the whole pavement structure.

They really needed a good hot-mix asphalt contractor because 1″ of hot produced asphalt does add to the pavement structure and may provide some protection to that "recycled" layer. But, no hot-mix asphalt contractor wants to risk his or her reputation by paving over the cracked, raveled, prematurely aged and virtually destroyed pavement.

---

At this point, Sammy Stringbender and Sally Stringbender realized they were in over their heads and had to reach out to the only paving contractor available to them, a microsurfacing contractor from Florida. Microsurfacing is essentially a mixture of sand and asphalt emulsion that is blended at ambient temperature and spread approximately 3/16″ – 5″16″ thick. While this thin layer may temporarily seal the surface of the "recycled" asphalt, it is not a structural layer. Therefore, it cannot bridge the many deficiencies in the "recycled" mix.

There were no quality control measures in place for the microsurfacing, and the result is \*\*\*\*\* County paid for Type II micro-surfacing, but got Type I micro-surfacing instead. The difference is that Type II has some aggregate particles the size of a pea and Type I is all sand.

---

*Asphalt Daddy*: Be aware that they are planning to apply parking lot sealer to our roads as well. This material is patented as HA5 by

359

Holbrook Asphalt of Utah (another out-of-state contractor). The generic name is "High Density Mineral Bond," but don't let the name fool you. It is nothing more than the stuff you see applied to the Hobby Lobby parking lot in Carrollton recently. It's black and is slick when wet.

## Transcript ends

Pure, uninformed evil, that is what I say. Also, I have a sneaky suspicion there may be a little foul play going on there. Did I just write that?

You see, our FHWA actually writes sustainability into their transportation bill, and pays to support the publishing of the **Basic Asphalt Recycling Manual (BARM),** and support the production of the NHI In-Place Asphalt Paving Technologies curriculum. That's one side of the coin.

Then, on the other side of the coin, you have local DOT employees, and some FHWA employees, contradicting all the good that is going on for mankind, and our economy. One has to ask one's self, "Why aren't they saying anything positive about sustainable options or any of the other tools in our proverbial toolbox?"

Clearly, by now, I have shown enough proof of this negative Naysayer influence in this book. By the time you receive the free bonus curriculum delivered to your inbox, you have seen that **The Three Legged Stool of Pavement Management** is a positive, proactive, proven system to resurrect our economy and save our crumbling roads.

I just drove another 3,000 miles to help one of our local agencies. The Airstream Interstate trailer bounced around so hard on our crumbling interstates that the spare tire for the trailer—that was hung securely on the inside wall of the Interstate Pro Series enclosed trailer—fell off the wall!

---

If you decide after registering your book that you want more training material outside of what we are sending you, I would encourage you to register for **IPMA Academy** (http://www.ipmaacademy. com/). But even if you don't want to take 70 hours of online training and become **APM Certified**, you can find more training materials over at the **IPMA Marketplace** at http://drivingamericaforbet-terroads.com/ .

---

* HYPHEN CAUTION: If a link includes a hyphen as it goes to the next line of text, when you retype the link into your computer **do not include the  hyphen**.

Before I close out this bonus chapter and get ready to set you free on your amazing journey, I want to share with you what my mentor Brendon Burchard reminded me a while back:

---

Compound interest is the eighth wonder of the world. He who understands it earns it . . . he who doesn't . . . pays it.
— ALBERT EINSTEIN

---

Thanks, Brendon! You see, with this one book, we can resurrect our failing economy and have better roads for everyone! All because of collaborative compounding! Thank you, Mr. Einstein, for that!

## Here is how it works:

You buy this book or someone hands you a copy. Then:

Assumption 1 – Everyone reading this book has a personal list of close friends and colleagues of about 300 folks.

Assumption 2 – You share this book, and let your 300 folks know about it so they will purchase it or somehow get their hands on it.

Paul Colligan, http://www.paulcolligan.com/, gave me a great idea at a conference where we shared the stage: Angry ratepayers can purchase boxes of the **Book on Better Roads** and have them shipped down to their Mayors' offices. They can let them keep stacking up in there until something actually gets done with the crumbling roads. (Thanks for that image, Paul!)

If you do decide to do this at your agency, and it becomes a big news extravaganza on local TV, please don't blame Paul!

Assumption 3 – Of the 300 folks you tell about the book, 10% actually purchase it and go on to tell their 300 close friends and colleagues about it.

Assumption 4 – Of the 10% that read the book, a mere 2% will go on to save their agency a modest one million dollars in their lifetime.

Assumption 5 – We sell an total of 500 copies of the Kindle version, print version and audio version in the first year, 2014.

You are about to see why the Naysayers don't stand a chance against the Stringbenders. Let's get started!

**2014** = 500 books x 300 friends = 150,000 x 10% = 15,000 books x 2% = **300 Stringbenders** x $1,000,000 = **$300,000,000 saved for local agencies**

**2015** = 15,000 books x 300 friends = 4,500,000 x 10% = 450,000 books x 2% = **9,000 Stringbenders** x $1,000,000. = **$9,000,000,000 saved for local agencies**

(You have to turn your iPhone sideways for this.)

**2016** = 450,000 books x 300 friends = 135,000,000 x 10% = 13,500,000 books x 2% = **270,000** x $1,000,000 = **$270,000,000,000 saved for local agencies**

**2017** = 13,500,000 books

(I have to stop now because my brain is hurting just thinking about how this win, win, win collaborative compounding effect can turn our economy around in a few short years. Everybody wins, so, get the hell out of the way, Naysayers!

## STRINGBENDERS UNITE!

Tell everyone you know about the book, share it, give it away, buy more cases. Just know that for the good of the planet, you deserve to have better roads for less money and less carbon footprint. The smart contractors will adapt to the changes in your pavement management program; the ones who don't . . .well, maybe the dinosaurs will roam the earth again one day?

# Bonus Chapter #11

# Left Side – Right Side + Stringbenders

When they see the **Better Roads Bus** parked at a conference or a truck stop or at Wal-Mart, a lot of folks ask me, "Are you a band? What does the music and guitars have to do with the roads?"

So, before the book goes out to the masses, let me explain, because at one point in this lifetime, the **Bus** is going to come through your city or county, no matter where you are, and you may be wondering the same thing.

Live musicians, such as myself, inside of Apple Garage Band, manufacture each and every note of music you hear on our continent! Often we **Stringbenders** who double, by day, as engineering types, will stay up all night singing, dancing and pickin' guitars! So, if one morning I am standing next to you, and you wonder what is going through my mind, just know that I suffer from the curse of the left side – right side syndrome (not sure if that is a medical condition or not).

You will better understand what I mean by reading this blog post that I did with Greg and the folks over at the SITE-K Construction Zone's Digging-for-Dirt site. You can click here http://www.site-kconstructionzone. com/?p=7486 on your Kindle or read it below.

See you over in the next bonus chapter!

# Transcript begins

### Guest Blog on Site-K Construction Zone:

### Left Side – Right Side and RockStars

Blair: Before I begin my first diatribe for the Site-K readership, let me first say hello, and proclaim how delighted I am that you are taking time out of your busy schedule to read this column. I promise never to put anyone to sleep, though I may provoke some interesting thoughts from you from time to time.

Strangers often stop me in the street, or on planes, and ask me what I do for a living. When I feel we have a little time together to kibitz, I chuckle and state emphatically that I never sleep because I have both an engineering mind and a creative mind vying for attention at all times. Certainly, I reason, it is not easy for me, having grown up playing the electric guitar for two score or more years, coupled with an engineering mind, for as long as I can remember. This situation is clearly a curse for me. So, there you have it, for 24 hours a day, 7 days a week, 365 days a year, the left side of my brain and the right side are constantly fighting for their piece of the action, so to speak.

If you happen to have this same curse, then you can empathize with me and know that while I am trying to play a simple game of golf whilst listening to my favorite MP3 blaring in my earphones, I'm wondering: Was reverb on the snare drum? Did they use a click track in the studio? And, can they play live as well as the recording? I am also simultaneously trying to get a grasp on: Is that breeze I feel a two-club wind? Is the grass on the greens growing toward the mountains or the water? Is my lie level with the ball hook because I am playing to an uphill green? Will I be able to stick my wedge in there for birdie? What if the collars are thick grass, and I short side myself? . . .

Okay, for those of you who have this same challenge, I want to hear from you. And for those who don't, count yourself lucky! So, where are you going with this, Blair, you ask? Perhaps you already know me, and, if you do, you would know that I only speak in broken sentences while my brain over-processes facts and sound bites literally nonstop.

Well, during my former years as a band guy, aka: Rock Star, not only did I lug gear across the floor of every club in the ATL, I also spent the better part of my waking hours (21 per day) teaching rock guitar to countless budding musicians. As part of my curriculum, I would attempt to overwhelm the would-be, future teenage rock stars with the first session. It was my effort to weed out those who did not have the drive and determination to persevere and succeed. In fact, one of the phrases that I put into the student's textbook for the first night of shenanigans was the quote:

Amateurs practice until they get it right; professionals practice until they can't play it wrong.

This simple phrase had mountains of meaning back then, not just for little rock guitarists, but also for anyone who has ever tried to be the best at what they do. Well, almost everyone, I suppose. What I found from experience was that the young musicians wanted to learn how to play the guitar, to get into bands, to get famous, get rich . . . all that stuff and more, because these, in fact, were the incentives—the very reasons why they would practice for hours on end, often until their fingertips bled. In fact, it is clear that those who try to get better at anything, whether it is race car driving, golf, tennis, or even an MBA, have a clear goal in mind with some sort of an incentive as the pay off.

In closing, I have one thought-provoking question: If are you are an agency pavement manager entrusted with millions of dollars in roadways to take care of — even the smallest of cities have several millions of paved asset — do you have an incentive to get better at what you do? Or, can you just keep doing the same old same old, because that is the way it has always been done? Are you implementing the latest in eco-efficient pavement preservation techniques coupled with cost-saving and faster in-place asphalt recycling? Are you constantly honing your craft through continuing education to find more effective ways to manage your pavements?

If you can answer "yes" to all of the above, then you are already a **Pavement Management ROCK STAR**, and I personally commend you for that! If you are not able to answer "yes" to the above questions, then, Houston, we have a problem!

---

If you would like to take part in a comprehensive online and instructor led pavement management program and receive your **APM Accredited Pavement Manager Certification**, or join the **International Pavement Management Association,** I have listed the link below. Note that enrollment for **IPMA Academy** is only open July 1-14th and December 1-14th. **IPMA** membership is open all year round. **IPMA Membership** is open to equipment suppliers, manufacturers, consultants, contractors, agencies, students and academia.

---

One of the coolest things we have going on at HQ is the **IPMA Bid Share.** Agencies will upload all their RFPs and Bids for all things related to pavement management. IPMA member consulting firms and contractors can then download them as part of their membership. This will save countless hours for chief estimators who often spend days seeking the perfect project to bid on. The site is loaded with videos about all of this, so, be sure to check it out at www.ipma.co

It's been a pleasure meeting everyone, and please feel free to e-mail me if you would like to jam sometime!

Thanks for reading!

---

See how www + six small letters can save billions for agencies across the globe . . . www.ipma.co

---

Blair: blair@ipma.co

## Transcript ends

# Bonus Chapter #12

## Your Only Quiz in the Book – Here you go, Lee!

I included this chapter just for fun, but especially for my BFF, Lee Sampson, because he is quite the trivia and music aficionado, among other things! Big thanks to Lee and his team of proofreaders here, too: Basem, Steve and Jon!

So, back in the days when I used to have spare time (yikes), I would go down once a week to Little Five Points, down in the ATL, and pick up a box of CDs. After a week, or so, of listening to the CDs of complete strangers and unknown bands, I would write 500-word CD reviews for **Southeast Performer Magazine**, now known simply as http://performermag.com/.

So, here is the quiz, and it has absolutely nothing to do with pavement management. There you have it. This is how my brain works! Enclosed is a transcript of the article I wrote for this musician — whom I had never heard of, I might add — back in 2001 from the seat of my Ford Explorer.

I want you to guess who this person is. No cheating either!

Turn off your computer so you aren't tempted to get on the Google thing, and don't call to ask a friend! The name of this now very, very, famous musician will appear upside down on a page somewhere between here and the end of your book. I have changed the name of the CD, and made up fictitious names for the musician and her band members. If anyone wants to see the original CD review as published I can e-mail it to you.

While I would like to take personal responsibility for "Sally's" career, and say to you that she won all of her Grammy awards because of this one single CD Review, I can't. Although, you have to admit, based on my previous track record of writing here and what has happened to Sally since then, this **Book on Better Roads** might actually have enough substance in it to actually do everything we say it can do! Just look at what happened to "Sally!" So, please share this book with everyone you know; comment wherever possible (positive or negative), and remember to JOIN us at www.stringbenders.org. Great things are about to happen to our roads and economy on our planet!

Okay, set your timer for 3 minutes; let's see if you get this one, Lee!

Her name is upside down on one of the next few pages. When you get the opportunity, refer our reader's to it, you know these engineers.

* **HYPHEN CAUTION:** If a link includes a hyphen as it goes to the next line of text, when you retype the link into your computer **do not include the hyphen.**

# Transcript Begins

From *Southeast Performer Magazine,* 2001 – Back Issues Available

Sally Stringbender Band – Pretty Pavements

Engineered by:        Bruce Bennett

Recorded at:          Exocet Productions

Mixed by:             Scott Patton and Shalom Aberle

How appropriate that I get a chance to review a compilation of songs from an artist whose songs I have never heard before. No chance for bias here people. According to the liner notes, this record is a compilation of songs written by **Stringbender** between 1984 and 1988. While her former band, **The Three Legged Stools** backed the original recordings of these songs; her present band—Scott Slurry, Mike Recycleski, Wes Asphalt and Brad Emulsion—performed the backing tracks for this disk.

In **Stringbender's** own words she decided to re-record them as both a "Thank-you for all their fans that have been with them throughout the years and as an opportunity for all of our new **Sally Stringbender Band** fans to hear their musical evolution."

Now with the preamble out of the way let's get to the music on "Pretty Pavements." From the Aretha-type delivery of the initial track, through the spine-tingling acapella, sixth song, and the balance of tight arrangements, this Sally Stringbender Band newbie was very impressive.

I am a sucker for the B-3, so the "With Me" song one warmed me up to the band instantly. I liked the tight ending in song two, an acoustic driven piece with persuasive percussion. **Stringbender's** sultry voice pours out like maple syrup in "Beautiful Song" making the listener think this woman has likely won every open mic contest she ever performed in. I especially liked the little tempo change at 1:45, the "difference between lovin' and bein' in love" lyrics and the way the arrangement resolves.

"Good For You" makes me think about Stones classic Heartbreaker — Do, Do, Do, Do, Do, Do with its cool guitars and keys. Was that a fretless bass tracked in the rhythm section!

Song five displays **Stringbender's** range quite well, but I found it a bit long with no apparent hook. Fortunately, I could looked past that as I fell swooned by the interesting chord changes of that wondrously tracked acoustic (Taylor influences?). BGVs would have been a nice touch on this track as well. "Shade of the Hand of Fear", Jennifer Nettles, I am speechless. Kudos' to you and your vocal coach — unless you are one of those few born with a mic in your cradle.

"Crossties" makes an awesome, alive song, with its tight rhythm section and breakdown. "Sometimes" was a bit long, but solid, while song nine utilized the borrowed keyboard tones of **YES** days gone by. "Know", has no hooks, but excellent radio length and awesome BGVs. Again, a bit long for this listener on song eleven, but good grouping of songs with the 2:55 groove song in the 12 spot. A finger-picked acoustic wraps up the disc for this new **Sally Stringbender** listener who rates this effort at a solid 8/10. Check out the band at their next show if you want to hear some heart-wrenching emotional writing delivered by superb musicians.

Contact:     www.sallystringbender.com
By:          Blair Barnhardt
(500 words)

# Transcript Ends

# Bonus Chapter #13
# Final Thoughts & The Fine Print

Please refer to the terms and conditions on our websites mentioned in this book as well as the short summary below. Thanks for reading our book! Our journey together has now officially started. Be sure to register your book at www.thebookonbetterroads.com/register to receive ongoing training delivered directly to your inbox.

Thanks to Mike and Paul for creating AEMM for folks just like me to share my knowledge with the world, and special thanks to Camper Bull for getting me off my butt to write this thing! Big shout out to Andy, Brendon, Brian, Chris, Darren, Frank, Jack, Jeff, Joe, Jon, Rick, Scott, Mary and Irene as well, for all you do over at EIA (Experts Industry Association: http://www.expertsindustryassociation.com/.

NY Times multiple best selling author and founder of Experts Academy, Brendon Burchard

'Chicken Soup for the Soul' NY Times best selling author Jack Canfield

* **HYPHEN CAUTION:** If a link includes a hyphen as it goes to the next line of text, when you retype the link into your computer **do not include the hyphen**.

'Project Everlasting'
author
Mathew Boggs

Joe Polish,
Piranha Marketing Inc.
Founder & President

Finally thanks to the Princess
for all that you do
- Number One Stringbender!

# What Our Attorney Wants Us to Share With You

The content, case studies and examples shared in this book do not in any way represent the "average" or "typical" learner or client experience. In fact, with any product or service, we know some clients purchase our products, services and intellectual knowledge and never use them. Therefore they get no results from their association with us whatsoever.

You should assume that following anything we discuss in any of our audio, printed, video, or any and all content, for that matter, will produce no results for your local agency, private sector firm, or you, yourself, personally.

Therefore, the case studies we are sharing can neither represent nor guarantee the current or future experience of other past, current or future readers, listeners, viewers and/or learners of our created content. Rather, these member case studies, and any and all results reported in these case studies by individuals, represent all that is possible by following our system and training available.

Each of these unique case studies, and any and all results reported in these case studies by individual persons, agencies, academic institutions, associations and/or private sector firms, are the culmination of numerous variables, many of which we cannot control or influence, including pricing, target market conditions, product/service quality, offers, customer service, personal initiative, and countless other tangible and intangible factors.

Any earnings (or income statements), savings (or anticipated savings), earning income or saving dollars examples, are only estimates of what we think you could either earn or save. There is no assurance you'll do as well. If you rely upon our figures, you must accept the risk of not doing as well.

Where specific income and savings figures are used and attributed to an individual or business, to the best of our knowledge those persons or businesses have actually earned or saved that amount. There is no assurance you'll do as well. If you rely upon our figures, you must accept the risk of not doing as well.

Any and all claims or representations regarding income earnings or dollar amount savings are not considered to be as average earnings. Likewise, any and all claims or representations, as to job promotion, career advancement, or similar, are not to be considered as average results. There can be no assurance that any prior successes, or past results, regarding income earnings or dollar savings results can be used as an indication of your future success or results.

Monetary and income results, as well as dollar savings results, are based on many factors. We have no way of knowing how well you will do, as we do not know you, your background, your work ethic, or your business skills or practices. Therefore, we do not guarantee, or imply, that you will either get rich, or save millions, nor that you will do as well, or, in fact, make or save any money.

Making decisions based on any information we share about our products, services, or on our website, should be done only with the knowledge that you could experience significant losses, make no money at all, save little or no money at all, and/or achieve no desired results regarding the products or services that we offer, whether fee based or non-fee based.

Our products are for educational and informational purposes only. Use caution and seek the advice of qualified professionals in their respective fields. Check with your accountant, lawyer, or professional advisor, before acting on this or any information in our products, services and websites.

Users of our products, services, and websites are advised to do their own due diligence when it comes to making business decisions. All information, products, and services that have been provided should be independently verified by your own qualified professionals.

You agree that our companies are not responsible for the success or failure of your business decisions, whether in the public or private sector, or academia or otherwise relating to any information presented in this book.

---

Thanks for reading! We are going out to do some pavement evaluation right now! Anything we can do to serve this amazing circle of pavement management **RockSTARS,** just let us know. Contact me at blair@ipma.co,

---

## The end . . .
## Our journey together has just begun!

# About the Author
## Blair Barnhardt, APM

An award winning National Highway Institute Instructor, serial entrepreneur, filmmaker, musician, speaker and Founder and Executive Director of the **International Pavement Management Association**, Blair Barnhardt has designed and delivered green, cost-saving pavement management, in-place asphalt recycling and preservation programs across North America over the last 2 decades.

His **Three Legged Stool System** of pavement management forms the basis for most all of the curriculum he teaches in the *Book on Better Roads*. In addition to his online **IPMA™ Academy Accredited Pavement Manger (APM™) Certification** training, Blair has also designed and delivered training for FHWA's NHI Workshops, Asphalt Institute, NWETC, APWA, LTAP, TTAP, Purdue Road School, Utah Road School, IACERS Road School, Utah Asphalt Association, University of Kansas, UC Berkeley ITS Department and Auburn University.

In addition to the above, Blair was involved with the most recent revision for one of the textbooks that is used in the **APM™ Certification** Program curriculum (ARRA/FHWA Basic Asphalt Recycling Manual) and Subject Matter Expert for the revamping of the NHI In-Place Asphalt Recycling Technologies Workshop.

Blair is a is a published author in every major related trade journal including *FHWA Public Roads, Public Works, Roads & Bridges, Asphalt Contractor, Army Engineer, Better Roads,* and *World Highways Magazine.* Blair Barnhardt and **The Barnhardt Group** are Founders Circle Lifetime Members of the Pavement Recycling & Reclaiming Center at CalPoly Pomona and Charter Members of **IPMA™**. His consulting firm, **The Barnhardt Group** provides pavement management services and training nationwide for struggling local agencies, private sector and army installations.

## About the Author - continued

Over his career of thirty years in heavy civil infrastructure, Blair has taught thousands of local agencies how to do more with less, while increasing their authority, expertise and income. Originally from Cambridge, Ontario, Canada, Blair and his family reside in Kennesaw, Georgia, USA. His home away from home is the RV, and he travels extensively across the nation with his mission to save our crumbling roads.

His vision and goal is to create a movement across this nation that will increase awareness and training for pavement managers, politicians and everyday people that will in turn resurrect our flailing roadway system with less money and less carbon footprint. He is one of the few individuals that recognize the enormity of the problem at hand, but also brings the practical solution to solving it, hence *The Book on Better Roads*.

**The Three-Legged Stool™ System of Pavement Management**